SO-ARM-844

PRAISE FOR *RAD FAMILIES* **AND** *RAD DAD*

"I miss the days when *Rad Dad* would be found in my mailbox and I would wait patiently for my turn to read it. It was mostly dads, fathers, and the frustrations and tenderness and amazement of fathering. As a mother, I needed those stories too. Now I can't wait to get *Rad Families* and share it with all my friends, parents or not. We all need to hear these stories if only for the diversity of experiences. We all need these stories because we need rad children. We need a rad future." —Nikki McClure, illustrator, author, parent

"I love this book! Wonderfully written, tenderly honest, unabashedly hilarious, deeply important stories from the messy-beautiful world of real-life parenting. Thank goodness it exists."
—Michelle Tea, author of *How to Grow Up*

"This collection takes the anaesthetized myth of parenting and reminds us that intimacy looks like menses on the toilet seat and the cramps you get when baby-making in a Safeway bathroom. The contributors describe the contours of family in a way that resonates."
—Virgie Tovar, editor of *Hot & Heavy: Fierce Fat Girls on Life, Love, and Fashion*

"Want a thriving family raising magical kids, building beloved community, and rooted in a vision of liberation that frees us all of white supremacist hetero-patriarchy? Read this book."
—Chris Crass, author of *Towards the "Other America"* and *Towards Collective Liberation: Anti-racist Organizing, Feminist Praxis, and Movement Building Strategy*

"When I first heard of the *Rad Dad* zine, my contrarian instinct was to roll my eyes. Of course throughout human time women have raised kids, but the moment a dad takes on a fraction of that responsibility we have to make it out that we're all 'rad' and shit. I vowed that if I became a dad I would just do the job and not be a 'Rad Dad.' Just a dad. But then I actually became a dad and read some *Rad Dad*. It was not at all what I thought it would be. The essays were self-reflective, literary, and important. And it was not all about dads! So I'm really excited about this project and expanding the framework to families is both apt and overdue. Full of deep insights, silly anecdotes, unique perspectives, but most of all great writing, *Rad Families* is the collection for all families."

     —Innosanto Nagara, author/illustrator of *A Is for Activist* and *Counting on Community*

RAD FAMILIES

A CELEBRATION

Edited by Tomas Moniz

PM Press | Oakland
Fernwood Publishing | Halifax & Winnipeg
2016

Rad Families: A Celebration
© 2016 PM Press
All rights reserved. No part of this book may be transmitted by any
means without permission in writing from the publisher.

ISBN: 978-1-62963-230-8
LCCN: 2016948141

10 9 8 7 6 5 4 3 2 1

Cover art by Thi Bui
Cover and interior design by Josh MacPhee/Antumbradesign.org

Published by PM Press
PO Box 23912, Oakland, CA 94623
www.pmpress.org

Published in Canada by Fernwood Publishing
32 Oceanvista Lane, Black Point, Nova Scotia, B0J 1B0
and 748 Broadway Avenue, Winnipeg, Manitoba, R3G 0X3
www.fernwoodpublishing.ca

Library and Archives Canada Cataloguing in Publication

    Rad families : a celebration / edited by Tomas Moniz.

Co-published by PM Press.
ISBN 978-1-55266-915-0 (paperback)

    1. Parenting. 2. Families. I. Moniz, Tomas, editor

HQ755.8.R33 2016   649'.1   C2016-904350-9

Fernwood Publishing Company Limited gratefully acknowledges the financial support of
the Government of Canada through the Canada Book Fund, the Manitoba Department
of Culture, Heritage and Tourism under the Manitoba Publishers Marketing Assistance
Program and the Province of Manitoba, through the Book Publishing Tax Credit, for
our publishing program. We are pleased to work in partnership with the Province of
Nova Scotia to develop and promote our creative industries for the benefit of all Nova
Scotians. We acknowledge the support of the Canada Council for the Arts, which last
year invested $153 million to bring the arts to Canadians throughout the country.

Contents

Calm the Fuck Down: A Foreword
Ariel Gore

A distant friend called this morning to ask me for parenting advice. "You're the only one I could think to call," she said, almost apologetically.

And it was true that when I'd seen her name glowing on my phone, my first thought had been, *she's got a lot of nerve*. The last I'd heard from her, she was publicly slamming me for my lackadaisical parenting.

"Adolescence," she whined now. "I didn't it would happen to my smart boy. Should I *spank* him?"

"No. Definitely not." But I didn't have much more for her in terms of advice.

To be honest, I've grown weary of most parenting advice.

I never went for the dumbed-down "how to" pieces and listicles that cluttered the baby magazines when I had my first kid twenty-five years ago—the "Twelve New Positions in Which to Simultaneously Do the Laundry and Burp the Baby" or the "Twenty-Five Ways to Spruce Up and Unattractive Toddler Using Big Hats." But even some kinds of essays I used to write (like "Raising Kids Who'll Change the World") can make me roll my eyes these days. I mean, most of us don't honestly know what kinds of chickens we're raising, let alone who our children will become.

So here's all I could suggest:

1. Be yourself.

2. Be yourself except when "yourself" wants to spank your kids, in which case stop being yourself and calm the fuck down. Call me if necessary.

Because more than advice or slams, we need support and we need community.

Sometimes that support and community happen in person, sometimes online, sometimes over the phone, and often, for me, they happen via the printed word. I write my experience and I forgive myself. I read your experience and I am at once unburdened and emboldened.

Since I first found an issue of *Rad Dad* in my Post Office box, it has been part of my support and my community. What I love about *Rad Dad* is that it's here for us without judgment and most times without advice.

"I am still learning myself through fathering," writes one father in *Rad Families*, and twenty-five years into this parenting thing, I'm still learning myself through it all, too. This is my community and yours. This book is a celebration of our community.

How and Why to Read *Rad Families*
Tomas Moniz

S tart anywhere. Skip around. Look for what you need. Make it yours. Pick up this book when you want to feel a little less anxious or worried. Not that these stories have answers, but they might remind you that you are not alone.

• • •

"Why 'Rad'?" someone asked me about the title. At the time, all I could say was because it's so hard sometimes. But what I meant was that sharing our stories, honestly, so that others may learn or feel consoled or less frazzled is one of the most radical things we can do.

• • •

Over a decade ago I started *Rad Dad* as a hand-stapled zine to trade with other people (most of whom were not parents) at the Bay Area Anarchist Book Fair, but I was desperate for help. It initially attempted to explore fathering differently than the mainstream patriarchally constructed narrative, all about discipline and hetero-normative masculinity. My goal: to silence Adam Sandler forever.

The zine evolved to include other genders, providing a space for marginalized voices in the parenting world, fathers and parents of color, the trans and queer, the step-parents, the allies and child care providers.

In 2011, the book *Rad Dad: Dispatches from the Frontiers of Fatherhood* came out like a manifesto, a call to men with babes in arms, testifying to our visibility, dispelling the stereotypes about bumbling, inept fathers.

But *Rad Families* feels different—less sequel, more evolution.

• • •

I like to think of *Rad Families* as "radical" because it has the gall, the arrogance, to celebrate; it laughs and smiles and trusts and doesn't hide; it honors the families that we choose to create and understand that parenting is difficult, painful work, but work that will sustain us and could, in fact, change the fucking world.

• • •

Here's the breakdown.

Think practical paired with metaphorical:

Part 1 is "Birth" and all its manifestations: trans pregnancy stories, infertility, loss, new family structures born from the old. Birth as metaphor. As threat. As goal. As welcome home.

Which leads to "Staying Connected," the myriad and disparate contexts in which we live and birth our families.

Part 2 is "Gender" and conversations around sex-positive parenting and feminism, riot grrrls and warrior princesses.

Which leads nicely to "Failing and Learning," stories and collaborations and musings on how we try and how, so often, we fail, but there's beauty, redemption, even radicalness in how we move on.

Part 3 is "Who We Are," the pain and beauty of parenting while black or brown or "othered," as well as stories from those who see themselves as white and are committed to dismantling racial oppression.

Which leads to "Advice" and the irony that so many of these stories come from failure, from fear, from doing the dirty, everyday work of being honest and human and imperfect and humble. Keep a poo journal—trust me, you'll miss them diaper days.

Part 4 wraps up with "Community and Allies," stories of parenting a child with special needs, parenting in the violence of police brutality, parenting outside of the gender spectrum, parenting through breakups and mental illness.

• • •

Read it during naptime, if you're not napping yourself. Read it with others so you can talk about it at the park because so much serious, revolutionary shit happens at parks (and make sure to welcome the dads if they are there!). Read it to your own kids.

• • •

If you're exhausted, just turn to the lists and the "Ask a Dad" columns and the Rad Parent Manifesto. You will feel less alone. If you like interviews, you'll like these woven throughout the book with Ian MacKaye, Allison Wolfe, Chris Crass, Carla Bergman, and Frances Hardinge.

• • •

Parenting teaches a little bit of wisdom and a whole lot of humility. It forces you to ask for help, makes clear your limitations, shows your own internalized baggage, provides you ample opportunities to learn to love without ownership, to understand the sublime beauty of life, to honor the moment, the quiet bike rides to school, the bath time, the homework helping, the silent watching from sidelines or bleachers as children become who they are: dancers, sports players, musicians. The pain of picking them up after midnight parties drunk and belligerent, the space you must give them when they refuse your comfort dealing with some teenage heartbreak.

Parenting has also taught me that what makes a parent has nothing to do with biology or gender and that family means so much more than living together.

Parenting has made me more fully human.

Parenting continues to be the hardest work I have ever done.

• • •

Of course, there are other paths to wisdom and humility and being more human, perhaps easier ones, definitely less messy ones, but for those who have faced the daunting, terrifying, stupefying reality of parenting and family building, this book and these stories, this celebration, is for you, my friends.

con safos
Tomas
PO Box 3555
Berkeley, CA 94703

Forgiveness and Wet Toilet Seats:
What Parenting Has Taught Me
Tomas Moniz

Recently I've realized that my day-to-day parenting is coming to an end, that I am probably without my kids more often than I am with them. This is a stunning revelation for me; it's like one of those statistics you refuse to accept: how often you drink, how little you exercise, how much time you waste on the internet.

It's a dirty secret, a deficiency, a failure.

It makes me feel like a pretty lame rad dad, to be honest.

And, yes, I realize that parenting at this developmental stage (my son is an adult and both my daughters are teenagers) is generally more difficult because the consequences they face can be more severe (legal, physical, sexual) and our ability to soothe our children, to alleviate their pain is tempered, perhaps even moot. A broken heart is so much harder to heal than a bruised knee, although ice cream does distract, at least temporarily, at any age. Today, my mistakes as a parent are more painful and glaring while the pleasures are more acute because I know that soon the time will arrive when I will not see them that often, when they will lean on others in their lives rather than me.

So what am I to do now, who have I become since I was that arrogant, ridiculous, naive twenty-year-old who discovered he was gonna be a dad?

Here are some of the things parenting has taught me.

I've learned that boys do tend to pee all over the toilet seat. Perhaps it's genetic, but they also can be taught to wipe it up. I've also learned, much to my initial confusion, that young women sometimes bleed on the toilet seat and having to ask them if they did so and can they wipe it up is a conversation no one is really prepared for.

In fact, I've learned to speak about menstrual blood with the same calm aplomb as I would about toothpaste, offering on one road trip to pocket one daughter's used tampon and dispose of it in a trash can because she was too afraid to flush it down a toilet at a rest-stop that had no wastebasket.

Give it to me, I said, reaching out my hand.

The look on her face: a mask of confusion and revulsion and a little bit of love.

I've learned the art of compromise on multiple levels and varying degrees of intensity: from the "yes, you can eat a pint of blueberries but you'll need to also eat six Brussels sprouts" to the "yes, you can have a party at my house and because I know there will be underage drinking you cannot have anyone driving home." And like I counted off each veggie, I sat patiently saying goodbye to drunk teenage boys and girls as they got picked up until well past my bedtime.

I've learned to work through really awkward conversations with other adults about the behaviors of our children, such as having to explain that my son pronounced ice cream like ass cream and so I'm sorry your son has started copying him. I know it's difficult to have them running around parks and stores singing "ass cream, ass cream, we all scream for ass cream."

I've learned that honesty cuts through all the denial, which we frequently hide behind. As parents, we front too often, we threaten when we are afraid, we punish when we hurt. Parenting teenagers has forced me to step through, or at least sit with, uncomfortable stuff: being called a hypocrite and knowing it's true, being asked why and not being able to say anything more than "because," being blatantly challenged on some point and having no effective retort.

Nothing is scarier than a cocky and correct angry teenager.

So I've learned to be honest from the start, to try to initially think through the implications of my parental proclamations and to recognize when I'm in a bad mood and own up to it.

I'm always shocked at how much of a difference it makes when I just say that I'm sorry that I'm feeling kinda grumpy, especially when I see my kids then doing the same thing. It disarms so many potentially explosive situations: the word *sorry*, the ability to be self-reflective, to be honest about where you're at.

I've learned to make amends and to apologize.

I've learned the importance of compartmentalizing. It's perhaps the most important thing parenting has taught me. It's taken me a number of relationships, raising one adult son and two teenaged daughters to learn and remember that being upset about one thing does not mean I should globalize the issue, making me angry about everything.

It saddens me to remember how often I'd get frustrated at my son for some transgression and have the anger taint the rest of the day or evening or sadly the next three days and evenings.

And, in retrospect, what was I so angry about?

A forgotten chore.

A missed time commitment.

A wet toilet seat.

These are all legitimate reasons to be frustrated, don't get me wrong, but not to hold on to, to let affect my interactions with him over homework, playing basketball in the street, or driving him to school. Perhaps I've learned to let the punishment fit the crime. In fact, I've learned now to ask what punishment or restitution they think fits the crime or transgression.

I've learned to watch my kids hurt deeply and not do anything about it. I've learned how to let them hurt and figure out how to heal themselves, how to sit with pain or disappointment or anger and work through it.

I've learned to give space, to step back, to let them go until they reach out to me.

Parenting has taught me about the power of forgiveness, about seeing those closest to me as complex, flawed, wonderful, imperfect, messy, beautiful people. Just like me. There is such liberation in acknowledging our weaknesses and loving ourselves regardless.

Yet, strangely, parenting has also enabled me to hold on to my own childish mentality, one that reminds me to get on the floor, to be ridiculous, to laugh at farts, to tickle and get tickled. To run down the sidewalk waving my arms in concentric circles for no other reason than to wave them in concentric circles. Because it makes my kids laugh, because it's simply fun, because we all are ridiculously human. Parenting continuously reminds me that I have license to celebrate and play and laugh and love like a child—fiercely, naively, uncompromisingly.

Parenting liberates.

I guess looking back on the things that have changed in me, I want to share with all the new parents as well as the people afraid of having kids because they believe parenting sedates or settles a person.

In my experience, it's done the exact opposite. Parenting can just as easily radicalize a person.

As a parent, I've come to realize the need to stand up for all children. No child should be hungry, abused, violated, bullied, intimidated. It's given me the energy when I've been down or exhausted; it's a constant reminder to stay focused, to push my boundaries, to work hard to create the community and families I want to be a part of. Parenting has made me a better person, more engaged, more loving, more connected.

Parenting ultimately has made me more human, and for that I am grateful even when I times I'm forced to wipe the toilet seat or pick up a gaggle of drunk teenagers; I know there will be a time when I will miss this work, when I wish I had to do these things. Until then, forgiveness and toilet paper I will keep in excess.

PART 1

Nipples

My mother never wore a bra; instead, she regularly wore shirts that said, *flat is beautiful* or *boobies are for babies*, her little breasts hanging low, her nipples arrogant, hard, always poking through the material. It embarrassed me. When I was fifteen, I asked her as she was getting dressed, "Why, Mom, why don't you even own a bra?" She turned to me shirtless and asked, "Do you know the reason men have nipples?" "No," I shrugged. She said, "To remind them of what they could have been."

Legacy

The first time my father saw me, arms chubby and legs fat like little sausages, he poked at me and said, "This one's a Chiconky." It was just like my father to mash two things together into a new thing: Chicano, Honky. Years later, he'd ask me like a dare, "What's the brown part of you?" When angry he'd growl, "That's the white part of you." When high or desperate or lonely, he'd whisper, "I love every part of you." Legacy is a thing passed on and a thing remembered. It's a tension. Because of my father, I learned to fret about the parts and the whole, piecing this to that, sorting out what belongs and what doesn't. But he also taught me to recognize that shit don't always make sense, so when I viewed my first child, squishy and little, I understood his desire to name that unknown, the weight of the past, the threat of the future, and call it a new thing.

BIRTH

Scars and Diamonds: A Birth Story
Jonas Cannon

All of the wonderful people in my life carry scars that show where they came from. Every single one of them. The people closest to my heart, the ones I admire, the ones who've inspired and continue to inspire me—none of them found a shortcut to the good times. There was domestic violence, sexual abuse, mental illness, physical illness, drug abuse, financial crisis, police brutality, alcohol abuse, loss of loved ones, racism, sexism, ageism, classism, homophobia, transphobia, physical disability, and so on and so on. They all suffered through it or suffer with it.

Sometimes, looking back on it all, I can't help but think that life has to crush us to get to the diamonds. Maybe you are the diamond. Maybe the diamond is what you will create. Whatever it is, you are going to take a bruising before you find it.

• • •

My kid wasn't due for another month. It was a Saturday night. My wife and I know how to party: we were going to spend the evening on the couch, watching bad television. Before I even turned on the TV, though, my wife suddenly looked confused and said, "Um, either I just peed my pants or my water broke."

I said, "Come on now. Let's be reasonable here. As an adult, have you ever peed your pants before?"

She said, "No, but I've never been pregnant before either."

"Touché," I said.

She went to the bathroom for a few minutes, then came back out holding up her pants and panties. She carried them over to me and said "Um . . . Smell this and tell me if you think it's pee or not."

I did not smell her underwear. I said, "You grab the car keys and I'll pack our bags."

• • •

My wife wanted a natural birth. My friend Teresa was her doula; a very brief phone call sent her speeding over to the hospital on her bike to meet us. Soon, the three of us were taken to the labor room, a pretty big space with a foldout bed.

And . . . we waited. Mostly in silence. My wife was nervous—no, she was downright terrified of the pain she was about to endure. Teresa and I took turns massaging her, speaking to her quietly to try to ease her mind a little.

I felt surprisingly calm through it all. Being at the hospital made it all seem very procedural, very normal. Also, I wasn't the one in the hospital bed.

After waiting in the labor room for a few hours, the nurses started my wife on Pitocin. When the Pitocin kicked in, it was goodbye natural birth, hello epidural.

There was a lot of pushing and then there was a lot of blood and then there was an emergency C-section. The nurses led me into an adjoining room to see the baby, lying on his back and screaming bloody murder.

I know that for some parents, the first sight of their child is a glorious moment, a precious, unforgettable blink in time. Some fathers are reduced to tears. Some are wide-eyed and speechless. Some collapse and faint. That's all sweet and touching—even the fainting part.

I didn't experience anything like that.

I looked down at the baby, the six pounds and seven ounces of brand new life. He'd spent the better part of the year taking it easy in a cozy little womb. Then, suddenly, a team of doctors came along and yanked him out, delivering him into a world that is mostly bad. It made the poor kid wail his little head off, and all I could think was, son, I don't blame you. I don't blame you one bit.

• • •

There are many ways to interpret a baby's cries after delivery. I picked the cynical one, the one that has nothing to do with babies and everything to do with the life I'd lived.

But there was my diamond: my son, my beautiful boy, right in front of me. I wanted to lead him to good times, but without all the pain it takes to get there. Only I didn't know how to send him down that road. I didn't even know if it was within my power to do so.

I still don't know.

Yes, I will teach my son as much as I can, by word and by example. He will join me at protests. He's going to be surrounded by books like Assata Shakur's autobiography and *King Kong Theory*. He'll be raised with strong feminist values. He'll be taught to embrace his own heritage while being aware and respectful of the beautiful cultures around him. Within my power, I'll try to shield him from the dangers I can foresee and prepare him for the ones he has to face without me.

It's overwhelming to consider. It feels as though I made it halfway up a mountain, then came down to hoist a child onto my shoulders and start climbing all over again.

A couple months before he was born, I got into a conversation on parenting with a few pals. In the middle of it, my friend Kristi said flat out that the first couple years of parenting were all about struggling to keep a fragile little person from not dying. She's not one to sugarcoat things.

At the time, I was horrified by this notion. Parenting sounded intimidating enough without defining it as an ongoing life-or-death situation.

I think about what she said, and I find it comforting. It's a long, overwhelming journey to help him fit into the shoes of a strong, intelligent, compassionate adult. Luckily, for the time being, I just have to figure out the difference between when he cries because he's hungry and when he cries because he shit his diapers. Right now, radical parenting simply involves cradling, feeding, burping, and making sure that this helpless, speechless human being does not stop breathing. Before I can guide him anywhere, I have to figure out how to swaddle him tightly enough so that the little stinker won't kick his way out two minutes later. Before I teach him any language, I first have to learn the language of his crying.

With a Child Is Born a Parent:
An Interview with Ian MacKaye

I an Mackaye shared his thoughts and experiences about becoming a father a few years ago for *Rad Dad* and coined what I thought was some astoundingly true advice to new parents: it's fucking natural. It's the one interview I always encourage new parents to read. I thought I'd check in with him again to see what other ideas and experiences he's had since becoming a father.

Your son is now five years old! I wonder how your view of parenting has changed.

You know, I still stand by what I said in the last interview. Really the biggest change is that now sometimes he'll do stuff that offends me or angers me or hurts my feelings and so the consequences are that we stop whatever we were doing. And he doesn't like that. That's hard. But I don't want him feeling comfortable doing things that offend or bother or hurt people. For example, if he wants to throw a snowball at me when we're playing that's fine. But if he throws it at me when I'm not ready or he hasn't let me know we're playing, then that's not cool. But I'm his father and I can handle it. One day he'll throw the snowball at the wrong person or at other kids or older kids and there are much different kinds of consequences he will have to face. But really it's as much a learning process for him as it is for me. I often say this: with a child is born a parent. Each of us is trying to figure it out for ourselves and figure it out together.

Perhaps a more daunting question: your son is certainly being influenced or coming into contact with mainstream pop culture and all that comes with it. How are you managing that in the MacKaye household?

Managing? That's a weird term. I don't wanna manage him. I want to give him the tools to manage himself. It's his life. But what I would like to give him is the ability or the freedom to be wrong, so that way he can figure out how to be right, how to get back to being right when he makes a mistake. I want to give him tools to do that. I feel that to manage a child or shield them from the mainstream is to marginalize or essentially create somebody who feels marginalized from the world by their parents.

What I'd rather do is to let him know it's up to him to figure it out and learn. For example, Amy and I are vegans. We have a vegan household. It's simple. That's what we eat at our home. We have told him when he's out in the world if he wants to eat something that's not vegan, it's up to him. This especially comes up at birthday parties. So we tend to have some vegan treats with us when we go out to events like that so he can join in if he chooses to not eat the cake. But it's up to him. He can choose. I don't want him to be a vegan because I am. I ultimately want him to choose for himself and I will respect it. I was raised in a family that gave me tools. My parents said trust yourself and do well. And to this day all of us who live in the area eat dinner every Sunday with my father who is not vegan but cooks a vegan meal every weekend for us because he respects us.

Does your family plan to participate in the public education system?

I'm psyched that he's going to be a part of the public school system. That's where I went. Yes, it's got the problems that public schools have: bureaucracy and lack of funding and just life in general. But I think though that public schools are so important because it is the only opportunity when a person will spend long extended time with other people from all walks of life. There is no other time in life when this happens so consistently. You learn how to be with each other. Public school gives you the opportunity to see that everyone is a person. That we are all people. I could give a damn about test scores. I care about socialization and learning to care about others. In public school you have to learn how to coexist, which I think is pretty good practice for being with other people in the world.

Lucas's Birth
Burke Stansbury

The day after Lucas's positive health reports and development, Krista and nurse Florence were at the hospital with Lucas for another routine visit. Getting off the elevator someone walked by, looked at Lucas in his chair, and let out a sad "awww." Then a moment later in the waiting room a man came up and said, "It must be really hard." Throughout the long wait Krista and Florence could feel the eyes in the room on them and Lucas, each time they fired up the suction machine to clear the saliva out of his mouth or adjust the vent circuit in a way that led to that familiar, loud beeping.

It's weird that the same day Lucas was getting compliments on his positive health reports, about how good he looks and the excitement of all the progress he's made from friends and family on our blog, people at the hospital were going out of their way to remind us of his dramatic limitations. We still haven't figured out how to get him comfortable in his new stroller/wheelchair, so he often looks pretty out of it when we're rolling around. And just a glance at the tracheostomy, the vent tube, and the monitor wire connected to his toe can be jarring, even at a children's hospital where difference is often on display.

But what you don't capture in a five-second snapshot of Lucas is everything. We're lucky—we get to spend lots of time with the little guy and see him at his best: when he's cracking up because someone is about to raspberry his tummy, when he's exploring a fascinating new toy and deliberating on how to best get it into his mouth, or when he's splashing his legs around in his undersized bathtub. With Lucas, patience is a virtue. The more time you spend with him and allow him to do his thing, the more remarkable he becomes.

So it wasn't surprising that it was Florence who immediately piped up when the man in the waiting room expressed his sympathy about Lucas's condition. "That's okay," she said, "actually, he's doing great!" The man eventually sat down and asked more questions about Lucas, spent some time talking with him as well as Krista and Florence, and it ended up being a very positive interaction.

In fact, even though it can be awkward at first, we usually appreciate it when people come up and ask about Lucas, as opposed to the more common reaction of quickly averting eyes in an attempt to avoid the reality of a child connected to a ventilator. We don't hold the latter reaction against anyone—we've had it ourselves when confronted with people who have disabilities. But as this curious man in the waiting room found out, there are great rewards to having the courage and patience to get to know someone like Lucas.

• • •

Lucas will be discharged tomorrow morning from the hospital and hopefully we'll make it safely home before the next big snowstorm hits in the afternoon. He's pretty much back to his old self, but there's still a few things that are weird, such as an occasionally high heart rate, some residual swelling, and a new, goofy eye twitch. There's so much going on with him sometimes that it's hard to know what is significant and what isn't, but we're confident along with the doctors that he's ready to come home.

We've taken advantage of our days in the pediatric ICU to access all the specialists that might be able to help tackle Lucas's broader challenges, and through the various consults and tests over the last week we may finally have an answer. It's not something that's easy to share, but Lucas underwent an electronic test of the muscles that confirmed that he has a congenital muscle disease, most likely a genetic disorder called Myotubular Myopathy. It's devastating news—hard to even write these words—but based on our own research over the weekend we're convinced he will ultimately be diagnosed with this particular disease.

Like us, you probably have lots of questions about what this means for Lucas and we won't try to answer them all right now. Many thoughts have been going through our minds over the last few days and it's impossible to sort through them when the realization is still so raw. In some ways the news wasn't a total shock:

Lucas's hypotonia has improved very slowly since he was born and we had begun to doubt the theory that a brain injury alone had caused his low muscle tone. Upon seeing Lucas the other day, the neuromuscular doctor quickly confirmed our fears, and the conversations we've had with this thoughtful, humble man over the past few days have helped begin our process of understanding Lucas's disease.

Mytobular Myopathy is a very rare muscular disorder that affects approximately 1 in every 50,000 boys. It is not degenerative like most muscle diseases, but nor is there a cure or treatment for it. Lucas may gain some strength and muscle tone in the months and years to come (especially with the help of therapy), but he will likely always need assistive technology to breathe, move from place to place, and communicate with the outside world. Research on this disease only really began in the 1990s; prior to that, it was assumed that anyone with Myotubular Myopathy would die in infancy. Since then some boys have survived into their teenage years, and some attend school—unlike some muscular diseases it does not affect cognition, and intelligence levels for those who survive tend to be high.

Right now, Lucas's future remains very much unknown, but we can say this: Lucas hasn't changed, just the information we know about him has changed. He's still the same beautiful, little fighter that we've been lucky enough to know and love over the last five and a half months. He has already taught us so much. We will continue to experience great joy together as a family. And we can't wait to have him home again.

· · ·

We still haven't heard any results about Lucas's blood that was sent to the University of Chicago to test for the genetic mutation that causes Myotubular Myopathy (MTM). However, since our meetings with Dr. Leshner we've been going about life as it were already confirmed that Lucas has the disease. That might sound odd, since of course it's not something we want, but our research so far has only reinforced the theory, and all the pieces seem to fit. It will be weeks before we hear back on the genetics test, which means it will be weeks before we can actually ask Dr. Leshner about some of our specific questions about possibilities for Lucas's future. In the meantime we continue to do our own research and learning.

Researching your baby's debilitating disease is not an easy thing. At times we find stories of other children exceeding expectations in life that give us a lot of hope; at other moments we learn things that present really difficult possibilities for Lucas's future. Our goal so far has not been to find out every piece of information possible by throwing ourselves entirely into the world of MTM and muscle disease. Rather, we're still adjusting to Lucas's diagnosis, holding in our hearts the many intense feelings that it brings, and adjusting our hopes for the future as we let go of some dreams and embrace new ones. All the while, Lucas is growing and changing and we get to keep enjoying the everyday wonders of just being with him.

While we're far from making any definitive conclusions, there are a few things we're already learning from our research and from stories people have shared with us. First, a diagnosis does not mean a definitive prognosis, since diseases like MTM manifest themselves in distinct ways with varying levels of severity. Reading about different young boys with MTM has reinforced that. Lucas likely has the x-linked form of Myotubular Myopathy, which is the most common and severe form, but still there is a lot of variation in how it manifests itself. There are over a hundred different mutations of the gene that can cause MTM, and it seems that the type of mutation and where it is on the gene strand can impact the prognosis.

Second, though there are organizations and foundations funding research on Myotubular Myopathy and groups of doctors carrying out that research, the knowledge and technology related to genetic disease don't seem to be at a place where a cure is likely anytime soon. There do seem to be possibilities related to treatment and therapy that could be helpful for Lucas in the future. The fact that we're not hopeful for a cure anytime soon means that we can be forthright about the likelihood that this disease will affect Lucas for his whole life, which in turn helps us accept the challenges that lay ahead.

We're also continuing to connect with new people, especially other parents of kids with disabilities, as well as communities of people who are living with life-altering physical differences and figuring out ways to embrace those differences. So far we've just begun to tap into the amazing knowledge and support of other parents of children who have MTM. We've found a couple different online support groups and joined some listservs and a Facebook group. We've also learned about the first ever MTM family conference, which happened last year right before Lucas was born. Perhaps most importantly, we've connected by e-mail with some parents of children with MTM and are excited about continuing to develop relationships with them.

And it's not just families that have kids with MTM that have a lot to teach us. A number of people have related stories about family members, friends or heroes who have dealt with muscle disease or other similar disabilities/different abilities, and that kind of support and solidarity has been incredibly helpful. We really appreciate that people are thinking about Lucas's disease right now, and we are grateful for all of you sharing stories, articles, and introductions to new people and paths to explore.

Letting Go
Danny Goot

"It's easy to hate and point out everything that is wrong with the world; it is the hardest and most important work in one's life to free oneself from the bonds of fear and attachment." —Noah Levine

There they were, swimming around like eager wannabe babies. I was looking at my sperm under a microscope. I guess it wasn't me that was the "weak link" in our attempt at creating a baby. But I wished in that moment that it was me. Instantly, I felt compassion for how Jenney, my partner, would feel. Of course, I didn't think that she was weak in any way, but this is how I feared she would ultimately feel about herself even though she had already birthed two kids previously, at home, completely and fully naturally. These aren't exactly "weak human" accomplishments.

We continued to try for months. Nothing was working. We tried all the tricks and myths that we had heard and read about throughout the years. You know the one trick that will get you knocked up for sure? Yes, we tried that embarrassing maneuver over and over and still nothing.

After a year of trying, we were tired of the disappointment and decided to just forget it. And of course, that's when it happened. We wanted this sooo bad and finally, after letting go just a bit, it happened. I was on my way to becoming a papa! Not only was I thrilled with this next stage of my life, but I was also extremely excited to be taking this step with the woman of my dreams.

The possible names of our future new baby were piling up. Morning sickness made its appearance. Everything was as we wanted it to be. But just as soon as this started to happen, it ended. Eight weeks into the pregnancy, we lost it. You hear of these things happening a lot, but when it happens to you, it's devastating. After all the love that we built up around this unborn child together . . . Fucking devastating.

It was hard to get out of bed and go to work. It was hard to tend to our kids' needs. Vida, who was seven, needed to be taken to school, and Ari, who was two, needed full attention from her mom while I went to work.

At this time in our lives, we used alcohol to help numb our pain. I was building up fear-based resentment because of our loss instead of trying to build a support system. I didn't want to be around Jenney because I believed that her pain was going to cause her to not want me anymore. I was afraid that she would blame herself and go into a deep depression. I convinced myself that nothing good would come of this. I didn't want to see her in pain; it made me scared and uncomfortable. I had no control to change what had happened. Once again I experienced how our thoughts can be our worst enemy. These were dark times in the Goot household.

When it happened again six months later, we tried not to get attached. Yeah, (laughing out loud) not getting attached to our unborn baby was going to happen for me. Yeah, right! It was scary for sure, but this time I slowed down my excitement just a bit. I was afraid to feel all that pain of loss again. But, there I was, thinking I had some kind of control over what would happen.

This baby was not going to let go, and this baby didn't!

The midwives came but were instructed by Jenney to stay in the back room. She was very clear that she was going to do this unassisted, all the way through. Jenney went into a room by herself to work through her first stages of labor. It was around 1 a.m. and I could not keep my eyes open. There was no way I was going to be able to stay awake. Under just about any circumstance I have the ability to stay awake for days. I have driven across the country and stayed awake the whole time. But for some reason, during one of the biggest events of my life, I passed out. A complete shutdown most likely caused by anxiety and emotional overload.

Jenney woke me up hours later to tell me it was time to fill the birth tub with water. Things were moving really fast and I began to silently panic. I now felt horrible for falling asleep. The midwives peeked in to check the baby's heart beat several times to make sure everything was going okay. This did not help with my anxiety at all. Throughout this whole pregnancy I felt pretty confident that things were going to be okay, but now it was all coming to a head (typical bad dad joke). Why were they checking the heartbeat so much at this point? Dear god, was this normal?

When the tub was full enough, Jenney climbed inside. Immediately after she slipped into the tub, our baby started making its way out of her. A couple of minutes went by and Jenney reached behind herself to feel if there was anything going on. She looked at me and said, "I feel an ear," which took me to a higher level of freaking out. All I could think about was the baby getting stuck and suffocating, head halfway out.

Taking a deep breath and listening to the air enter and exit my lungs brought me back down, but only for a second because there was the baby. I scooped this baby up and held the warm, wet body in my hands. We'd had an ultrasound, which had informed us the baby had a penis, but I just could not convince myself that it was true. Although my kiddo's gender is not for me or a penis to decide, he indeed had a penis. He was out now and I handed him into his mama's arms. All that time, all that anxiety and all that waiting had come to an end. Wondering what he was going to look like, daydreaming about the color of his skin and the color of his hair and what he would feel like was all over. There he was.

This birth story doesn't end after Jerome, my sweet love, was born. It's only the beginning of a whole new chapter of being a papa. Today, Jerome is almost five years old. This fall he will begin kindergarten, which brings a whole new birthing process. All the fears and anxiety about the unknown haunt my mind. All the sorrow and disappointment with trying to make a baby turned into fear and anxiety to keep that baby safe. "Will the kids in school like him? Will he be smart enough? What will his struggles be?" and on and on. It never stops.

Well, Jerome doesn't share my fears at all. He just wants to learn and grow every day. He wants to play in the sun. He wants to laugh and eat "potissucoles" (popsicles). He wants to watch Hayao Miyazaki films. He doesn't worry about tomorrow so much; he's only thinking in the moment. What a gift, to only be focused in the moment.

I don't have control over anything; I only think I do. Letting go of the "control" I think I have with my family is a practice that never ends. And it's incredibly fucking tough to let go. If only I could stop trying so hard to teach my kids how to act and exist in this life. If I took more time to learn from them instead of attempting to control their situations, they would be great at teaching me how I could be a better papa.

Trans Pregnancy
Simon Knaphus

The first time my partner and I tried to conceive, we waited until I tested positive on an ovulation testing stick and rushed off to pick up a syringe for giving medicine to babies, which we would use to inseminate. We tracked down our donor, and he put his sperm in a little plastic condiment cup while we admired the view of the Castro through the wall of windows of the condo he was crashing at. I wondered about what it would be like for my baby to grow up in a posh condo with a big piano and a view. He would learn to crawl perched on the side of a steep hill with nothing but glass for walls and it was comforting to imagine my baby putting hand over hand and pulling up to peer out a window, cradled in a nest of worn-out Victorian moldings, walls and color, toys and curtains.

It was the middle of the workday, so we rushed back down the hill to the store where my partner worked and tried getting pregnant on a bathroom counter. It felt like we were getting away with something, we were adults making a baby like teenagers going off to make out in an alley. The lighting was all wrong and the counter was not long enough for me to lie down on properly. My foot was in the sink and I had to hold my head at a weird angle because the wall was in the way. After finding the most reasonable position, my partner transferred the sperm from cup to syringe and syringe to body. We kissed and grinned and gazed lovingly at each other. I tried to rest there for a few minutes while gravity was in my favor. The absurdity of it all struck me and I began to giggle, I got a cramp in my neck that only made the situation more hilarious. All the tension and excitement and nervousness and daydreaming and planning started to pour out of me in a fit of hysterical laughter. I decided that any conception-related advantage from my horizontal position was cancelled out by my body-quake of jubilation so I got up, pulled on my drawers and jeans from where they were bunched at my ankles around the top of my boots, splashed some water on my face, hugged my partner fiercely, and walked out of the bathroom into the sunlight of a different world—a world with our baby.

I had a spring in my step, and I wanted to sing to the birds in the trees and dance with the old ladies walking down the street. Later, when I was finally pregnant, I was struck by how much I could love someone I hadn't met yet. I wonder if that feeling is similar to how people feel who have fallen in love with someone by correspondence but haven't ever been with them in real life. The day I first tried to get pregnant I got my initial dose of that feeling.

About a week later I took a pregnancy test on the first possible day the box said it could show a positive result. It was negative. The bathroom walls were bright pink and reflected on the shiny plastic where the one-line-negative two-lines-positive appeared. The reflection looked like the glimmer of a line, but no matter how I squinted I knew there was just one. I took more tests the next day and the next day. I went back to the drugstore to buy another three-pack, but they were all negative. I started noticing stories of people who had become pregnant by accident and the world seemed a little more unfair than it had before. We tried again and again, but at home. We were parents without a child. My body was pregnant without a baby. Our world was different, but the change was still in the future. It got to be more routine, but always carried that charge of love.

I finally conceived my oldest child when I was twenty-four, after over a year of artificially inseminating and counting my life in two-week cycles. Since then, I've learned a lot from the other parents in my world, parents by choice and by chance. I appreciate more and more that I was able to have my two kids and that true reproductive choice means not only that we get to avoid pregnancy when we don't want kids, but also that we are able to have them when we want. So many of my fellow queer and trans people aren't able to build the families we want, while others are sterilized against their will. I wonder if it is possible for us to build a society in which having kids isn't the expected social norm (so that people who are ambivalent about parenthood don't have to do it) but also where families with children are supported, valued, validated. It is a hardship that my heart lives outside my body, it's a risk to be spread out that way, and it's hard to do my best for them all the time, even to figure out what the best is. Raising kids, especially on my own, is a whirlwind of chaos and brilliance and pee and silliness beyond what I could have imagined back in that condo over ten years ago. I'm always grateful to the friend who ended up being our donor and his gift of love and trust. The spark I first felt became a wildfire of a child, a conflagration of love, a family.

Daddy's Tangled Apparatus: On Infertility
Daniel Muro LaMere

I'm in a busy diner during the lunch rush, waiting for a friend to finish paying. I'm struggling to manage the weight of my infant son's car seat. He's not terribly heavy, but the seat is tricky to maneuver in tight spaces. It's pouring rain outside, and I'm trying to remember where we parked when the restaurant staff starts doting over my son.

To be fair, he's adorable. We share no biology so I can take no credit for his incredible cuteness. For most of my marriage, I wasn't sure I wanted kids. It wasn't a tough decision to make as we were usually broke. If we were going to have kids, it would have to be when we were financially secure enough to swing it; if that never happened, we could take all of that extra money we didn't have in the first place and do a bunch of traveling. Either way, it seemed we'd be able to find a happy outcome.

But then I got the bug. All it took was seeing dads and kids at Target and Home Depot and I was gone. I'd see these tiny people, barely up to their dads' knees, teetering along, slowly, deliberately. And they were holding hands with Daddy.

I was stricken.

Completely.

My wife and I soon began trying. This was a revelation for me: despite what you may think, trying-to-conceive-a-baby sex is some of the silliest sex there is. In place of passion, spontaneity, and romance are pressure, obligation, and a foreboding sense of timing.

It becomes rote, and both of you are aware of how strange that is, and maybe feel guilty about it, but still, the show must go on. And then you try to change it up, and next thing you know, you've got blankets spread out on the bathroom floor (which really sounds so very disgusting in retrospect), but the sink is running because it's cold outside and the pipes are frozen (!) and halfway through you're both getting splashed in the face with sink water, and who can take any of that seriously at all? Not the guy who's complaining about the cramp in his back, I can promise you that.

As it turned out, all of our trying was in vain, and so eventually I went in for a test. In an interesting twist of medical nomenclature, what could have been dressed up in jargon, couched in all kinds of Greek and Latin terms, is instead called by the somewhat undignified moniker of "semen analysis," probably to avoid giving the mistaken impression that there would be any self-respect happening anywhere in the process.

The office was decorated in dark oak and oriental rugs, something like an alpine hunting lodge. This overt expression of masculinity struck me as incredibly transparent, rooted in the idea that men in my position might need some sort of testosterone-based reinforcement. But just because I could see through their design choices didn't mean that I was immune to the inherent discomfort of my situation.

A nurse led me back to a small room. She was older, maternal, in the gruff all-business way of so many older, maternal women. The room's main feature was a reclining lounge chair covered in coarse medical paper, but she also made sure to let me know about the fertility-friendly lubricant that wouldn't mess with my count, the dimmer switch "for mood lighting," the pornography in the cupboard, and where to put my sample when I was done.

A few days later I got a call from another nurse. She said that the volume of the sample I produced looked good, and so was the motility (movement of the sperm within the sample), but there was a problem.

There was a problem, yet her voice was so detached from the gravity of this news and the effect it was having upon me. She would, I supposed, have more of these calls to make that afternoon, piled up in the days to come for as long as she cared to imagine.

But there was a problem.

Conservatively speaking, she explained, there are usually at least fifteen million sperm swimming around in one milliliter of ejaculate—occasionally even ten times that number. Mine had sixteen.

"As in, six more than ten?"

It turns out that's what sixteen means.

People will tell you that "it only takes one," and, you know, I saw *Look Who's Talking*, I know how it works, but on a line graph with 150 million on the top and zero on the bottom, sixteen is effectively zero. All those "it only takes one" optimists might as well buy me a Powerball ticket while they're at it—I'd spend my winnings on reproductive surgery.

I hadn't expected this news. I was devastated. I walked the dog, shuffling through a gray day in my neighborhood, trying to get my head together. I passed by the gas station, busy with customers, and was aware of how disconnected we all are from the problems of others.

I think I knew that there were options available to me. I just hadn't expected to need them and wasn't sure yet how I felt about them. More troubling than anything was the overwhelming knowledge that I had no idea what I was going to do. The doctors encouraged me to go see a specialist. This proved to be problematic; my wife and I had been operating on a somewhat specific timeline, one that was predicated upon academic and professional responsibilities. We now found ourselves working within a rapidly closing window of time, and the specialist scheduled appointments two months out. After months of charting temperatures and mucus quality, and all that overwrought sex, this was a new level of anxiety I hadn't anticipated.

I realized that I had even fewer options than before, compounding my disappointment. I felt lost. Any move I made seemed to negate other, plausible-seeming moves.

Eventually, we also stumbled upon a probable cause for my near-sterility. When I was an infant, I had a hernia. I grew up hearing the story about how I was blue from the legs down, like a Smurf in reverse. Our working theory, although never confirmed, is that when the doctors went in to fix me up, they may have accidentally snipped this, knotted that, and given me the inspiration for my upcoming children's book, *Daddy's Tangled Apparatus*. I was relieved to have something resembling an explanation, especially one that made so much sense.

Working on this assumption, we decided to pursue a sperm donor. I think some people find this to be a reckless decision, like I gave up and quit on myself. Who knows, right? Maybe I could have been untangled, reattached, or otherwise had my fecundity restored. And I don't want to be cavalier about this at all—it was an incredibly difficult decision to be sure. There was a lot of insecurity and second-guessing.

But my goal was to have a baby in the house, not to cultivate a biological legacy. Allowing that goal to really take primacy over everything else was very liberating, once I got there. Given the choice, I would have preferred not to have any infertility issues, but that preference didn't seem worth putting my goal on hold indefinitely.

Not only that, but we have a lot of gay friends who are starting families. Same-sex parents have no choice but to begin with a donor of some sort, and I'm not sure how productive it is for the nonbiological parent to lament the lack of shared DNA once the baby arrives. Any self-pity others would foist upon me seemed strictly a function of straight privilege.

We began to research donor agencies so that we could begin to research donors. I was, of course, grateful for the chance to become a father at all. When my wife walked into the bedroom with a positive pregnancy test in her hand, it was the happiest moment in my life up to that point, and one I'll never forget.

During the pregnancy we talked some about how I might react when the baby finally came. His in utero name was New Guy, and I was pretty sure I wouldn't feel any less connected to him than if he were the fruit of my own loins. Still, we both knew that this was one of those big life things for which you just can't predict a reaction. Not until you've lived it.

I'm happy to report that after a long and difficult labor, my son finally arrived, and when he did, I cried tears of joy like never before. He's seven weeks old now, and while there are difficult times, reflux-induced sleepless nights, diaper blowouts, and moments of self-doubt and insecurity, I have no misgivings whatsoever about my decision. Quite the contrary, the levies of my heart are struggling against levels of love and joy I could never have imagined. He is altogether mine, and I am his daddy, and like parents everywhere, biological or otherwise, the task now falls to me to be the best parent that I can possibly be.

Sperm donation can be a taboo topic, to be sure, tied up as it is in notions of masculinity, virility, and manhood, and this upsets me. I have never thought for a second that my low sperm count made me less of a man. I don't bring it up during casual conversation at cocktail parties ("well, you know we had to use a donor because I can barely make sperm"), mostly because I imagine it would make other people uncomfortable, but a little bit I wish I could. I love my son, and I wouldn't know him otherwise, and that's why I'm proud that we chose to use a donor. I look forward to having lots of conversations with him about all the different kinds of families in the world.

But maybe the rest of the world isn't ready. In the meantime, back at the diner, a member of the staff says "Oh, you're just so handsome like your daddy." And of course I know it's me, but I still can't help myself. I pick up the car seat, smile wryly, and whisper, "Who is your daddy, anyway?"

The Long Pause: A Conception Story
Artnoose

I was barely in my mid-twenties when I first wanted to have a kid. I looked ahead in my life and imagined I'd have a partner of some sort by the end of my twenties and have at least one kid by the time I was thirty. I didn't believe then that having a kid meant the end of one's life. I wasn't, however, looking to single parent. And I definitely didn't want to start having kids after thirty.

Suddenly I was thirty with no kids and no partner. I continued the search for an anarchist baby-daddy. I was sure that if I didn't end up with a kid by the age of thirty I'd call off the search and do something else with my life. I still didn't want to single parent.

Then I was thirty-five, still with no kids and with a partner who vehemently did not want a biological relationship to any child. However, he sincerely encouraged me to have a baby with someone else, coming up with two people who he'd be excited for me to have a baby with. It was the first time that I had really considered having a baby outside a romantic relationship.

I went back to California to visit friends, including Jim, one of the people on my baby-daddy list. On my last night in town I went to a party in a warehouse space in San Francisco and saw him on the dance floor just as I was about to go catch the last BART train. I straight-up asked him if he wanted to have a baby with me sometime. I had to shout over the music and gesticulate towards my belly to get him to understand what I was saying. He was speechless. I admitted it was an unorthodox place to ask a question like that and told him he could think about it. A couple weeks later he wrote me a very nice letter politely declining the offer.

The next person on the list was Roland, whom I had only hung out with once at that point, but he came so highly recommended by my partner—"one of my favorite people in the world"—that I decided to ask him. I told him that I had a project I wanted to work on with him and when his band came through on tour I wanted to run it by him. To step up my game, I made a really awesome mixtape of '80s Goth and industrial music, with elaborate packaging that opened up into a small booklet where I had drawn little pictures of his future kid's life—diaper changes on book fair tables, walks in the woods, snow people, etc.

"So," I began when I got him alone, "I want to know if you'll have a baby with me."

You know that pause, that long pause right after you say for the first time something like, "I really like you a lot," or, "You could spend the night here if you want," or, "I'm falling in love with you"? Let me tell you, it's nothing compared to the pause that follows, "I want to know if you'll have a baby with me."

"Uh, I thought this was a music project you were talking about," he finally said. "I mean . . . I've had a vasectomy. I'm sterile."

Then it was my turn for the long pause as tears welled in my eyes and I fumbled with the plastic box in my hands. "But . . . I made you this sweet mix tape."

There's no arguing with the cauterizing and clamping of the vas deferens. Although we spent months exploring the possibility of a reversal, ultimately Roland had the clarity of mind to decide that the money would be better spent on the kid and not a vasectomy reversal that he would eventually get unreversed.

People had by now asked why I didn't just pay a sperm bank. My answer was that I wanted to give my kid a better origin story than, "I flipped through the book until I found the biochemist on page 45." Besides, once you have both dance party and mix tape propositions under your belt, your idea of what is acceptable is somewhat skewed.

During the months that Roland and I were in negotiations about the vasectomy reversal, we were on tour with his band, and this is when I met Nicholas. One night while waiting for the band to set up, Nicholas and I got to talking about what we wanted to do in the near future.

"Well," he said, "I'd like to have a kid, but I can't find anyone to have one with me."

"That's weird," I said, "me too."

In a few months, Nicholas had packed up his van and was on his way to my city. In the cruelest stroke of fate, though, his vehicle broke as he stopped in Roland's town for a visit. Nicholas had to find a job to pay for the extensive repairs before he could go anywhere. This led to him finding a room in a collective house. Several months later, he and I discussed the baby option and which city we might potentially raise the kid in. Instead, though, he went on tour, and negotiations more or less ended.

As luck would have it, right around this time I met Flint, a twenty-year-old queer boy who looked like he had quit his modeling career to become a punk. The first time that he and I ever had a conversation, he said he had heard that I was looking for sperm, and that he could help.

"I mean," he added, "if no better offer comes along." I was surprised because at this point in the process I wasn't used to other people being more reckless than I was.

Despite his motivation, it still took a little over a year before I decided that no other offer was coming along. We came to the decision that we would start actively trying to conceive once his upcoming trial was over. After being found guilty, he was taken into custody immediately. When they led him away in handcuffs, I knew that this was the person I wanted to make a baby with. I don't know how to explain it, but that's how it was. Unfortunately I then had to wait for his sentence to be up.

I started charting my ovulation, even taking my temperature every morning. We did the responsible thing and got tested, which was funny because the nurses kept asking us if we were together, and we had a hard time configuring our nuanced relationship into a yes-or-no answer.

One thing we didn't take into account before trying this was how difficult it would be for us to actually do the dang thing. You'd think that two attractive and sensual people wouldn't have a hard time having sex with each other. As it turns out, scheduling units of conception time with a nonromantic friend is horribly awkward. In true DIY problem-solving style, we overcame this by scheduling meetings of Porn Watcher's Club, membership of two.

Five months later, during the hottest heat wave of the summer and Flint's discovery of a brand-new lover, I thought for sure it would be a wasted cycle for us. "You couldn't possibly have a single living sperm in your body right now," I said. Somehow though, after that last 103 degree afternoon, I had the sneaking suspicion that it had worked. Not much later, I woke up feeling a little woozy and got a home pregnancy test immediately.

"You'll never believe it," I said to him on the phone, "It's positive."

Sometimes during this long process I had bemoaned my own ill luck that I never met that romantic partner to be father to my kid. Instead, I created other options. I was lucky to meet someone who was just adventurous enough to attempt something ridiculous and just open enough to get through all those sessions of awkward nudity while still being able to laugh about it over lunch afterwards.

Flint ended up getting arrested again not long after I discovered I was pregnant. I had an added reason to hope the embryo stuck: my source of sperm was being held hostage by the state for an unknown period of time. To repeat the procedure would mean waiting for the courts to arrive at a decision in their own time, and rest assured that my fertility was not one of their concerns.

Say what you will about the choices that I made to bring this kid into being, but you have to admit that if nothing else I secured a pretty good origin story to tell. Scotty always told me how the kid comes into being doesn't matter—it's what happens after they're here that's significant. And of course he's right. Maybe it's my desire to see my own life as an adventure novel that prompted me to go to such great lengths to provide my kid with an interesting first narrative.

To be fair though, traditional blueprints of how to live a life have never really worked for me in the past. My goal was clear as the horizon, but there were no signposts because there were no roads.

There was my heart as a compass
There was my word alone as bond.
There was the full moon.
There were stars in the sky.

• • •

For the next several months, however, the world continued to turn.

My feet walked the earth. I rode my bicycle to prenatal appointments. I walked through the cemetery by my house, at all hours of the day and night.

My feet were at sea. I spent a short bit of autumn learning to sail, off the coast of North Carolina. My morning sickness transitioned to seasickness. I witnessed a pod of dolphins racing our boat in the dark, green and sparkly from bioluminescence. I used an old peanut jar as a toilet or else just peed off the side of the moving sailboat. Once, during a solo shift at the helm in the middle of the night, I felt the first fluttering of the tiny stowaway in my abdomen.

My feet again walked the earth. I began packing. The house I was living in was being sold, and I knew I'd have to move sometime around my due date. While other expectant parents would have nested, I renovated a small room in yet another punk house, including installing laminate flooring. It seemed sometimes as if the work would never be done, yet there was this other preparation to make. I had successfully gotten this baby into my belly; now I just had to get it out of there.

The Lamaze Class
Welch Canavan

Would I be attending the Lamaze classes simply so it would be less awkward for my friend, Artnoose (a single mother), or would she be expecting me to put the knowledge to use during her labor? Initially I was so blindsided by the request that I didn't think to ask any clarifying questions. Despite being twenty-seven, I had never been in the proximity of any friends or relatives who were having children. The invitation to be present for the birth of her child was unexpected, as the idea of being present for the birth of any child was foreign.

I have eschewed much of the commitment that most of my peers have taken on by this age; I don't have a mortgage, a career, or even a long-term partner. The one thing that felt clear to me was that regardless of the exact role I was being asked to play this was one of the most "adult" things I had ever been asked to do.

Though I was willing and even excited—if not nervous—to take the classes with Artnoose, it was hard to figure out what role I would play; setting our unorthodox arrangement aside we didn't even know what was traditionally expected. Artnoose later confided in me that she initially asked me because she didn't think she would be allowed to attend alone, and that when the instructor began to talk about the large role the fathers were expected to play she felt bad about roping me in.

Anxious about what I had agreed to do, I told a lot of people. As expected my friends were excited for me, but I was nervous to tell my mother. Would she understand? Would she even believe that the child was not mine? My fears, however, were unfounded. Not only was she not suspicious or critical, she was supportive and proud, and she said it was "a very nice thing to do." Having set aside my minor concerns about the perceptions of my friends and family I was freed up to worry about what the other people in the class would think.

I was convinced that our classmates would not only be able to peg us as impostors—not a real couple—I had gotten so paranoid that I thought they would actively attempt to root out anyone who did not "belong." As Artnoose and I are a bit of an odd couple ourselves, and cultural outliers from what we anticipated would be the typical Lamaze class attendee, I thought our cover would be blown instantly. I was bracing myself for all manner of awkward encounters and preparing my antisocial answers.

It turns out that Lamaze classes are not attended by high-school movie archetypes. The demographic of those willing to volunteer two entire Saturdays to help ensure that their childbirth goes as smoothly as possible consists of kind and thoughtful people. It's unclear to me now why I let my imagination get the best of me; I'm still not sure what exactly I thought was going to happen. On the rare occasion that we did interact with other couples they were nothing but friendly. The one person who did ask enough questions to discover that I was not the father took it in stride and kept the conversation moving right along.

My preconceptions (based largely on movie portrayals) of what the class would be like were way off base. I expected it to be mainly a series of awkward physical exercises, but the vast majority of what we learned was the Lamaze philosophy of childbirth. It was one of the more educational experiences I've had in recent years. It began with the history of Western childbirth and ultimately arrived at conclusions that were in line with those of the most radical doulas I know: that medical interventions are used too commonly and can adversely affect the health of the mother and child. The instructor was not at all hesitant to acknowledge or bring up sexuality. (Did you know semen can help induce labor?) The language and materials (even the videos) made no assumptions that the partner of the pregnant person would be a man. The ideas set forth were surprisingly and comfortingly progressive. I left the class feeling like I had spent my time well.

• • •

Artnoose labored for forty hours and I was present for most of the waking ones. While I had prepared myself to support Artnoose in her effort to stick to her birthing plan—to avoid medical interventions and have a vaginal birth—it turned out to be unnecessary; as circumstances forced Artnoose to deviate from her plan the staff were incredibly supportive of her wishes and never pushed her or let on if they were impatient.

My father often told me of his cousin who suffered second-degree burns over most of his body after his crop duster had crashed. The old skin had to be pulled away so that new skin could grow, and my father, who was present for all of these sessions, said that he could feel the pain of the procedure. I hadn't thought about this story in years, but as Artnoose endured painful examinations and gripped my hand tightly I found tears welling in my eyes.

It was also mentally exhausting when the doctors, midwives, and attendants who remained hopeful that a vaginal birth would be possible were also careful to remind Artnoose that intervention might be necessary. It was a painful back-and-forth between hopeful signs and cautioning to not get our hopes up. It was hard to watch Artnoose's hopes get dashed and even harder to watch her begin to blame herself. I did all I could to remind her of what I knew to be true: that she had gone above and beyond in her effort to ensure a healthy birth and—as our Lamaze teacher said—despite these efforts sometimes interventions can not be avoided.

What all of the nurses, midwives, and Artnoose's sister Kelly said was true: none of it mattered once she was holding her healthy child. Bernard is here, he is beautiful, and I am rapt with attention as he grows before our eyes.

And Now, an Epilogue
Artnoose

Three years later, I sit typing in my dark bedroom, the sound of my son sleeping ever so slightly overpowering the noises from the occasional passing train, plane, or bus. This is one of the magical hours between my son's bedtime and mine, precious time spent having tea with housemates, reading, writing, or catching up on the towering mass of unfinished tasks for the day. Sometimes I am so exhausted that I fall asleep while putting my son to bed and wake up fully clothed in the middle of the night. Sometimes the magical hours linger for too long as I spiral into stress-induced insomnia that drags me into the early hours of the morning.

When I look back at my writings on the conception story and Welch's description of the birth, I am struck by how little I knew about things—about babies, about parenting, about anything. Who was it that casually hit up friends and acquaintances for sperm—was that me? How did I think I couldn't attend a Lamaze class by myself?

At the point during my son's birth when it became clear that a C-section was more or less inevitable, I cried because it was to be my only experience with childbirth, and I wasn't going to be a bad-ass punk goddess shoving a baby out of my vagina with nothing more than a positive mental attitude and black metal vocalizing. There was a flip side to intentionally having one kid though, and I remember telling Welch just before I was wheeled into the operating room, "I can do this once, and then I never have to do it again."

A fair chunk of my brain got used up learning parenting tasks that I may never need to know again. Just when I got kind of okay at swaddling my newborn into a neat burrito, he outgrew the need. I could cloth diaper my son half-asleep in the dark, and then we embarked on the road to potty training. When my son was using a toilet during the day and waking up every morning with a dry diaper, I realized that he wasn't the only one moving into a new phase.

In a few weeks my son starts preschool, and we both move into new chapters of our lives. Despite my misgivings about education, I feel like I'm in view of a finish line of some sort. I have spent the past three years of my life full-time solo parenting while also working. With no child support and very little child care, even. Do the math, and then throw your calculations away because somehow I made it work when it really shouldn't have. Although I have to toss my only kid into the sausage grinder of formal public schooling in order to get the child care I need to work enough to someday afford the luxury of separate bedrooms, I am about to have an amount of kid-free time each week that boggles my mind.

And I'll probably look back on this in a few years and laugh about how little I knew.

The Beating
Jennifer Lewis

'm lying on the operating table crucifix-style with leather straps binding my arms. The needle in my spine has erased my body. I am only a head.

"You won't be able to feel your lungs," my doctor says, "but you're still breathing."

Just then, something holds my breath. It feels as if I'm underwater. I can't wait to blindly touch the wall, but there is no coming up. I'm suffocating. The beeping intensifies. An alarm goes off. My eyes flutter into the fluorescent lights.

"Is she okay?" my husband asks.

"Her vitals are fine," my doctor replies.

I turn my head away from them and clench my face. I wonder if my body is sobbing, if my heart is beating.

"Can we untie one of her hands?" my doula begs. "So she can at least feel her breath?"

"I guess," the doctor says.

Someone unbuckles my right hand. I watch my fingers wiggle. I cover my mouth and miraculously, I feel the tiniest *hah* on my palm. I'm breathing as if I'm fogging up a mirror. My hand is a piece of glass. Suddenly, my temperature drops. A freezing sensation envelops me as if they were putting me on ice. I hear a knocking sound that is louder than the beeping and buzzing. I listen to it as I *hah*, *hah*, *hah* into my hand.

"Is there anything you can do about her shaking?" my husband asks.

"The shaking is normal," the doctor says.

I look at my husband, who is wearing scrubs but not a mask, and he looks incredibly young, too young to see his wife quivering on a table.

"Can we put a blanket under her elbow?" my doula suggests. "Her elbow is banging the table."

The doctor's face behind her mask is unfazed by my clamoring. She sighs. A nurse appears. Two folded sheets are placed under my arm. The beating stops, and strangely, I miss it.

"I'm going to make the incision now," the doctor says.

She cuts through my tissues, slowly carving her way to my uterus. When she reaches my abdominal muscles, she separates them with her hands like my mother, who is waiting outside, used to unbraid my hair.

"We have the baby's feet," says the doctor. "You're going to feel some pressure."

I am so grateful to feel anything that I almost say, "Hurt me." The doctor's hands knead my stomach like dough. She rises on her toes as she flattens me out. I can only feel the pressure. When the pressing stops, the pulling begins. Deadlock. The doctor versus the strength that's harboring inside of me. Its stubborn head stuck underneath my right rib. Its unwillingness to turn is why I'm being cut open. I don't know how I know this or even if it's true, but I know the doctor's hands are around the baby's ankles and I can feel her shimmying life out of my incision. The doctor takes one step back and pulls out something the size of the universe.

AAAAH, I breathe into my hand. I am an empty vessel.

The doctor lifts up this white mass of pulsing flesh, high above the blue sheet like a sacrifice, and asks my husband, not me, "Do you want to announce the sex?"

No one responds.

She repeats herself. She holds the baby that is not bloody but covered in toothpaste under the bright lights. Its white face tightens but doesn't make a sound.

"It's . . . it's a . . . ?" She angles its swollen genitals to my husband.

"Girl?" he says, and the doctor nods, yes. Color rushes to my husband's face. I had only thought it was an expression, but he looks like he might actually jump with joy. I close my eyes. I know somewhere I am deeply happy, but I cannot feel exhilaration—yet. My heart is cold. Even colder than the ice bath my girlhood is drowning in. Tears fall from my eyes.

"Why is she white?" I ask in the thinnest voice. "Is she okay? She hasn't cried. She isn't moving."

"It's called vernix," the doctor replies. "Babies that are early are still covered in it."

Somebody wraps her up. They hold her white goo to my face. I turn my neck. She has huge purple lips. My husband's lips. They hand her to him. His entire being grins into her barely opened eyes. The genetic blueprint passes, and it's instant love for them. I perform a smile and watch my husband, whose abdomen is still intact, bleed with happiness, while I bleed somewhere behind the blue sheet. And instead of being moved, I think: *I transformed, while you, you only watched*.

A team of eager scrubs come in and takes her to a plastic case. Somebody tells me that they are checking her vitals. Her vitals are good. My husband follows them. Leaves me. Rolls the baby outside to my mother. My mother is waving and holding the baby. She will still be holding the baby when I'm rolled into post-op, waiting for my body to unthaw. But for now, I'm left with the women—the doula, two doctors, and a nurse.

"That was thirteen minutes," my doctor says. "We have about thirty more."

I remove my hand from my mouth and sink to the bottom. I watch my doctor as if she is working on someone else. Her movements are small and her eyes are intense but not unkind. She tells me she is removing my placenta. I hear something wet drop into a bucket, splashing. She rearranges my organs, cupping them with her hands, and glues me back together. The doula begins rubbing my scalp, pulling me out by my hair.

I am closed up.

My husband walks beside me as they wheel my bed into another room. My nose itches from the morphine the nurse has injected, but I can't scratch yet. I still can't lift my arms or wiggle my toes. I see my mother rocking the baby, who is wrapped in a footprint blanket. Someone has placed a tiny pink-and-blue-striped cap on her hairless head. I look down at my limbs as if the heat of my stare will melt the anesthesia away. It doesn't. Someone could stick a knitting needle through my thigh and I wouldn't even know.

My doctor swoops in. She lifts up my gown, removes the maxi pad that one of the nurses has placed on top of my wound to absorb my blood, and smiles at my incision. She's pleased with her work.

"She's the best," the nurse says. "You'll hardly scar."

I narrow my eyes at the nurse and look at my doctor, who, two years from now, will remove her mask and kiss my cheek after she delivers my second daughter, vaginally. Two years after that, she will save my son, who will be born with the umbilical cord so tightly around his neck that his face is blue and bruised like a boxer. But at this moment, she asks, "Would you like to have him circumcised?"

I look at her so intensely that she catches her mistake. "I'm sorry," she says, "that was my fourth C-section today." She places my folder in the pocket on the door and walks away down the hall.

A lifetime later, my lungs start to take shape. I flutter kick my feet. Roll my ankles. Bend my knees. I flip my palms to the ceiling and make a fist. I bring my hands to my shoulders like I'm lifting an imaginary barbell. I open my jaw, one last *hah*.

"I'm ready," I say to my mom and my husband.

My mother hands me Grace, and I look at my daughter as if it's the first time.

Patchwork Family
Tomas Moniz

> "We understand the world by how we retrieve memories,
> re-order information into stories to justify how we feel."
> —Stephen Elliott

June 5, 1969

My story technically begins on June 5, 1969. The day of my birth.

I used to try to recreate the particulars of that day in my mind. Here's what I've been told: my mother in the hospital, alone, my grandparents waiting in the room beyond the delivery room doors. My father hundreds of miles away finishing up the last few classes of his junior year in high school.

No matter how I tell it, it feels like such an incomplete story, so instead I search for other beginnings.

Perhaps the story begins nine months earlier.

But the story of my conception is something I have to invent. I imagine asking, "Mom, do you recall the weather on the day you and my father created me? What were you wearing? What time of day was it? What did you feel like moments after?"

Awkward.

So instead, I tell it this way: in northern New Mexico, mid-September, it can be hot, the final clutches of summer, or it can be brisk, the first punches of fall knocking summer into memory. It was late in the evening. The sky clear. There is a lake just outside of town with picnic tables. Let's say, it happened there.

Why should I ask my mother? It's my story after all. Do I want to know her answers, her version of the story of my origins?

Maybe she can't remember details because they were like bunnies, one hot tryst blending into another. Maybe it was an ugly

41

experience for her, fraught with guilt, shame, coercion; perhaps my origin is a regret she still bears, perhaps it was an accident.

So I rewrite and reinvent the facts, the narrative, but no matter how I tell it, I can't avoid certain outcomes. I was born, my father was absent, my mother eventually left the state and his family behind.

Somewhere in all that, my story starts; it's what leads to the story of my family now: three kids, an ex-partner, some great years together, some painful ones, some regrets, some anger. But there's more to it than that.

I tell stories to try to make sense of it all, to explain how we got from there to here.

Summer 2012

There is a scene in the movie *Beasts of the Southern Wild*, in the midst of some reverie during the storm, the father leans back and looks at his child sitting off to the side, watching the adults play, and he asks, "Did I ever tell you the story of your conception?" It seems clear that he has, many times, but the child looks on waiting for the story, eager. You can see it in her eyes.

My children get that same look.

Their mother and I have been separated for years now. My youngest child probably remembers little of us together. The way we used to love each other, the way we cared for each other. I asked her recently if she did, and she shook her head no and then asked me, "Do you?"

It was a strange question I thought, but then, I realized the profundity of it. For me at least. Do I remember?

I do.

I used to believe I told the stories of my children's beginnings for them, so they could know where they came from, that though their family has changed and evolved, they were always loved, fiercely and without question. But I tell these stories for myself as well.

September 1997

Ella, you were born so quickly I barely had time to cry. Your mother wanted the Cadillac Birth, she boasted months ahead of her due date. After two natural births, she wanted to get the drugs! We'd high-five each other. What the hell could I say; I simply tried to be supportive.

We waited to the last minute to prepare for your birth. In fact, it was on the day of our hospital tour, your mother noticed weird contractions; she assumed it was just Braxton-Hicks or something. Eight hours later we were back in the hospital, being wheeled into the delivery room, and it was then she was told she was too far along for drugs; you were coming.

And you did. It wasn't until I held you and touched your cheeks that I cried. And you joined in as if on cue, screaming and crying with such determination and anger, a lot like how you are today.

September 2005

We sit all the kids on our bed one night in September. It's there we tell them their mother will be moving out in a few weeks. It's then we explain our family will be changing dramatically. Life will be changing. Our son nods like he understands. Our middle daughter just sits there. Our youngest immediately starts crying. Then we all do. It's the first and last time we all cry, together, as a family.

Sometime in 1980

After my mother found a place to live in another state, after my brothers and I started new schools, after we struggled to fit into our new neighborhoods and make new friends, my mother one night handed me the phone; it was our father. We hadn't seen him in a few months. He told me then that he would not be moving in with us like we were promised when we first moved. He was going to remain thousands of miles away in Hawaii but he'd come visit soon. My mom stood off to the side and couldn't really look at me. I passed the phone to my younger brothers. I walked to my room trying not to cry. It's all I really remember.

September 1990

I have told this story many times before. But it bears repeating. Making family is not something that just happens. It's a choice; it takes intention, dedication, perseverance. I sat in my car idling at the first intersection I came to on my way to get food for my girlfriend who was back at our house trying desperately to breastfeed our first child. She was twenty. I was twenty-one. Somehow that is important. Perhaps it explains why I sat there wondering what to do. Perhaps sitting there, I thought of my father and the distance there always seemed to be between us. Perhaps, I remembered my mother's face as I left her room that night, her look of anger and shame at not telling us the true story of our family's breakup until it was too late, her silence her only apology. Perhaps, I thought of the look on my girlfriend's face right after our son slid from her body, the wide-eyed look of a person who just discovered the meaning of life. Whatever it was I thought of, I decided then, right there, that I would not let my fear of fucking things up prevent me from trying to make this family work.

October 2005

We gathered all the kids together in their mother's new living room. Her face a mask of apprehension and fear. I choked down my anger at feeling left behind, at the fear that my family was breaking.

Families don't break, I told myself. Over and over.

I gathered them together. I put a candle in the center of us. I asked my partner, the mother of my children, the woman who was now choosing to start something new, to light her match, the long stemmed strike-anywhere kind. Then each of the children lit theirs, and then I did. We all lit two candles, one for her house and one for mine.

By the candle light I could see the kids' faces, both sad and unsure, but in the orange glow, I could see they felt safe. We all looked at each other and then blew out the matches.

October 2012

This is my story.

I was born on June 5, 1969. I am a father of three. But there is more to it than that.

I have a large extended family, a network of friends and a loving girlfriend. I've learned now that family is not static, not limited to one or two or ten possibilities; family is nebulous, shifting, consensual. It's difficult, can hurt, can push you out of your comfort zone. Family is the stories we tell to give ourselves roots, to make connections, to foster new possibilities. It's a patchwork quilt, a collage of hushed conversations, a montage of fading memories. Family continues to grow and change.

Here's an example, a new story I am working on.

My son decided to leave, needing, I think, his own space from his mother and his father. He lived a year in NYC and now has returned to his own apartment in west Oakland. We hang out weekly, sometimes sharing a beer, sometimes eating a meal, generally talking about the Oakland Raiders, but slowly we are moving towards more personal, difficult subjects. I am trying to close the distance between us. I want to ask him what he remembers of his youth, of the way our family used to be, of the way it is now. What all these things mean to him?

I want to hear his stories.

Just as, someday soon, I hope to hear my daughters' stories, who will be embarking on their own journey in a few years.

In fact, I can't wait to hear the stories they tell of what family means to them. And just as I have my own story, the stories they tell will be their own.

I'm sure their beginnings and endings and what it all means will be so different.

And shocking.

And surprising.

STAYING CONNECTED

Unlike the Brady Bunch
Zach Ellis

"We're all a little weird, and life is a little weird. And when we find someone whose weirdness is compatible with ours, we join up with them and fall in mutual weirdness and call it love." —Robert Fulghum

I live in a house with a front porch and a porch swing. I live in a neighborhood where cars slow down for people in crosswalks and drivers wave to one another.

In my neighborhood, families gather at the frozen yogurt shop. Kids play on the street together and parents e-mail one another to set up playdates at some godforsaken indoor play arena. At the park, parents bring extra things for their kids, just in case. Extra scarf or hat in case there's wind. Extra snacks in case there's hunger. Extra tissues or wet wipes in case there's dirt.

I live in a very sweet house with my partner and one and a half kids. The half kid is mine, because she's with her mom half of the time.

We are what's known as a blended family. For four people, there's a whole lot going on. I'm an Arabic, recovering alcoholic, wildly hirsute, unemployed queer transgender man. My partner is a Jewish queer social worker who is a single mother by choice and likes to think she's more high maintenance than she really is. Her daughter is a fierce seven-year-old, who could convince a bear to come out of hibernation, wrestle it to the ground in one fell swoop, and then gently tend to any wounds it might have. My daughter, also seven, cries a lot. She is very sensitive and would most likely be eaten by the bear. She feels everything deeply. She prefers reading Shel Silverstein and drawing ethnic princesses with special powers that usually involve a cat.

I imagined that we might become a queer Brady Bunch when we decide to move in together. I would be a combination of Carol,

Alice, and Sam the Butcher, while my partner would be Mike. Everyday would bring some dilemma to one of us, and by dinnertime, we would have logically figured out a solution as a family. End of story. Most days, the dilemmas are the same. Why can't these damn kids get out of bed on time? Why can't we all eat the same food for dinner? If I have to serve macaroni and cheese one more time, I may have to shoot myself. What part of the bedtime routine you've been doing for the last four years do you suddenly find so hard to do? Why *wouldn't* you want to wear a warm coat? It's twenty-seven degrees out. When did everything become so unfair *to you*?

Some days, we want to trade the girls in for an older model. A bookish twelve-year-old, who is interested in helping others and wears shirts that say things like "Girl Power" or "Queer Families Rule." A girl who wants to watch PBS instead of *My Little Pony*. A girl who can recognize Barack Obama faster than Strawberry Shortcake.

Some days we roll our eyes a lot. The parents anxiously awaiting bedtime, the kids annoyed at being asked to pee yet again.

We are very much unlike the Brady Bunch. Cindy never got ass rash because she forgot to wipe. Bobby did not mumble when he was trying to speak up for himself. Carol never needed alone time in the bathroom to inject herself with testosterone. And Mike never had to remind anyone not to flush the wet wipes down the toilet.

I come from a long line of shouters. People who feel they aren't really being heard or understood, so they raise their voices. My father communicated mostly with facial or hand gestures. The worst insult my father could give was to call someone "dummy" followed by the dreaded cutis gesture. It translates roughly to "screw your whole family." I was an expert with this gesture by the time I was seven. My mother communicated mostly through babysitters and 10 p.m. trips to Baskin-Robbins after an AA meeting.

I did not grow up in a family where anything seemed possible. The future did not really exist because surviving the present was the priority. I didn't know choosing my family was an option.

Dummy. Greasy Little Kid. Fatso. These were the names my birth family gave me and I've spent my life trying to escape them.

Zacho. Pacho. The Bald Guy. Daddy. Babe. Love. These are the names my chosen family has given me and I adore each one.

Dear Stranger, Thank You
Alicia Dornadic

Dear woman at the park who picked up and consoled my toddler when she fell off the slide. Thank you.

Dear stranger in the coffee shop who gave me a knowing look and half smile when G threw a fit in the middle of the floor and refused to get up. Thanks.

Dear another mother who held my baby at the trailhead while I peed in the portapotty (and whose kid serenaded us with the recorder). I owe you one.

To the woman who rolled down her car window and yelled at us in the crosswalk when she was making a right turn in her huge SUV . . . well fuck you, actually.

Dear twenty-something guy next to us on the train, thanks for being understanding when G wiggled, fidgeted, poked, hit, and overall consumed your personal space.

To the lady in Apt 3B who came to our aid when I was tear-streaked in the parking garage because G would just. NOT. get. into. the. car seat. In a Zen-like manner, "Do you have to go where you are going?" she asked me. And my answer, "Well no, actually." Thank you.

To my neighbor at the end of the hall ("the watchdog" I call her) thanks for always keeping "eyes on the street" and wholeheartedly commiserating, "Isn't it just *so* hard?!"

To the little old Armenian lady who lives a few blocks away and goes for walks with her hand-knit-sweater-wearing dog in the evening, thanks for looking out, thanks for chatting, thanks for being so warm and reminding me of my grandma.

Thank you to all the little kids who stop us in the street and say "hi" (really all little kids love babies), and to one in particular who won my heart by adding, "hi, I like your baby."

To the other moms I barely know, who are overworked and underslept, and return my 3 a.m. texts with an "I've been there too." What would I do without you?

And finally, to future strangers whose paths I will cross, the ones who hold the door, share a story or snack, help out in some other small way. Thank you.

Learning to Be Human
Jesse Palmer

When I became a father I discovered that the most precious things I'm learning aren't about babies or being a parent but about what it means to be human and what is important about life.

People treat you differently when you walk around carrying a cute infant. From the grizzled hardware store workers to the homeless guy spare-changing to the people in line at the grocery store—people's faces light up with happiness when they see Fern. Absolute strangers who would normally scowl or ignore me walk right up and want to talk. They are kind and even loving.

I keep thinking, "Why can't strangers on the street treat each other like this all the time?" Spending time with Fern offers a window into the kind of world I want to help build—a world organized around human interaction, caring and community—not the mainstream world which is so ground down by corporations and the state with all their inequality, violence, and misery that people avoid each other.

Watching how hard my partner Kristi works nursing Fern is humbling. Soon after Fern arrived, I started seeing all the adults I met in a different light—imagining each of us as a tiny baby being nurtured day and night by someone. Realizing how much energy and love went into each one of us, I started having floods of compassion for other people—complete strangers. Without wanting to repeat a cliché, Fern helps me see everyone around me as valuable members of a huge family.

So far we've raised Fern without a car because we live in an area where we can get by without one. Because she is still too little to go on a bicycle, I've mostly been walking for the last nine months. Moving slowly on foot gives me a lot of time to notice the world around me, what's going on with Fern, and what's going on with myself.

But moving slowly so you have time to notice things is increasingly rare these days. The capitalist/industrial machine is constantly speeding everything up and overwhelming all of us with sensory overload. As assembly lines and computers move faster and faster, the speed and inattention bleeds over to everything about how we live our lives.

Fast transportation is symbolic of this shift but also propels it. Raising Fern without a car makes life slower and more complex. We've redefined both what is possible and what is desirable. When the modern world makes so many things possible, it is up to us to figure out whether we want all that speed and power, or whether those kinds of freedoms are really cages.

Caring for a baby means a lot more hanging around than I'm used to and not being able to get as much done as I could without a kid, or having to get it done more slowly because I only have one hand free. Because of how I was raised, I've always felt a constant internal psychological pressure to be productive. By contrast, Fern is just about being. She doesn't feel that she has to justify her right to exist. She just gradually grows up. Spending time with Fern helps me kill the boss in my head and realize that I'm no different from her, or the cat, or a rock floating in space. We all exist and are legitimate because we exist. None of us have to prove anything to anyone.

At the same time, mainstream society sees babies not as tiny subversives bringing anti-capitalist inspiration to their parents but as a huge market for consumerism. It is amazing to see all the plastic bullshit that suddenly seems necessary to raise a baby in a modern industrial context.

The best part of spending time with Fern is watching her joyfully unrestrained face when she hears music, sees my face, or looks up in the sky. Seeing the happy and loving way Fern relates to the people and animals around us underscores how the world we live in as adults—organized around stress, ownership, competition, scarcity, consumerism, and shame—is imposed on us by cultural, political, and economic systems. These qualities aren't natural or inherent to humans as animals—we're born way better than the world we grow up in and eventually inhabit. Radicals and the counterculture are struggling to defeat these oppressive systems and create new structures aimed at supporting the underlying humanity I see in Fern, which prioritize the search for pleasure, engagement, and love. Spending time with Fern makes it easier to imagine a future where we'll all be more present and full of wonder and joy.

Only Bits and Pieces: On Adoption and Parenting
Mindi J.

This is my third attempt at writing this essay. I can be kind of a perfectionist when it comes to writing. It's what I put most of my energy into and what I basically revolve my life around. Perhaps a ramification of living under what could be deemed a capitalist regime, I want my writing to be "good." I want it to convey intelligence and wit. I want my articulation to be striking and insightful. I want to be seen as "a writer." I want people to be impressed.

I'm in what will positively be a never-ending process of unlearning these attitudes; I am a fucking writer. It's what I do. An extensive vocabulary and knack for weaving words together doesn't constitute "good" writing—but an ability to convey voice, be relatable, and find validation in self. To initiate and perpetuate internal growth of one's own self and the self of individual readers is of much higher value.

Despite trusting all of this to be true and accurate, in my previous attempts at constructing this essay, I've approached the project with the tact indoctrinated into me by public school, persinal study, and extensive reading. But adoption, indeed parenthood in all of its forms, can't be honestly reflected in such a way, and thus my attempts at crafting some well formulated essay describing these actualities were not only entirely in vain, but a disservice to the beauty of raw humin emotion.

This is a messay about adoption.

Another thing I've struggled with in regards to writing this is finding a balance between telling the story I want to tell, and feeling this inexplicable inner obligation to tell the whole story. The story I want to tell isn't the whole story, only bits and pieces of it. But telling the whole story is so tempting for me because I want so badly for people to understand, to the extent that I can offer, the choice of adoption.

Amerika, among other things, is the land of baseless, action-less opinion. When I mention adoption to different people, they all have something to say about it, even though they themselves usually have no experience or immediate persinal relation with it. And while many are supportive, many still are incredibly judgmental and insensitive.

I won't be telling the whole story here. There's not enough space in this publication or enough energy in my heart to regurgitate it all over again. Consequently, I have a few humble requests of you, dear reader:

I ask that you read on with an open mind and an open heart. I ask you to be patient. I ask you to trust the instinct of a mother and her love for her child, trust in her ability to make what she knows is the safest decision for her baby. I ask you to realize and respect and appreciate the immense amount of strength and selfless sacrifice it takes to make such an extremely heart-wrenching and difficult decision.

You may be thinking, "Shit, she sure is asking a lot. What do I get out of all this?" Regardless of my resistance and deep detestation to the capitalist state under which we exist, I insure that you will not be giving something for nothing.

If you consider all that I ask of you, much will be gained. If you continue reading with an open mind and an open heart, you will learn from someone who may have very different experiences than those of your own. If you practice the virtue of patience, you will become more humane and loving than you already are. If you trust me as a mother, perhaps it will enable you to trust other mothers in your life. And if you're a mother yourself, perhaps you'll find solidarity in my desire for trust, and be assured that despite not being perfect (as no mother fortunately is), you'll feel confident in knowing that you deserve this trust as well. If you realize, respect, and appreciate the immense amount of strength and selfless sacrifice it takes to choose adoption, the hope is that perspective will be gained. That a little faith in the capacity of a mother's love, a humin's love, might be restored. And if you can revel in the joy of wanting more, rather than feel cheated by me not telling you the whole story, maybe you can be reminded of the excitement that is life. Living another day unquenched yet enthusiastic for the zeal of being alive.

For the fear of sounding like I'm selling something to you, let the messay begin.

. . .

My son was adopted by two of the most spectacular people I've ever known when he was five weeks old. Up until that point, I cared for him primarily by myself. I breastfed exclusively and on cue, never giving him a bottle and never giving him a pacifier. I safely slept with him every night. And I cloth diapered him, washing the dirty diapers in the bathtub with homemade soap and hung them to dry by the heating vent.

Adoption was something I contemplated throughout my pregnancy. Not because of my youth, not because of a lack of money, not because of drug problems, and sure as fuck not because I "couldn't handle being a parent." These are all the reasons many people assume I myself chose adoption and also assume why other mothers choose adoption. People who don't even know me have asserted these things about me. This last one particularly hits a nerve, considering my care for myself during my pregnancy and care for my son once I gave birth. I was dedicated to a model of care that most average amerikans conclude is "too difficult" or even "impossible" and often "unrealistic" or flat-out "dangerous."

I considered adoption, and ultimately chose it, because I want my son to have a healthy, loving extended family. This is something I couldn't offer him outside of myself and a few of my close friends. I grew up with an alcoholic single mother who was and continues to be verbally and emotionally abusive. I suffered incest as a toddler. The majority of my extended family are either drug addicts or alcoholics or are abusive in some way or another.

Although I am a generally happy persin, feel I have a "good head on my shoulders," and am very excited and optimistic about my life and my future, it bothers me every day that I don't have a blood family to turn to for support, advice, or company. Although I felt confident in my ability to be a parent and a mother to my son, I did not want Burko to experience anything remotely similar to the feelings of hurt and abandonment that I felt growing up and continue to feel.

Despite all of this, I focused less on adoption during my pregnancy and devoted myself fully to my baby. I loved being pregnant, loved my growing fetus, loved the idea of being a badass radical mama.

I was hell bent on not only being absolutely nothing like my own parents, but also being as politically conscious as possible regarding parenting. I devoured "alternative" parenting books. I learned practically everything I know about caring for a baby from Dr. William and Martha Sears and from Jessica Mills. Just about everything else was firsthand experience with my newborn, Burko. He was the first baby I've ever held.

George and Nina flew from Oregon to Muskegon, Michigan. They came to my house and we met for the first time. It was the day before Thanksgiving. I thought that was a romantic time for an adoption to take place.

They stayed for about four hours, and I pretty much talked the whole time. I talk a lot when I'm nervous, and I wanted them to know all about Burko and his routines, cues, and preferences and maybe even to let me convert them to anarchist vegans.

I described to them Burko's sleeping schedule, his interests, his taste in music. I showed them how to use a cloth diaper. I discussed and encouraged induced lactation with Nina, showing her how to get Burko latched onto her breast. I told them all about Burko's rapidly developing persinality and described his temperament and physical abilities thus far. I showed them how to lay him down for a nap so he wouldn't quickly awaken and reviewed safe co-sleeping arrangements.

I described in greater detail than we had previously discussed (I corresponded with George and Nina about a week prior to the day they arrived for the adoption) my political beliefs and moral values, and how that related to my care for Burko and the ways in which I anticipated it would be integrated into the way he would continue to be cared for and parented. They didn't agree with me on every single detail but are on the same page for the most part and remain very sensitive, respectful, and considerate of my values and my hopes for Burko's upbringing.

In my pursuit for being understood by George and Nina as both a mother and an individual, as well as my mildly selfish desire to recruit them for the cause, I gave them a lot to read. Countless books and zines. *My Mother Wears Combat Boots*; *The Womanly Art of Breastfeeding*; *Eating Animals*; *Anarchism: Arguments For and Against*; *Witches, Midwives & Nurses*, and so many more. They had to ship two medium/large boxes back to Portland before leaving. In retrospect it was probably a little overwhelming for them, but I felt like, "Of course! These are my son's parents! They gotta know this stuff!"

We've continued dialogue about gentrification, gender socialization, white privilege, veganism, activism, and much else. I continue to share my feelings and fears and admiration and gratitude. I feel comfortable asking questions and making suggestions. We have an intentionally very open line of communication with each other about both our comforts and our discomforts. George and Nina have been two of my biggest supports regarding my grieving for Burko. They are there to lend a listening ear during my struggles and to celebrate in my achievements. They even put my report card on their fridge.

The evolution of our relationship has been miraculous. Watching them come into themselves as parents has truly been a pleasure. I talk to George and Nina several times a week. There is no script for an open adoption, but navigating this new terrain has thus far been a smooth and enjoyable road (although not without some heartache); we are becoming a family, and a pretty fuckin' radical one if you ask me. Creating this family with them has made me feel so blessed by the Universe, and I am beyond excited to continue this journey with them.

Reflecting on the last five months of my life conjures up a vast array of thoughts and emotions, but there is one thing that I especially want to mention.

At the time of my son's adoption, I was a month shy of twenty-one years old. I've lived my whole life in a small, very conservative city in the rust belt of Michigan. I haven't traveled anywhere besides southeast Missouri and a family vacation to Florida. I didn't graduate high school. I grew up in poverty, in an abusive home, and have lived in foster care as a ward of the state. I'm someone who fell through a crack in the system at an early age and apparently is still living there.

George and Nina are both in their late thirties. They grew up in relatively affluent homes, in Eugene, Oregon, and Northern

California, respectively. They both have master's degrees and progressive, professional careers. They've traveled around the world.

Generally, my attitude is to resist and combat social constructs, power dynamics, classism, and elitist bullshit of the like. However, I think there is an importance in recognizing and acknowledging these realities. I have lived an extremely different life than both George and Nina on many levels. Some might say a much less privileged life, a life with less opportunity and access. Nonetheless, I had a major part in teaching them the most valuable and essential skill a humin can possess and demonstrate: the skill of caring for a new, helpless persin. A persin putting all of their trust and optimism into their caregivers. Throughout all adversity, I helped George and Nina become parents not only in a literal/physical sense but in every sense.

This reality is incredibly profound to me. It is something I consider and attempt to learn from constantly. We live in a world infested with fierce competition, which teaches us that if we help someone or teach someone something we should either receive something in return or gain some kind of righteous social recognition. In the world we live in, we are witness to horrendous atrocities committed by humins on humins, a fact that is ingrained in virtually every aspect of our lives. However, the lessons I've shared with George and Nina are timeless. They transcend class and race and even age. Our ability to teach and to learn how to care for our babies and our children is proof to me that we're still humin. It's hope that we'll be okay. These truths and also the love that all three of us have the capacity to feel for Burko is evidence that the Universe hasn't given up on us yet. She's sanctioning us to teach, learn, bond, and to love each other. It is an inconceivable injustice to this gift she is entrusting us with to not pass it on.

Building a Community of Parents:
An Interview with Carla Bergman
Tasnim Nathoo

When I first met Carla seven years ago, I knew pretty much nothing about diverse movements to create communities of mutual aid, unschooling, alternatives to traditional models of education, or great zines like *Rad Dad*. Carla was the director of the Purple Thistle, a youth-run arts and activist space in East Vancouver, British Columbia. She lives with her partner, Chris, and their two kids, Zach and Lilah, and is involved in a bunch of projects related to building communities and creating counterinstitutions. She's the coeditor of *Stay Solid! A Radical Handbook for Youth* (AK Press, 2013).

When did you first realize that parents shouldn't have to do it alone?

When I was a kid, I realized, from my own family situation, that I needed mentors or adults other than my parents. Later, when I had my son, Zach, I brought that childhood awareness to my parenting—the idea that kids need more than their parents to guide, nourish, and inspire them. And, as a parent, I needed my own mentors—people to learn from and share ideas and struggles with. My first introduction to a community of parents was at a parent-participation democratic school.

How does your work at the Purple Thistle Centre connect to your parenting?

When my son, Zach, was eleven years old, I wanted to develop a community of peers for him as part of his own interests and development. Over time, many of the youth at the Thistle have been involved with my family, and my partner and I have supported many of the youth. This has built a community where, in many ways, my home is an extension of the Purple Thistle Centre. In part, this reflects a desire to deepen and broaden what the role of adults can be in caring for youth in our communities.

Can you tell me about one or two of your inspirations or guides as a parent?

That's a tough question because I have met so many amazing people over my fifteen years of community-building. But I will say that the folks that have resonated with me most are the ones who reflect what John Holt talked about many years ago. Holt is credited with coining the term "unschooling" and supported youth rights and liberation. I always return to a quote of his in my parenting and in my work: "Trust Children. Nothing could be more simple— or more difficult. Difficult because to trust children we must first learn to trust ourselves—and most of us were taught as children that we could not be trusted."

How would you describe your family?

On the surface, my family looks pretty "mainstream": nuclear, hetero-, white, two kids, a dog . . . But, once you look deeper, you'll see an extended family of about ten youths and adults who have keys to our home, a small community of friends engaged in care and mutual aid. I've come to define family as "a group of people who always have your back."

What's one thing you're proud of with respect to your parenting?

Making the decision to participate in a bigger community with my kids, I think, has helped me strive to be a better parent. I think it's important to get away from feeling like parenting is a private act that happens behind closed doors. By parenting in public, I've had to show both the good parts and challenging parts of being a parent. I think this has helped me remain accountable to myself and my values and that my kids have also deeply benefited from this. In the past few years, I've had a number of youths in their twenties come to me and say that they're inspired to be parents after witnessing my very public and politically informed parenting.

What's something you're still figuring out?

A lot! I tell other parents all the time, "Be kind to yourself. You will fuck up." I see it in myself and many other rad parents—getting caught in parenting guilt. We need to get over ourselves. We all make mistakes—let's recognize it, apologize, learn, and move on. In general, I am constantly reminding myself that there is more to learn and that the sign of a good parent is someone who is open, flexible, and responsive to the ever-changing needs of their kids.

Any tips for parents who are looking for ways to build a stronger community of parents?

Just do it—you won't regret it. Developing a community of any sort will benefit you and your kids. Start something, anything—a book club, a community choir, a dinner co-op, a child care co-op, an arts-based weekly class for all ages. Start small and see what happens. I think it's really important that we don't isolate ourselves and our kids. We need communities of folks of all ages and to get away from spending time solely with people who are our own age or our kids' ages. It continues to be super-helpful for me to meet parents who are raising kids who are slightly older than mine. They have been some of my strongest mentors and guideposts.

(Birth) Mothering from Prison
Rachel Galindo

Note from V. Law: This originally appeared in the zine *Tenacious: Art & Writings from Women in Prison* (issue 22). Each year, to recognize that over two-thirds of women in prison are mothers to children under the age of eighteen, *Tenacious* publishes a Mother's Day themed issue. Some facts to remember when reading this story (and other stories about mothers in prison):

—In 2007, over 147,000 children under the age of eighteen had mothers in prison in the United States.

—Children of incarcerated mothers are five times more likely than children of incarcerated fathers to end up in foster care.

—In 1997, Congress passed the federal Adoption and Safe Families Act (ASFA) requiring that if a child is in foster care for fifteen of the past twenty-two months, the state must begin proceedings to terminate the parent's legal rights. These terminations are irrevocable, meaning that the parent will have no more rights to the child than a stranger in the grocery store. Only three states make exceptions in the case of incarcerated parents.

—Given these circumstances, one can see open adoption as one of the few ways that incarcerated mothers might be able to maintain long-term contact with their child(ren).

To get a copy of *Tenacious*, send $3 (well-concealed cash or a check/money order made out to V. Law) to:
V. Law
PO Box 20388
Tompkins Square Station
New York, NY 10009

Though I have a son, I have never had to roll up my sleeves for diaper duty or bribe him to eat certain foods. I was not the one to decide what kind of classroom he will sit in for the next few years, and I am not able to cheer for him as he runs up and down the soccer field. Because I have been incarcerated since early pregnancy, and since I chose for my now-six-year-old son to be raised in an open adoption before he was born, I have not had many common experiences of motherhood.

Technically I am a birth mother, a title I was slow to warm up to. For a long time, it sounded to me like the name for a baby-producing robot. Although my son knows me as "Rachel," simply enough I have played my role as mother in choosing adoption. I was able to choose an open adoption, which allows me and his father (and our families) to keep in contact with him and his parents. My incarceration was a large factor in our adoption process and still influences our relationship. Along every step of the way, we have had to take into consideration how my separation and imprisonment plays into how much we are able to be involved in each others' lives and in what ways.

Like other mothers in prison, I deal with severely limited contact with my child. I have to limit expensive phone calls ($4.60 for ten minutes), send/receive written messages, mail out crafted gifts as special gestures, and rely on updates from others. Since my son lives a few states away, he and his parents are able to visit every couple of years. This situation is frustrating, can be depressing, and sometimes I grieve for a lot of experiences I don't get to have with my son because I am locked up.

It is largely in mind, thoughts, and memories that my son remains a part of my daily life. A ten-minute conversation with him lasts for weeks! Every form of contact I can have with him is valuable and that encourages me to be active within the confines of my position as a birth mother in prison. Even in limited forms, my efforts to connect reinforce a bond with my son and his parents. I believe this is true for other incarcerated mothers. We must fight to reach out to our children despite state-imposed barriers. While sometimes this involves directly challenging policy, it always means doing what we can to connect. We must know that we are worthy of being called mother, even with felony convictions.

Some may not perceive the ways we can parent. Others may not believe we should play a role in our kids' lives because we are in prison. However, it should be acknowledged that we should, can, and do parent from prison. There are challenges, but our being in prison is a more urgent reason to be consciously active in reaching out to our kids. Parenting from prison may include cooperating and communicating with our kids' current caretakers. Also, I encourage those who are in the lives of children with incarcerated parents to be supportive of efforts to cultivate and maintain parent-child relationships.

If being incarcerated is traumatic, and if having a loved one in prison is traumatic, imagine how it is for children with parents in prison. Imagine what it means to children to experience their parents as a sustained presence in their lives, even with the given limits of prison. Regardless of what we have done, and whether we are serving a few months or twenty years, we still have a place of significance in the minds and hearts of our children. We can parent from prison by offering honesty, love, support, and open communication. This is crucial in ensuring a foundation with our kids, whose role in our daily lives may grow once we are released, or in one way or another in the future.

As a birthmother, I say this: We each have our own set of circumstances to contend with, but we should not let the additional difficulties and conditions of being an incarcerated parent keep us from doing whatever we can to connect with our children.

Daddy Thoughts: Lose Yourself!
Robert Liu-Trujillo

You know that feeling of actually letting go? It is the feeling of writing so many words that you can barely get them out fast enough. It is the feeling of making a jump with your bike so high you're afraid and in awe at the same time. It's the feeling of hearing a song that changes you. You can't explain it, but you want to hear it again. You want to learn the words, the melody, and the chord changes. I have been afraid for my life and the happiest I've ever felt all at once. I've smiled, cried, and shouted at that feeling of discovering something that instantly was me.

I feel pretty happy to have seen a glimpse of that happiness in my son. As he played "air guitar" to his favorite song, I stopped to realize he was "letting go" and finding himself in this song. But wait, let me back up.

Music is a universal language. Almost every culture on this planet shares a form of melodic genealogy. We play music that shares stories. We play music to mourn or when we are sad. And we play music that makes us elated and engulfed in the moment. I come from a musical family. We don't have any famous musicians that you would know of, but we listened to, danced to, sang along with, or played some form of music for a very long time. I know this to be true because when I was a kid it was all around me. In the car stereos of relatives, the voice of my parents, the hum of my grandfather, and the backdrop to so many memories. I have a love for music from many places and I have always sung to my son, whether he wanted to hear it or not. I played CDs, mp3s, and records for him. I let him put the record on the turntable, scratch it, stop it, and let it play again—much to his delight.

His mom and I always played music for him, so do his grandparents. But it wasn't until he heard Hendrix that he began to repeat the words back to his mother and I. His great uncle bought him a guitar and he learned a bit about playing it. He lost interest for a while and then picked it up again later by way of animation and commercials that made use of old '80s pop songs. One song in particular he could not get out of his head and would sing it, look for it on YouTube, and ask me if I knew the band. So, I decided I would take him to the record store, as my dad took me many times (thanks, Dad), to look for this song. I knew it but hadn't heard it since the '80s.

The record is "We're Not Gonna Take It" by Twisted Sister, a New Jersey group that got its start in New York clubs in the late '70s. Whenever he hears the record he loses himself. He shouts, he nods his head, he hits his hands against whatever is nearby. Several times he's invited my fiancée Joy and me to his room (after I got him a CD player to play the record) to "rock" as he calls it. He hands me a tennis racket and proceeds to rock out. And it was in one of these rocking out sessions I was so happy to see him just lose himself, to enjoy the song without any reservations. It was another lesson from this little one to enjoy the moment, the song, and life. Right now.

Sometimes I get tired after a day working or just from life and just want to sit and do nothing. But he reminds me that there is still much out there to discover, to love, and to celebrate. It makes me daydream of those afternoons when I pedaled as fast as I possibly could, rode down a huge hill, or heard the original sample for a beat I'd had on repeat. It is "losing yourself" even if just for a moment.

Deep Roots, Wide Branches, and a Place in the Sun
Dawn Caprice

Raising children is an uncertain undertaking at best. For those of us whose gardens grow on the edges of our society and in its cracks, in its margins and borders and queer spaces, it's more uncertain still. I don't need to tell you that the world we inhabit is vastly different from the world our parents knew when we were young, and theirs from the world of their own parents. Our children's world will be far different still, in ways we likely can't even imagine.

My own family, faithful Mormons, did their best to resist what they saw as the tempests of a world on the brink of their god's Second Coming. They avoided television and microwaves but were early adopters of the personal computer. They soundly condemned all forms of "immorality," up to and including the spandex-clad Amazons of supermarket fitness magazines, and insisted that women's work was to birth babies while men wielded the power of god. But they taught, by word and example, that all people were brothers and sisters regardless of class or race or culture. They homeschooled several of their children—including me for many years—in part to ensure that their faith was an integral part of our education. I don't agree with many of their choices, but they made them with courage and a burning desire to raise their children as best they knew how.

I'm far from the sheltered orchards of my childhood now, and though I'm not looking for any deus ex machina ending, it's clear that the winds of change are blowing hard. My own children are little more than saplings now, and like many others, I wrestle with how best to nourish their growth through the coming storms. As trees in a forest share resources through their roots and gossip through the birds in their branches, I offer these meditations in the hope that my children and yours will benefit from the exchange.

A storm of my own began a few weeks ago when I went with my daughter to visit her kindergarten, drop off her supplies, and meet her teacher. Sending kids off to school is enough to raise any parent's protective hackles, but the daggers in the other parents' eyes when they caught sight of me were sharp enough to skin a bear. Despite my best efforts to present as a sober, respectable citizen, the suburban moms of Beaverton, Oregon, just aren't ready for a world in which a parent can wear both a dress and a beard. Their eyes seemed to carve fears of kidnappers, child molesters, and worse in letters of fire and ice on my transgressive skin.

I cried all the way home, across two counties (my daughter's school is located near her mother's house). It wasn't the other parents' reactions that bothered me—I know how to keep my head high—but I worry that my daughter will face teasing for having a dad who wears skirts. I have other fears, too—of the grinding tedium that my daughter faces under those fluorescent lights, of the soul-crushing hours she'll spend learning the hundreds of tasks that Oregon's Common Core standards dictate she must master in kindergarten, of the dangers she faces in navigating the cattle-chute of public education with her oh-so-magical soul intact. And I'm afraid that at the end, she'll have been prepared for adulthood in a world that no longer exists.

So why is she going to school? Her older brother has never gone. His curriculum, for what would be fourth grade, contains exactly zero standards. He has never taken a standardized test, but he reads voraciously, explores his world with a scientist's careful eye, and asks questions—about physics, history, biology, and philosophy—that even my own endless reading leaves me hard-pressed to answer. He's never wanted to go to school, and so there's never been a reason to send him. I worry about his social life, of course, but he's polite, gentle, and makes friends easily, so I don't worry too much.

My daughter is going to school because it's been her dream since she knew what school was. She's going because her mother and I know we can rely on each other to give her the support she'll need. She's going because we both believe that all children sense what they need and reach for it, that they can feel the subtle shifts of the world and respond to them instinctively.

Adults are thick-barked and more firmly rooted; it is our job to provide shelter, but our children must find their own light, growing out of our shade. All our theories, self-grown or developed by experts and ancestors, can only tell us what's worked in the past, but our children grow for the future. We and the communities we form are the forest that shields them from the wind; our own roots are the matrix that secures the soil; our ancestors—and theirs—are the soil itself. The deeper our roots sink toward bedrock, the more firmly our children are held.

For me, this means owning my own stories and the stories of my family and my culture, respecting our strengths as I recognize our failings, and passing these stories on to my children. It means maintaining a stable lifestyle even as my heart yearns to chase my horizons. It means learning to live in harmony with the land around me and beneath my feet, and lending my voice to the forces that would prevent its destruction.

And just as healthy ecosystems rely on the integration of countless species, our children thrive on the richness and diversity of our own social networks. This is one of the lessons the mass culture is currently struggling to learn; for those on the margins, it's a reality of survival. In my life, that means actively seeking connections with those whose stories are different from my own. It means getting to know my neighbors despite my natural reclusiveness. It means helping those who ask for help, so far as I am able, and asking for help when I know I can't handle things on my own. It means learning from and respecting every culture on its own terms, and lending my voice to prevent others' from being silenced.

Finally, children, like trees, need space in the sun, and this is a hard lesson for any parent to learn: how to step back, how to give our children room to breathe, to experiment, to make mistakes, to reach for the skies in their own way, to live their own truth. For me, this means that my son wears camouflage T-shirts while my daughter wears pink skirts and sparkly boots, because that's what they want to wear. It means swallowing my fears and sending my daughter to kindergarten, as well as wearing my most masculine clothes on her first day so she could make her own first impression. It means exposing my kids to other worldviews and beliefs than mine and letting them make their own choices. It means letting them see me fail, see me try, see me reach toward my own light. It means dealing with my own demons and working with those who would heal the world's.

I don't know what the world will be in ten or fifteen years, as my children become adults. Some things are relatively certain: the climate will continue to change; fossil fuels will continue to run out; people will live their lives and adjust as they can; they will die. Beyond that, who can say whether my children will be better served learning the STEM subjects or survival skills, witchcraft or computers? They know better than I what they need, and my job is to show them what's available and give them what I can.

Wide branches, deep roots, and a place in the sun—these are the best gifts I can give my children to help them weather the coming storms.

List 1:
How Fathers Can Help Fight Patriarchy

1   Believe in other men's ability to parent. Talk to other men about fathering.

2   Strive to do more than half of the labor of raising a kid, building a family, and maintaining a home. This is part of living our feminist values in our family and being a good role model for our kids and their friends.

3   Do your kid's hair, cook, clean, and other responsibilities that "women" usually do that are also intimate bonding experiences.

4   Pick flowers for your little boy and fix stuff around the house with your little girl.

5   Play pretend.

6   Listen when a child says stop. Then stop!

7   Encourage the boys in your life to enter the worlds created by girls during play, and encourage them to invite girls into theirs. The invitation is the key. Stop them if they try to impose their worlds.

8   Teach your kids how to do the stuff you know how to do, regardless of gender.

9   Talk with other parents about how they practice feminism in their parenting and families. This is useful both to gather insights and to help normalize the conversation between parents, particularly for dads.

10 Talk with your kids about mainstream beauty standards.

11 Vocalize your support of breastfeeding moms.

12 Read books about feminism, to your kids and to yourself.

13 Say "Everyone gets to choose for their own body" often enough that your kids think of it as one of your catchphrases.

14 Use "feminism," "patriarchy," "misogyny," "sexism," and related words in your everyday conversations with kids, and take

time to listen to their use of those words. They have brilliant insights about the oppression they see.

15 Talk to your kids about how women used to be treated when talking about history (and about how a lot of change is still needed).

16 Commit to eliminating violence, aggression, and force with women and children.

17 Teach your kids about mansplaining and male entitlement and why it hurts all of us.

18 Teach them about male privilege at an early age. Teach them to use their privilege in the service of others until the time they are ready to attempt to eradicate it.

19 Let your kids hear you defend your feminism. At first you might feel like your talk about feminism is forced and mechanical, like swimming against the current; in time, we will find our own voices, develop our confidence, and speak from our hearts in ways that are both healing and empowering to ourselves and our families.

20 Once a day or once a week, talk about an example you saw of patriarchy or sexism.

21 Don't shame kids of any gender for being girly. Feminine gender expression is as valuable and wonderful as any other! Read books like *Princess Boy* to help normalize and celebrate boys who wear dresses and embrace feminine gender expressions. While "tomboys" are generally accepted, it's good for all kids to see that boys like girly things too.

22 Don't let your kids hear you make generalizations about people based on gender. "It's a boy thing" and "It's a girl thing" harm kids of all genders. If and when you do say it, be honest and compassionate with yourself, saying something like, "Why did I say that? Is that actually true? I don't think so."

23 Reject the pink/blue color code.

24 Do not assign female gender/sex traits to inanimate objects. Your car is a car. Do not refer to it as "her" or "she" or any other anthropomorphized designation.

25 Talk about stereotypes with your kids.

26 Combat images of bumbling fathers in the media. Talk to your kids as you encounter these stereotypes. Dadcott Adam Sandler movies!

27 Make a point to ask if there are changing tables in the men's restrooms everywhere you go.

28 Speak up when you see unwanted tickling.

29 Teach consent every day. Teach your child that we need permission to touch each other's bodies. Raise our daughters to be safety conscious and to have a healthy self-esteem against the onslaught of sexism and misogyny. Raise our sons to promote consent culture.

30 Make a plan for how you are going to teach your kids about rape. Men, have conversations with other dads about this and ask them what they're thinking of doing. Be ready to share about why you think it's so important that we talk with all our kids about it. Again, our goal is to create a culture of men working together to support each other to end misogyny and generate feminist power.

31 Men: tell your kids when patriarchy hurts you. Be emotionally open about challenges and difficulties—times when you were told "act like a man, don't cry"—and how they impacted you. Our example of taking emotional risks will speak louder than encouraging our kids to do it.

32 When you do something wrong, let your kids see you own up to it rather than blaming someone else.

33 Don't argue or get defensive when women talk about their experiences.

34 Listen when women are talking.

35 Teach sons (and daughters, too) to listen and ask questions.

36 Sex positive is a family value. When sex comes up, be open, honest, and positive.

37 Work with your child to write a letter to a politician, local newspaper, or blog about an issue that affects women in your community.

38 Figure out how you are going to talk to you kids about abortion and reproductive justice.

39 Explain to your teenager why you are pro-choice.

40 Talk to your kids about how to stand up when they see someone treated badly.

41 Discuss unfair power with your kids.

42 Teach your kids about a feminist activist, famous or not.

43 Learn and teach each your kids about Mujeres Libres, the Combahee River Collective, Riot Grrrls, and other movements for women's liberation.

44 Don't be an asshole to women or girls. It is not calculus. Treat women/girls with respect, always, but especially in the presence of young boys. You'll be all the example the boys in your life need.

45 Teach them that sensitivity, caring, and empathy make you strong.

46 Call out gender/sex-based discrimination in public—if it is safe to do so. If it is not acceptable in the home, it damn well shouldn't be acceptable in the world.

47 As a family go to demonstrations and community events that support feminist politics and use the experience to talk with your kids. Think about ways to make it as enjoyable for your kids as possible, whether that's going with friends or getting a special treat afterwards that makes it part of a fun family outing.

48 Talk with one or two close friends about ways you can support each other and share in the joys, difficulties, heartbreaks, and beauty of liberation parenting.

49 Strive to be compassionate, forgiving, and reliable in doing this work. Beating yourself up for mistakes and missed opportunities will lead to burnout and self-hatred, neither of which we want for ourselves or to model for our kids. Be the parent to yourself that you are for your kid, believing in yourself, ready to pick yourself back up with a pep talk about what we learned so as to be better prepared next time.

50 Men, be expressive with your love and tenderness. Strive to be emotionally open and fluent in love, appreciation, and gratitude. Patriarchy teaches men to be fiercely competitive with other men and to be oblivious to the contributions of women. Naming and speaking our love, appreciation, and gratitude helps counter this.

Ask a Dad

Dear Rad Dad collective: What is your advice on how to talk to kids about sex in a feminist, sex-positive, loving, developmentally appropriate, and safe way?

Robert: The way I had the talk with my son (age nine) was on a normal family day with him, his mom, and me. I plan to have the talk continually because sometimes he'll mention things or we encounter it in a movie or something. We told him we had similar talks with our parents about sex and that his mother and I are here to answer questions about anything sexual anytime. Some of the topics we talked about are personal space, private parts, how our bodies change, safe sex, what consent means, the difference between making love and sex. His mother and I talked about our experience as a heterosexual couple and how he was created, what went where, and how. I gently stated that sexual relationships are between adults, but that we could talk about it no matter what age he is. I try to let him know that both him and the act are super special.

Tomas: Honestly, playfully, respectfully. Those three words are what I ask myself about any difficult parenting situation—drugs, violence, schoolwork, friendship drama, sex. I remind myself to be honest, playful, respectful. Let me explain. Honest. I know how loaded and scary and sex-negative our culture is, which doesn't mean I pretend sex isn't a complicated, scary thing. But it's also a natural thing. A wonderful thing. A significant experience in the growth from adolescent to adult. I want to be honest with my children about it, to encourage them to research and seek out information, to feel empowered by asking questions rather than feel shameful or silent. I want them to recognize the sexual violence that our culture is plagued with and how to protect and inform themselves about their choices and their voice. Playful. Sometimes parenting is so serious, as if all we do is dispense wisdom or warnings from on high. I want to use my mistakes, my assumptions, my own struggles as an opportunity to model and share. I've done some stupid shit and I remind myself to lighten up. Respectful conversations, though, are the key. I respect their boundaries, their interest level (I try not to lecture but converse). I try to ask what they want to know and what they already know or think they know. I think this actually doesn't answer your question. But I hope it encourages you to trust yourself and your child and begin those important conversations.

Fivel: I love this question because it essentially answers itself. That said, we should talk *with*, not to, kids about sex and sexuality in a feminist, sex-positive, loving, developmentally appropriate, and safe way. Developing a solid foundation of trust is key, and encouraging your child to ask questions is ideal. Try asking them questions about what they are curious about. Or read a book together that fits your kid's developmental stage. And despite developmental similarities between kids, age-wise, children are obviously unique in their ability to understand certain material, so I would keep that in my mind. Fortunately for rad parents with kids of all ages, there are great resources out there. I have personally used these books and websites with my son, at various times in his life:

    X: A Fabulous Child's Story by Lois Gould (out of print but fabulous because it breaks the gender/sex norm in kids' books)

    What's the Big Secret? by Laurie Kransy Brown and Marc Brown (hetero/cisgender-focused but otherwise good for the younger set)

    Everything You Never Wanted Your Kids to Know about Sex (But Were Afraid They'd Ask) by Justin Richardson and Mark Schuster

    Scarleteen.com (sex ed geared toward teens as the title suggests)

    S.E.X.: The All-You-Need-to-Know Progressive Sexuality Guide to Get You through High School and College by Heather Corrina (Corrina founded and runs Scarleteen.com)

    Sex: A Book for Teens by Nikol Hasler (Funny and accessible writing style)

Jonas: I have a bit of a journey ahead of me yet (my son is almost seven months old as I type this), but it's one that I often consider. Admittedly, the smallest part of me hopes that he's going to be a shy little nerd like his papa was, and this talk doesn't come up until, oh, about when he's ready for college. Realistically, whenever the talk happens, I'd want to him to know that sex is a wonderful act but one to be accompanied by total respect and consent. I'd want him to know that there's no shame at all in exploring his body and sexual needs, but that exploring them with another person requires from each a great deal of maturity. I'd follow with a long talk juggling both sex positivity and the rape culture we have to dismantle. I'd do my best to put it in a way that didn't scare him but made him aware of the weight his actions could carry—emotionally, physically, and socially.

PART 2

Redwoods

When I was young, I dreamed of being tall, big, and arrogant like all the men of my family. I wanted to be the one who presided over those who were smaller, the one who chided others to pull it together when they were weak, the one who never ever fell down. But walking in the redwoods, I feel childish, ashamed at my misguided sense of height, of what makes something tall or big or a man. These trees find power in giving: protecting what is smaller with their canopy, housing safely in their branches whole ecosystems like a father's hug, and even when they fall, even in their demise, new life, little things, take root, seek shelter, find a home in their decaying bodies.

Toenails

My daughter wanted blue and green on every other nail. "Of course," I agreed like it was something everyone would want. "We all should have different color nails," I professed and painted green toe, pink finger, pink toe, green finger. It was when she asked me if she could paint mine that I balked. "No," I said, "because . . ." And I stopped. I looked at her. I thought, because I'm chickenshit, because of playing basketball at the park, because of drinking at bars, because of talking to other men. "Okay," she said and walked away like she realized everything about me was a lie.

GENDER

Warrior Training Starts Young:
On the 20th Anniversary of Riot Grrrl
Shawn Taylor

Then: Riot Grrrl did not hit me like it did the women in the crew. For them, it was an (albeit lily-white) explosion. It was a profound shifting in how they publicly expressed culture. I noticed it in bits and pieces. The women who once were the backbone of our zine-making and distribution empires now could not be found to bum a ride to Insty-Prints to make copies. They used to emcee—introducing the bands. They now had bands of their own, and they were playing better and with more ferocity than the dudes they once supported. It wasn't like it was an all-out gender mutiny. It was not a split, but a forced reckoning—we had to notice the girls. They were no longer support staff to the indie/punk-culture male ego DIY-industrial complex. They were Riot Grrrls.

Well, not exactly Riot Grrrls. Many of the women of the crew were waiting for a critical race element that barely manifested. They were Riot Grrrls, but they were also young women of color. Many of them had a difficult time reconciling the two. They were at a crossroads between bell hooks and Bratmobile, having a difficult time discerning which had the greater pull, and which would be a more useful politics for their futures.

Needless to say, this played havoc with trying to hook up. Tattoos, Doc Martens, and being surly were no longer enough. To step correctly to a woman, we had to be versed in women-centered politics and cultural implication. We just couldn't know about certain bands or artists, we had to know why they were important. And if these bands or artists had even a tangential tendril of misogyny dangling, they got the boot. They were excised from the new cultural canon, only to be spoken of in whispers of disgust.

This new reality forced me to understand what a feminist-politic meant. Having grown up in a profoundly matriarchal environment was not the education you might think. It was a given that my aunts, mother, and the over-boss that was my grand-mother were running shit. It was just how it was. But when con-fronted, or asked for support, I had no idea what I could do to back up this phoenix rising among many of the women in my life. But I would learn. I had to learn. I had to act. It was Revolution Girl Style Now, for real.

I do not feel that I am in any way qualified to talk about what feminism is. What I am qualified to impart is how I learned to be an effective ally (and eventual feminist). This consciousness trans-formation was not as hard as it sounds. I started with a few simple rules:

1   I removed woman/girl-demeaning language from my vocabu-lary. This was the most demanding piece of my transforma-tion. Hate and disrespect are so insidious because they colo-nize your language and reify their negative influences every time you speak.
2   If anyone around spoke disrespectfully to or about women and girls, I'd speak up. If speaking up didn't work, I'd knuckle up.
3   I shut up and let the women in my life be the experts on their own existence. I followed their lead to address their needs.

I still follow these rules to this day—well, I don't knuckle up as much as I used to because my ally vocabulary is light-years more so-phisticated than it used to be. But I will put foot-to-ass if I need to.

In retrospect, I can experience the effects of the Riot Grrrl explosion as advanced training in how to be a good partner and a good father to my daughter.

• • •

Now: I'm writing this circa twenty years since my initial encounter with Riot Grrrl (and three days after my daughter's fourth birth-day). I write this with an aching nostalgia. There was an urgency that popped off back then, a sense of kicking norms in the crotch and striking out into wholly brand new territories. New maps of expression were being drawn, a new language being spoken. I don't feel that now. My daughter came home one day singing Justin

Bieber, talking about wanting to be a princess, and knowing who Nicki Minaj was. Are you kidding me? What happened to all the Bodysnatchers, the Selecter, Bad Brains, and M.I.A. that I've been feeding you? I felt all of who I was, who I wanted my daughter to be, spill out into a murky puddle of senseless pop stool. I know she's only four, but still. Warrior training starts young.

It is a very difficult parental realization when you have to come to terms with the idea that your children are people. People with their own wills, desires, and tastes in everything from food to the culture they consume. Parents are also in constant battle with the influences that your kid runs into when you are not around them—when there are at school, friends' homes, or child care. You can expose them to all you want, but they are in charge of whether or not they give a damn about your recommendations.

This was a bit disheartening, but I no longer have to worry about this, or about going overboard with trying to expose her to all of the things that I think are vital and necessary. The only two things that I have to do are act and speak with respect and integrity. My only mission is that every word I utter, every action I take, affirms her as a girl but does not lock her into being so. She sees and hears how I speak to her mother, and the other women in her life, and finds comfort and solace in this. I am in no way a saint. My latent misogyny can flare up from time to time (usually when I'm not in love with myself or jealous of my wife's accomplishments) but I think I walk the feminist ally line often enough because my daughter will tell me how different I am compared to other daddies. She says this with a smile and a headbutt. No more validation is needed. My daughter shows me daily that what I say and what I do matter to her. She reaffirms that I am having both an affect and effect on her life. While she may have ripped my musical heart out by singing Justin Bieber, she repaired it—instantly—by singing "Monkey Man," the version by the Specials. Here is a different accounting of what I mean:

Once upon a time, my daughter wore dresses. Nothing too frilly, or pink, or taupe, just nice little sun dresses. Then, as she got older and started to have a say in what she wore, the great dress-rebellion of 2011–2012 began. After showing her photos of her in dresses (and noticing the turned-up nose as she perused the pictures) I asked her, "Why don't you like dresses anymore?" With no beat missed, she stared at me, "How am I supposed to save the world in a dress? I need a bow and arrow and a tiger." Revolution Girl Style Now. For real.

A Woman Who Is a Daddy to Her Kids
D.A. Begay

I was well into my thirties when my partner of six years and I signed ourselves up for parenting. And it was a signing up for, too. Since we are in a same-sex partnership, we didn't have the benefit of sperm whenever we wanted, so we opted for the foster care/adoption route. Our first child came to us as a two-year-old boy. We presented both of ourselves as his mothers, with the names Mama and Mommy. I tried on the Mommy title, but I was never quite at home with it. So, three years ago when we were given the opportunity to adopt a baby boy from my tribe, the Navajo Nation, I chose to become Daddy instead. To this day, my youngest son has never called me anything but "Da-da." This distinction put me in the "edgy" category with friends and my community. What was I doing? Was I aware that I was blending the gender gap? To be honest, I did what felt right for me. I didn't sit and ponder about the social and political implications of my decision as I am doing now.

I grew up in a very traditional home, what kids today would refer to as "old school": my mother stayed at home, while my father trudged off to work each day. My parents had defined roles, and they were not subject to revision. Both my parents succumbed to society's parental labels before they themselves had any children. My mother is a carbon copy of my grandmother; her role as Mommy meant she was responsible to feed us, clothe us, check our schoolwork, and make sure we were all clean by the time my father arrived home from work. My father started working when he was twelve to support his mother and sisters, so it was clear to him that a daddy's role was to work, to bring home the money so we could enjoy our standard of living. He would often use this phrase, "standard of living," with me and my brothers in passing, but he never took the time to explain what it meant, so I had only a vague sense that it was important and that we were under someone's standard.

As I unravel my own beliefs about what a mommy and daddy are supposed to be, I am jettisoned back to my childhood. Until the age of twelve, my mother considered me a mommy-in-training. However, my father was also more understanding than my mother when it came to my identity and sense of self. It sickened my mother that I was a tomboy, but my father took it in stride. He would even call me Sam when I thought I wanted to be a cowboy. I took it so seriously that I would write Sam as my name on my school papers. This concerned my mother because Sam was incongruent with the label she had attached to the inside of the little dresses she'd send me to school in. My father saw it all as harmless and necessary in figuring out who I was. My mother believed that a parent's role was to tell their child who and what they were.

My life's work has brought me to this incredible place of self-acceptance. I can go against the social fabric and be Daddy to my kids. In our own ways, my partner and I have roles, and we do not blend them. However, the difference is that we define what is encased in the roles and do not rely on society to tell us who is who and what is what. For example, I have a law degree and have had vast experience in the professional world, yet I chose to stay home full-time and raise the kids. This means I do the laundry, feed them, clothe them, and decide what activities consume their days. My partner travels all over the country and makes our standard of living possible. Yet she is Mama and I am Daddy. I will put my kids on the baseball field as my daddy did, but I will not brand my beliefs onto my kids. My oldest son wore a velvet dress around the house for a time when he was four because he was curious as to what it meant to be a girl. My youngest boy has hair almost as long as mine and is often referred to as a girl. I most often don't correct people. To me, at his age there is no distinction really.

I have never wanted to be someone who was overtly political. Yet as I grow older, I realize how crucial politics have become to our sense of identity. Everything seems to need a label in order to be understood. My partner remarked the other day how she was impressed that I was so proud to be a daddy. My son, who is almost three now, "outs" me wherever we go. While at his gym, where there are dozens of mommies with their children, he calls out "Dada," and immediately the moms begin to look around for a man. To him, I am Daddy. I am who he looks to for toughness and also for tenderness. We wrestle all the time. I try to teach him to take risks at every opportunity. I always try to be a courageous daddy to him. I am still afraid of spiders, yet my idea of courage includes being able to admit when you are afraid. So I step back whenever spiders are involved and let his Mama do the removal job.

We live in a system that seems bent on understanding through labeling. The problem is that we don't have the right labels or enough of them. Our labels seek to divide, not unite. Our labels seek to cause fear, not courage. Our labels seek to elicit shame, not pride. Our labels seek to domesticate the spirit in us that can only grow by being free. I've only recently realized, mostly through the reflection of my partner, that it takes courage to be a daddy to my kids. I see people unable to comprehend exactly what that means, which translates to me that I am not yet accepted. I am not accepted because they are unable to comprehend exactly what I mean, or what I stand for. Fortunately, my reality is not contingent on their acceptance, and my life is not suspended on someone else's belief system. I stand for freedom. True freedom has to do with the human spirit. Who stops us from being truly free? We stop ourselves. What does it mean to be truly free? I learn everyday that I have the power to believe whatever I want. I choose everyday to believe that I am free. I want to teach my kids this concept as well. I want them to know that to be truly free means to be truly ourselves. Like an undomesticated flower, I grow in the direction of the sun and have no worries about the past or fears about the future. I am in the present moment. And in this moment, I am a woman who is a daddy to her kids.

My Sex-Positive Parenting
Philana Dollin

I like to think of myself as a sexually-confident, queer cis-woman raising two children with my partner. I love my body and I have always been happy to use it in ways that are pleasurable to me and my partner(s). I recognize that I am privileged in this way. This privilege, to feel confident in my body, aware of feminist principles to guide my choices, comes in part from the way my mother raised me, and is something I want to pass on to my children.

To provide some context, a bit of background on my family growing up: It was common practice for my mother, sister and I to walk around naked in the house. We also used to feel perfectly comfortable climbing into bed with our parents in the mornings. Even with this openness, I was not prepared for this life-changing conversation. When I was nearly ten years old (a long while after all the typical anatomy lessons), my mother pulled me aside and asked me if I masturbated. "Ew, Mom!" I was both disgusted and fascinated by what she would say next.

"Well, it's a good idea. People enjoy pleasure. They enjoy pleasuring each other. But if you don't know what feels good to you, then it's hard for someone to help you feel good." Wow—still disgusted and fascinated. Like a car crash: something so awful you can't pull yourself away from it. Your curiosity gets the better of you despite feelings of fear, discomfort, or what have you. "When I was a girl, I was afraid that masturbating might mark me. Might change the look of my vulva or make me not a virgin. I didn't have anyone to tell me it was okay. I just wanted to tell you, it's okay." This talk was followed by a quick thank you, a red-faced blush, and a very brisk run as far away as I could get. However, I was also extremely grateful for the terribly awkward encounter. Cool! We feel pleasure and it's not just okay, it's good. Although I was not yet aware of the love-hate relationship that society has with women's sexuality, I still knew that some things were considered taboo and I had still experienced strange and negative conversations about masturbation in the schoolyard. What a relief that a reliable source should say that sex is supposed to feel good and that the notion of "practice-makes-perfect" applies to sex as well.

The notion of being sexually confident—a confidence I went on to develop through the knowledge I had gained about myself since that conversation with my mother, as well as an appreciation of my body and all it could do—is something I wanted to pass along to my daughter. In fact, I was so keen on it, that I decided to start "sex education" even earlier at my house, since the opportunity presented itself so easily.

When my daughter was two years old, she was openly exploring her body parts. Sometimes, in the bath, this would end with a sore vagina, stinging from soap. Or a small scrape from nails that I neglected to keep short enough. And when I would explain why her vulva or vagina was ouchy, my daughter hung on to my words with utter amazement.

My (female) partner is a nurse and I work in environmental health. So in our house there have always been a lot of biologically/scientifically correct dialogues of illness, bodies, etc. My daughter has always been very interested in her health and could be reasoned with on a good number of subjects if health was brought into the discussion.

On this particular day, she was zoned out with the fingers of one hand exploring her vulva in the bath while the other was holding her toothbrush to her mouth. I asked her if it felt good and if she wanted privacy for what she was doing. Yes and yes, was her response. So I closed the shower curtain and let her continue. Then, ouch, I opened the curtain to find her with her toothbrush between her legs. That's when I got the idea . . . I pulled out a little handheld mirror and told her to lie on her back. If she was interested, I would show her what it all looked like down there. She grinned from ear to ear as I pointed out her clitoris, urethra, vagina, labia, and anus. We reviewed it at least six times because she was so excited.

"Girls have three holes between their legs?!"

Pure amazement. I couldn't pry the mirror out of her hands if I tried. And for the next month or so, every bath became exploration time. She had so many questions. I provided answers the best I could. Since then, and ongoing, we have had amazing discussions about everything from consent, body autonomy and anatomy, to reproduction and digestion.

The arrival of our son brought a whole new dimension to these discussions. First, among many layers, it has involved learning to discuss male genitalia with proper words. Second, more important and more challenging (as my daughter's curiosity is very strong and my son is still too young to tell us what he is okay with), has been discussions about getting consent before touching another person in a way that might be uncomfortable to them. For example, the two kids bathe together and my daughter is constantly trying to find excuses to touch her brother's penis. In our house, this applies to everything from hitting to gentle touches of body parts that could be considered special. We use the simple phrase "it's my body" (and encourage our kids to do the same) for everything from unwanted tickling to hair brushing that is causing pain. We hope that this phrase will stick with them both as they grow and are (hopefully never) exposed to unwanted attention or touching. We have encouraged our daughter to use this phrase with her friends. We have also explained that sometimes people use other words to express their discomfort and that something as simple as "no" can mean the same thing and must be respected.

I sincerely hope that our discussions will continue and that both kids feel comfortable talking with me as they go through some of the more complicated changes and issues that accompany puberty. I have vowed to never shy away from a discussion of sex, even if I can't stand the thought of them doing it. I have promised myself not to judge, but to provide support, love and information, if I should be so lucky as to be asked for it when the time comes. In the meantime, my daughter (now almost four) and I will continue to enjoy talking about anything and everything that comes up. I hope the same for my son and will do everything in my power to foster this type of relationship with him as well.

Dear Vivian
Zach Ellis

I've had to learn a thing or two on my own about how to be in this world. I don't want to parent you like I was parented. I want you to have the things I never had (self-esteem and confidence, for example). I used to wish for a guidebook that would tell me how to act in certain situations or how to deal with unfamiliar things. I hope that I can be that guidebook for you to share some of the important things I desperately needed my mom and dad to tell me when I was growing up. I hope it helps you if you ever need it.

1   7–11 is not a restaurant. I don't care how much allowance you have saved, you are not allowed to count a Slurpee and a bag of Doritos as dinner. Blueberry Slurpees do not count as a serving of fruit, and the orange stuff on Nacho Cheese Doritos is not actually cheese and therefore does not count as a protein. Anything in a box with the word "Helper" tacked on is also not dinner. If you need a helper to make you dinner, you let me know and I will gladly help you.

2   I wanted to raise you as an indoor child. It's true. I didn't want the world to hurt you. Forgive me if I hover too closely at the park when you're climbing on the play structures or utter the phrase "Is that safe?" once too often.

3   There will probably be a time, or four or five, when I embarrass you. I'd like to think it might be because I know the lyrics to so many musicals or because I still can't remember if it's Snow White or Sleeping Beauty that eats the poison apple, and have to ask you why Sleeping Beauty has three names anyway. I worry a lot that what will embarrass you most about me is that, like you, I used to be a little girl. I know that having

a dad who understands "that time of the month" is probably not something that you would have chosen. If and when you become embarrassed by me because I am transgender, I want you to know that I will understand. I know how it feels to want normal. I might not be able to teach you about princesses or fairies, but I can teach you how to be brave. There will be times when you have to stand up for yourself, when you have to make choices that you know other people might not understand or agree with, but you have to act because your heart and soul and guts tell you to. I hope that when those times come, you will remember to call me and I will tell you about bravery and remind you that no matter what, your life and happiness are worth standing up for.

3   Just because I understand "that time of the month" all too well, don't worry. I'm not going to talk about Midol or cramps. I would freak out if my father had done that to me, regardless of his biological origins.

4   There is no rush to be an adult. You only have one childhood. There will be plenty of time for schedules and anxiety. This is the time to play with your toys. To be fascinated instead of embarrassed. To be excited about anything that's new. The words "hip" and "cool" should only refer to body parts and temperature at your age. Like whatever the hell you want to like, even if it's Disney princesses. You're allowed.

5   I go to AA meetings because I have a strong suspicion that I would completely suck as a father if I were drinking. That said, if I ever have to take you to an AA meeting, I promise not to make you memorize the slogans hanging on the wall. I will get you as many cups of hot chocolate as you need (one), and if there's a cake to celebrate someone's sobriety anniversary, I will always share my piece with you.

6   I have dreams that include traveling to England someday. I enjoy opera, though I don't always understand what's being said. I like *Masterpiece Theatre*, doing the Sunday *New York Times* crossword puzzle in pen, using a bookmark rather than

dog earring a book, and I happen to know a shocking amount about a group of women referred to as "The Real Housewives." I promise not to push any of my interests on you. There will be a time in your life when you might not have a clue why I enjoy the things I do, and I will equally scratch my head at whatever interests you. That's just part of what parents and kids do. I loved KISS when I was young (I'll explain them to you another time) and I'm sure my parents did not understand why I wanted to paint my face like a cat when I was learning to play the drums.

7   Love your body despite what the world might say. Your value has nothing to do with the shape or size of your body. Value has to do with the heart and the mind, and kindness and love. You are perfect from head to toe.

8   I have loved you from the moment I knew you existed. I couldn't speak for almost fifteen minutes after you were born. You should know by now that for me to be silent that long is pretty unusual. I was silent because from the first second I saw you, I couldn't believe that I would get to be your dad. There were no words to equal the joy I felt when those big brown eyes of yours looked at me. Please try and remember, when you're a teenager and feeling like a misfit or feeling unloved for whatever reason, that no matter what, you were wanted and hoped for, and I am so grateful for you.

9   Ask me anything without fear. I won't leave. If I do, it's probably just to go to the next room to find a book that might have the answer if I don't.

10   Princesses can fall in love with other princesses and have just as good a time at the ball.

Slut-Shaming on the Playground
Airial Clark

My older son is now eleven and wow . . . the sex negativity is increasing exponentially. It's a sneaky value system, like a creeping vine or oozing pore. My son is getting anxious about when he is going to have his first kiss. He thinks about it a lot. I wasn't sure exactly how much it mattered to him that some of his friends are at the kissing phase while he obviously is not.

"Mom, I'm a nerd," he said to me as he climbed in the backseat of our car. He sounded resolute. Like, some deal had been sealed and all there was left to do was accept the consequences. But, really, being a nerd has never bothered him before.

His version of nerd has a lil' swagger to it. But today there was none of that. "Girls don't like me. I'm too nerdy. I'm not cool enough. Not dangerous. Not s—" and that is when the gush of words stopped abruptly.

"Were you about to say sexy? You're worried about not being sexy? Really, E, are you supposed to be sexy in the fifth grade?"

"Some people are!"

"Ya? Like who?"

After making me promise I wouldn't call the school and make a deal about it, he confided in me that some of his classmates were kissing after school. He then told me about a girl in his class, Z, and how she had kissed three boys this year. "Three, Mom! Can you imagine? And everybody knows. She just kisses whoever she wants and her sister is so embarrassed. I don't blame her, I would be ashamed to have my sister act like that! Sheesh."

Wait? What? This is where it gets interesting for me as a sex-positive parent. My son just went from wishing he was sexy to shaming a girl for being just that? I rolled up my sleeves and got ready to do some unpacking.

"Um, so what about the boys she is kissing, should they be ashamed too? She's not kissing herself . . ."

"Well, no, uh, they just go with it. It's like she comes after them. She's forceful."

"So you don't think they want to kiss her. Do they seem uncomfortable? Do they say no but she does it anyway?"

"Uh, no, they seem happy about it. The first two boys stopped being friends after she kissed the second guy."

Try not to roll your eyes. Try not to roll your eyes. Try really really hard to not roll your eyes. Deep breath. I continue, "So, okay, it doesn't sound like she's pushing them into kissing her, so can we assume they want to kiss her as much as she wants to kiss them? Unless, you've heard or seen different?"

"Ya, I guess so, okay. But still, Mom, don't you think three is a lot for a girl? Her sister even said so."

"Honey, I'm not concerned about the sister, I'm concerned that you are judging someone for doing something that you yourself wish you were doing, and I'm also a little upset that you're making this about her being a girl."

"Oh."

"People develop at different speeds. People are comfortable with their bodies and with intimacy at different stages. You're not there yet and that's totally okay. You will be when the time is right for you. If I was her mom, would I be a little worried about this behavior? Yes, but not because she is a girl but because she is young. I would want to make sure I had all the talks with her that you and I have had."

"So, it's obvious I'm jealous?" Cue the ego deflation.

"Uh, yes. Majorly. You're anxious about when you're going to be ready, you're anxious for a girl to like you, and you're angry that this person in your class is doing what you can't, and you're probably a little pissed that she isn't doing it with you."

Did I just unpack slut-shaming for the eleven-year-old? Yes, I think I did. It would have been easy for me to demonize this girl's behavior in order to make him feel better and also to try to control his future sexual behavior. Slut-shaming is a time-tested tool in our culture. We use it under the guises of keeping kids from doing some sexually inappropriate thing. But does that work? No. Does it cause a lot more harm than good? Yes. I don't want to raise a hypocritical judgmental misogynist. Which means I have to have these conversations with him *now*, not when he's twenty-one and in college.

I'm learning that what goes down in the dorm room starts on the playground. And Mama ain't havin' it.

Radical Role Models
Riot Grrrl and Parent Allies:
A Conversation with Allison Wolfe

Allison Wolfe said she's not a parent, but she's a cool aunt! Clearly an understatement! Allison Wolfe has been an example of what Cindy Crabb calls the kind of older role models we need to have in our lives to show us it is possible to live a radical life and survive. We spoke briefly over the phone about Riot Grrrl, rad families, and Birkenstocks!

How has your involvement in the Riot Grrrl movement influenced your relationship with the women and men in your life who have become parents?

I started out with an alternative upbringing, which impacted the way I thought about families and about being female. I was raised by a radical, feminist, lesbian mother, so I had an understanding of different ways of living. She opened the first women's health clinic in Olympia while raising three kids on her own; I guess I learned to never take parenthood or families for granted. However, every summer my sisters and I would go to my father's side of the family in Tennessee and experience the polar opposite way of thinking about families. We were the bad kids; my relatives kept trying to force us into these really traditional feminine roles, which we simply refused to abide by.

That dichotomy was intense.

And then as a young punk the community tended to be really anti-religion, anti-marriage, anti-kid. We were just kind of against it all. And in many ways I still am kinda anti-religion but I've come back to appreciate all kinds of families, though there are still a lot of things that need to change. For example, I know people who have become parents yet benefit from so much privilege without ever being aware of it or taking responsibility for it.

I've also been in relationships with people who are still against kids. It was so bad that in one instance I just had to leave the situation and all that bad energy.

Yes, I know what you mean; often parents or young children are really not welcomed in spaces. One project I love is Vikki Law and China Martens's Don't Leave Your Friends Behind, *a book about supporting parents in various radical communities. I'm wondering what your experience is with parents in your community?*

It's funny, I think I've experienced a little of this from the other side. A lot of the people I knew in the DC scene got paired up or started having kids and became very exclusive with other parents or couples. I discovered there was no place for a single person or someone without kids. The older I got, the less I was invited to events; I guess they thought I wouldn't want to hang out with them at the park. But I do. I mean, hell, I want to go to Target with you and the kid. I want to be invited to the dinner party.

When my younger sister got pregnant and had her son, I really learned a lot about how to support and connect with families and kids as a parent ally. She had a bad situation with her son's father, and so I would try to go visit; it's hard to do that as frequently as I want to, but when I was able to, I realized how attached I was to him and my sister, how good it felt to help them out, and when I'd leave I'd feel this strange thing like guilt.

There's nothing worse than parental guilt.

Watching my sister struggle, I'm reminded again of how such traditional gender roles still impact so much of our communities. The father refuses to try to parent in an equal or respectful way. I've seen this enough to know it's not just an isolated incident.

I appreciate you talking with me. I guess I wanted to end by saying thank you for the countless ways you have influenced me as I parent young teen women and how you continue to influence them with Girls Rock Camps and other such events.

Well, this is an around the way story but just recently the boy I French-kissed for the first time contacted me. He was telling me that his daughter is starting to get into girl punk rock bands and when Bratmobile came up, he told her we kinda went out, she was blown away; of course, this was also the boy that broke up with me the day before Valentine's Day because I was kinda freaked out by making out and that's what he wanted to do. I had just saved up and bought this huge Hershey's kiss.

He then asked me for advice on how to support his daughter.

What'd you tell him? Because I play your music for my daughters all the time though they say they prefer more current musicians and all, but I figure that some of it gets through.

I told him about various Girls Rock Camps in his area. But I also know that kids need to separate from their parents like your daughters are doing. My mom had all these Joan Baez albums, and I liked them, but I had to find things out for myself, which led me to new wave and punk. In fact, my mom even tried to give me her Birkenstocks to wear! I guess we all have to find our way. It is amazing to me though to hear stories of people who are influenced by Riot Grrrl; it feels like I was part of something important that will be written about, like I was part of a continuum of a valid feminist movement.

Riot Parent, Riot Kids: Reflections on Teen Sexuality, Becoming a Feminist, and Riot Grrrl
Tomas Moniz

The other day I found myself exclaiming to my two daughters, sixteen and fourteen respectively: Don't have sex until you're in your twenties, but here are some condoms.

I'm not sure if there is a better example of sending a mixed message.

I should explain. Recently, I discovered my oldest daughter had spent the night with her boyfriend.

I have consistently brought up sex with them and with their older brother, who now lives on his own with a gaggle of twenty-something young men in west Oakland. And I have consistently been rebuffed, scoffed at, silenced by their stares, punctuated with a rolling of the eyes or a sigh of exhaustion.

"Dad, please . . ."

But I don't let it stop me. I know I'm not someone they want to confide in, and I actually cringe thinking about it if they did. But I want to approach the discussion of their bodies, their rights, sex in general differently than the terse warning I received from my father to keep my dick in my pants or the silence around the subject from my mother.

There is nothing wrong with sex; it's powerful and beautiful and a profound ritual of entering adulthood.

Clearly, it's also something they see all around them so to pretend they aren't aware of it, even that they don't have opportunities to engage in it, would be blatant denial.

And parenting by denial is never a good approach to raising children.

However, even though I broach the subject any chance I get, we don't actually talk as directly as I'd like. And that's why I know I need help: from other adults in our lives, from examples of people or movements reclaiming the body, all offering other ways to view sex, that might empower young women.

Sadly, there doesn't seem to be a lot out there for them; besides a few adult women in their lives whom they can turn to in need, there is almost nothing in mainstream society that speaks to young women about their growth and desires in sex-positive yet realistic and honest ways.

So I find myself saying things like, I don't think you should have sex until you're older, but here are condoms.

Now I also add every chance I get, "And remember . . ."

Remember . . .

Please, remember . . .

. . . you can always stop, you can always say no, even after you're in the car, in the room, out of your clothes, in the bed.

No means no.

Stop means stop.

So in an attempt to provide those positive examples of body ownership and empowerment, I searched out zines about self-defense, about sexual abuse, about sex-positive experiences, things written by other young women.

And then it hit me: Riot Grrrl.

Let me back up.

Fathering made me a feminist. I was twenty-one when my son was born. I remember being served papers by the county of Santa Barbara to officially notify me that I must "provide" for my child. I was served those papers, of course, while I was rocking him in my arms, cleaning up the house I shared with my girlfriend. The cop stood there, scolding me that I should be out getting a job. At twenty-one, I said nothing back to him, afraid of his power and authority.

Okay, I said and shut the door.

But I was fucking angry. I was a full-time student. So was my girlfriend. We both had part-time jobs. We took turns doing what needed to get done; we switched it up when one of us got tired of, say, balancing the checkbook (or more likely made too many mistakes). We argued and fought, but loved and spent a lot of time focusing on what was important, our son. We sacrificed our autonomy or ability to participate in things other twenty-year-olds were doing.

We were a tight, angry fist of domesticity.

We struggled with the decision to send our six-week-old child to an illegal child care center that clearly had way too many children for one woman.

But we had no other choice; she was what we could afford.

Even then, when I would walk up to drop him off the sitter would tell me I was carrying him wrong. Time went on, but the attitudes towards men as parents never seemed to change.

On the weekends, I would bike around Santa Barbara with my son letting his mother sleep because she was out till two in the morning selling roses to drinking partiers at the bars along State Street.

Of course, I will admit that balancing him, a year-old baby, on the handlebars sans helmet may not have been the smartest move a father could make. But the number of times I was told I couldn't parent was infuriating. I was told I hadn't dressed him properly, leaving home socks and shoes, or that I knew nothing about his well-being, despite being the one to take him to many doctor's appointments, or that I would hurt him or drop him, which I sometimes did, but not because I was a man.

I was determined to prove them all wrong.

I took him a few times to various classes during my first year at UCSB not because I had some point to prove about young parents but because I had no child care and a number of my teachers made no exceptions about attendance.

I remember having to change him on one teacher's desk after class, her face full of disdain, her body recoiling. I apologized, afraid I was being disrespectful. I thought of my mother, who did the same thing ten years earlier, telling me, a twelve-year-old, to stay in the car and watch my brothers while she ran in to take her final test to pass some class she was taking at the community college.

I realized the strength she must have needed, a single mom, to continue her studies, to persist despite the intense judgment society throws at parents, especially poor, single moms on welfare like she was at the time.

Shit needed to change. Even then, I wanted role models. People unwilling to bend, brazen, arrogant, relentless.

I was becoming more radical in my politics and trying to figure out my place in the world, my mixed-race heritage, my sense of class, and perhaps most profoundly my definitions of manhood, of fatherhood, of gender.

How to relearn gender?

After all, I was parenting a boy who would grow to be a man.

What kinda man would he be? What kinda man was I?

My girlfriend was a powerful, hardworking woman from a poor background. She had that poverty mentality: work yourself to the bone and never ask for handouts. But what was more stunning was that she had 100 percent trust in me as a parent, as capable of soothing, calming, protecting, loving our son.

She never doubted even when I made mistakes.

No one else had that kind of trust.

After two years in Santa Barbara, we were leaving, heading for the Bay Area. For my last semester in the spring of 1992, I signed up for a feminist studies class; one of my last assignments was to share with the class how the ideas we addressed might impact our daily lives. It was a good assignment.

For it, I walked in with my son and a diaper bag filled with bottles and food.

This is how, I said.

I got a B.

But another student walked in with a bunch of zines, some 7-inches, and one bad attitude.

Riot Grrrl found me.

It has stayed with me all these years as I meandered through graduate school, as I reexamined gender relations in my own relationships with women, as I became a father to two girls, and as my children have grown up.

Because of Riot Grrrl, I was forced to think closely about what I let my son do at ten and what I let my daughters do at the same age. Because of them, I challenged myself to address sex in positive, open ways; I encouraged my son and my daughters to speak with other adults in their lives if they couldn't speak to their mother or me.

As I have rediscovered Riot Grrrl while looking for things that might help my daughters navigate their world today, I was reminded about their courage to speak up, to risk saying what needed to be said.

Because I know that remaining silent, like Audre Lorde said, is dangerous; it'll come back and punch you in the mouth from the inside.

I know now what she means by that; she means that what matters is communication, is taking those risks to share the stories of who we are and what we believe.

So I work hard to see my daughters both as young women and as individual people, not limited to their gender, but not disconnected from it, to respect my children's autonomy and privacy as young people.

I am learning to let go of my kids and trust their power.

I am learning to keep on talking despite feeling uncomfortable.

I am learning to listen to them.

I am still learning about myself through fathering.

Perhaps none of this is about sex education or being a man in society today or about Riot Grrrl. It's about one person simply learning to see himself and those around him as the complex people they are: full of contradictions, fickle to a fault, sometimes brave, sometimes fearful and trying to live a life worth living. And of course, it's about trying to hand my daughters condoms.

List 2

RIOT PARENT

because so many political, artistic, and literary movements left out parents.

because xnot all parents have the same struggles, but all children deserve the same support and safety.

because we want to create spaces where kids are seen and heard.

because we will not be silent about race & class & gender privilege.

because we all are the future.

because poor parents should not be seen or labeled as inferior simply because they lack $$$.

because we want all of our children, of all sexes and genders, to know that when it comes to their bodies, they decide.

because our resistance is an example for our children.

because we know what society thinks and we want our kids to think for themselves.

because ANGER in the face of opression isx righteous for adults and children.

because we teach our children that it is possible to have morals and be ethical without organized religion.

because all children are beautiful.

because as children we were told to shut up and watch TV.

because our sons deserve to explore allxsix sides of themselves not just the macho bullshit.

because our daughters deserve to be outspoken & stand up for themselves.

because we believe with all of our hearts that radical families can change the fucking world.

Ask a Dad

Hey Rad Dad collective, I needed some advice on how to address an issue with my son. Not a few minutes ago, my wife had him sitting down, eating dinner but talking to him about what he has to do for homework. He is five and is sometimes difficult when it comes to doing homework, but it bothered me that my wife told me that he was showing disapproval of doing his work and he then told my wife, "Mom, stop acting gay."

I was totally floored because while I always assumed I'd know what to say, I am at a loss for words on how to actually address the topic and how using "gay" as a slur or derogatory term is incorrect. Any ideas on how to talk to him so that he understands and refrains from saying or thinking this again? Any help would be greatly appreciated.

In solidarity, Ramon Mejia

Chris: Ramon, thanks for reaching out. My first advice is not to take it as any kind of failure as a dad or family. Homophobia and all these systems are so deep in our society and kids just pick stuff up. So I'd say to not get heavy on him for saying it, but bring curiosity to find out what he thinks gay is, where he heard someone say that, and what he thinks he's saying. I'd also say talking with him, in a playful way, about how being gay is awesome—maybe people in your community whom he knows who are gay/queer, or pop stars or anyone he might relate to—so "gay" becomes associated with real people. Love to you and it's inspiring being in community with beautiful parents and comrades like you.

Robert: Kids say stuff. Sometimes they say it just because they heard another kid say it. Sometimes it's because they want to see what you will say or do. My best advice is to calmly explain to him your beliefs, especially what you and your wife agree on. I'd try to talk about the fact that there are many types of relationships between adults and that being gay is not bad. I would also let him know that it is okay for him to ask questions about what it means or about other families and sexuality in general.

Jeremy: My first advice is to be mindful of your own ego. A question like this triggers anxieties because we have fantasies of parental omnipotence. We have a false belief that we can stage-manage everything in the child's life so that they never encounter a negative thing, and they will therefore turn out perfect. We see the child as an extension of ourselves, and we dream of making them perfect versions of ourselves. When something isn't perfect—when the child says or does something that reflects the world at large instead of our own fantasies of perfection—then we are quick to blame ourselves, however subconsciously, for being bad parents. That's all ego, really. It's us thinking we're more important than we are, or have more control than we do. Putting aside the self-blame and the self-centeredness opens the door to us seeing our children as separate human beings—and respecting them as such. Part of that is respecting their development as it happens over time. "Gay" doesn't mean the same thing to a five-year-old than it does to someone older, who has seen the harm caused by homophobia. So you have to meet them where they're at—and start by asking, "What does 'gay' mean to you?" and then share what it means for you to hear the word. That's the beginning of a dialogue that will hopefully go on for years and will change as your child experiences more of the world. Who knows? Someday you may say something that will shock him, and you may have to let yourself be schooled!

Craig: I agree that this is shocking when we hear these (and other) words come from our children's mouths. In hindsight, it is a reminder to me that our kids are their own people rather than extensions of ourselves. I agree with the great advice above: it is a chance to dialogue with your son, help him explore this strange new world, and help him develop his own foundation for navigating language. Discussing how people use language to hurt others and what he can do about it can help reinforce both how hurtful words are and the power of resistance. It is also a chance to role model love—love for him and love for people in our communities. Lastly, making a difference in our kids' lives is not a one-off event; it is ongoing. So in addition to talking with your son, showing him how you and your wife live your values can be the most powerful influence. Good luck.

Simon: I agree with the others who are saying not to worry too much and to just open up a conversation. It's very likely that he doesn't even know that "gay" means "homosexual." He probably heard it from other kids and was either trying it out to see if he could find out what it means at home, a safe place for him, or he was just saying it because that's the way the kids around him say "Stop acting in a way I don't like."

There's a record-screech moment that happens sometimes when one of my kids says something that just can't slide, and this would be one of those situations for me. I hope I would say, "That's a word we don't use as an insult, and we're going to talk about it when we're all calm." (Because I might need to sort my thoughts, and because it sounds like he was already in a not-calm state of mind himself.) I try to explain to my kids that there are better ways of dealing with other people than to use insults and that some insults end up being more harmful to other people (like gay people) than they are to the subject of the insult. I let them know that I love them even when they make mistakes and that mistakes are part of learning. I tell them that in addition to not using hateful language, they have a lot of opportunities to speak up and be an ally when they hear other kids talking like that. Kids may be separate people, but as parents we do have a lot of influence and responsibility. Families and family culture are a major part of the foundation of communities and cultures. It doesn't mean there is something wrong with us as families or parents when our kids bring home reflections of problems with the world, it just gives us an opportunity to help them learn skills to deal with a world full of problems, reinforce social justice as a core value, and hopefully make change.

FAILING AND LEARNING

A Reinterpretation of Tears
Roger Porter

learned shortly after my daughter's mother and I separated that by continuing to be in my daughter's life I was committing a highly subversive act. It felt as though my ex-girlfriend wasn't prepared to deal with my continued presence, my picking our daughter up on weekends, my asking for her on holidays. It felt as though I wasn't following the script and she, as well as her family, couldn't understand why I didn't just leave. After all as a black man wasn't that what I was supposed to do?

My parents' marriage disintegrated not long after I came into the world. I have absolutely no recollection of them being together but my older brother and sister insist that this was indeed the case for several years. I rarely if ever saw my father. And when I did he was always very serious, even when he smiled. And every time I saw him he was always in a suit and tie. Occasionally he would pick us up on a Saturday afternoon and take us out to eat. Then we would often go several weeks at a time without seeing him.

Shortly after I turned seven years old, my father came over to our house one evening and called my two older siblings and me into the living room. Like always he was wearing a collared shirt and a tie, and like always he was very prideful. He told us that he would be moving back to his home state of Tennessee with his new wife to be the pastor of his own church. We didn't believe him. We made him place his hand on the holy bible and say it again. After he obliged, we knew it was true. He only stayed for a few minutes then he left. We smiled and waved goodbye to our father through the window never fully realizing what was taking place.

After that night sometimes we would see him once a year, other years we wouldn't see him at all. In the beginning he would call but then the calls began to come in a lot less frequent. I never called him. As a matter of fact, by the time I was a teenager I became a lot more comfortable with his absence than I was with his presence. In the public schools that I attended not having a father was trendy. It made you normal.

In junior high school, whenever I was hanging out with my friends in the hallway or in the gym and the subject of our fathers came up we all chimed in with different reasons as to why we hated our dads. Why dude was a coward. At least one of us declared that he would beat his father to the ground for what he did to his mother—if he ever saw him again. There could have been a whole room full of black boys and you wouldn't find one of them that wanted to be like his father. No one ever tried to understand his father. We all depended solely on our mothers, or in some cases grandmothers, for our daily representation of what a man was supposed to be. And we were able to infer from these women's stories that a "real man" was everything that our fathers were not.

At the age of nineteen, I fell in love with a woman. Three years later she gave birth to my child. About six months after that she broke up with me. She confronted me one evening and said that she could tell that I was unhappy with the relationship. I couldn't find the words to disagree with her. Two days later she moved out of my house and took my baby girl with her. It was at that point that I realized I had no idea what being a father meant. I needed to find out in a hurry but there really weren't a lot of role models in my family.

My mother's father was shot in the face the day that she was born and died in the hospital a few days later. The only thing I know about my paternal grandfather is that he and my father didn't get along. He died before I was born and I have never so much as seen a photograph of him. My mother once said that he was the overbearing type but I've never been able to confirm this with my father. My father has never brought him up.

So each week I would approach my ex-girlfriend's house to pick up my daughter, I would be completely confused. I wanted to be in my daughter's life so she could know what it was like to have a father, but I didn't know how to do it. I had nothing to draw on. My rides to her apartment complex were painful, my walks to her front door were swift, my knocks were violent, and we always exchanged the baby in a visceral silence.

My daughter felt the negative energy. Before I could buckle her down in her car seat for the nearly one-hour drive, she would break out screaming and crying until she lost her breath. After I strapped her in and turned onto Main Street heading toward the freeway, the crying would persist. I would look at my baby through the rearview mirror, she'd make eye contact with me and scream louder. One day, I became unraveled.

I demanded that she stop crying and told her how much I sacrificed for her. That I had gotten a college degree so I could provide for her. That I was being degraded on a daily basis at a job that I couldn't stand just so I could have enough money to come get her, and she had the nerve to disrespect me. Cut it out! I told her. Stop it! But she continued to cry. This little brown-skinned girl, with light brown eyes like mine and full eyebrows like mine, was in her car seat openly expressing all of the sacred things that I had learned to forget, like trips to the barbershop.

I never liked to get my hair cut as a child. About once every few months my father would take my brother and me to the barbershop for a haircut. By this time, I had a small unkempt afro with patches of tiny naps on the back of my neck. In preparation for my trip to the barbershop, my mother would gently comb my hair with a little plastic comb. She would spray water on the tougher spots so the comb would go through nice and easy and so I wouldn't squirm as much because I was severely tender headed. But I still squirmed and all of my mother's careful strokes and tedious labor were irrelevant by the time I got to the barber's chair because the water had dried up, making my hair harder and nappier than ever.

The barber was my father's friend. He was an old guy with thick glasses named Will. He never showed me any mercy. My father was always first to get a haircut and it always amazed me how he used the barber's chair like a pulpit. He carefully directed the general conversation of the shop to topics that interested him. Somehow he was able to redirect all conversations about sports— which he has always abhorred—to the need for black people to support black businesses. Conversations about women somehow ended up being about Christianity. My father, although small in stature, was the unofficial maestro of the barbershop. And he never once had to raise his voice.

My brother would go next. He never let his hair get as long and kinky as mine. His hair was so soft and thick the barber almost thanked him for letting him touch it. Then it was my turn to go. While my father continued to direct conversation and my brother sat in his seat glowing with all of the adulation he had just received, Will the barber ripped through my hair with a torturing device known as a "natural comb." A natural comb is a long black comb with metal teeth designed specifically for taming the most savage, unruly naps. As he ran the comb through my hair with so much force that it snapped my head back and I could literally hear the naps popping, I tried so hard to keep it together, but I could feel the tears coming. I knew that he had to comb my hair so that it wouldn't damage his clippers but I couldn't understand why he had to be so brutal. Why didn't he ask me if I was tender-headed? If he did, then maybe he would be able to comb my hair gently like my mother did. Why didn't it bother him that he was hurting me? I could no longer stop the water from trickling down my cheek. I looked at my father, the great composer of conversation, through blurred eyes as I cried. And I remember him finally looking up at me. He did not say anything. He was ashamed.

And now this little being was in my backseat screaming so loud and for so long that she lost her breath. I hadn't made it to the freeway before I cracked. She broke me down. I pulled the car into the nearest parking lot, unbuckled her, and held her close to my chest. I let her cry and she did for several minutes. I rocked her and shushed her gently while telling her over and over again that everything was going to be okay. I kissed her tears away until no more fell, until she went to sleep in my arms.

That was the day I learned to transcend my manhood in order to be a good father. I promised to listen to her cries in order to interpret exactly what she needed. Sometimes it was a bottle, sometimes it was reassurance, and sometimes it was a hug, while other times it was a song. Indeed my daughter was the first female I learned how to effectively communicate with. She became my entire weekend, she was my focus, and she became my identity.

That was the day I promised I would never leave her.

Binge Parenting and Bad Advice
Tomas Moniz

I used to be a good parent.

I was so focused, determined, undaunted. Perhaps even arrogant, self-righteous, unabashedly proud of my wild kids running naked down sidewalks as toddlers or expressing themselves a bit too loudly in libraries or grocery stores or classrooms as tweens. I even welcomed the moment they eventually found their own passion and anger and confidence as teenagers. I listened to them. I let them have their feelings. I think I even offered decent advice.

Not that I was a perfect parent. Believe me, I wasn't. (And if you don't believe me, feel free to peruse the pages of *Rad Dad* back issues: specifically 3, 12, and 18). To this day I have regrets about some of my parenting choices: banning what my son enjoyed doing, as a punishment; using guilt or shame to get my kids to do what I wanted; not immediately stopping when a child said stop while we were roughhousing or tickling.

Actually that is my biggest regret.

If I could do anything different, it would be to always, always listen to their words.

But this is not an essay about regret; it's an essay about the realization of how much my parenting has evolved since I welcomed my son into the world.

It seems obvious, but let me state that as kids have stages of development, perhaps then so do parents.

There is the OMG Phase, wherein you say to yourself: ohmygod what the hell am I doing with a kid and do they really just let you leave the hospital not knowing what the fuck to do? Then there's the Hover Phase, wherein you become the hyper-vigilant, tad-too-concerned intermediary between your child and the big bad evil world. Then the Buddha Phase, wherein you try to discover how to let go yet hold on, how to trust your children's own abilities to make it on their own during school, riding the bus, just hanging out in the real world.

And then there's what I am going to call the Binge Parenting Phase.

This is me now, either smothering my youngest and last child who lives with me with way too much affection, attention, food, personal problems, and household chores; or I'm expecting her to do everything for herself, forgetting that she indeed is still young and not fully the young adult she so often proclaims to be.

Of course, all these phases are different for every parent and perhaps this phase is particular to the last child. (Clearly my two older kids would have loved a little less attention lavished on them when they least wanted it.)

So let me start off by saying sorry to my youngest daughter who bears the brunt of this Binge Parenting. There are nights I desperately want to have her come into my bed and curl up with me like we used to do, all snuggly and warm and content to be held. I holler at her from my room asking what she's doing. I, of course, do this about every ten minutes, which annoys the shit out of her. There are days I ask to see the homework she needs to do and she looks at me like I'm crazy because I haven't asked her about homework for weeks (according to her it's been since middle school). I say, "My asking to see your homework isn't contingent on the last time I asked to see it." But she has a point because there are also times when I have some event or date or reading that I just have to go to and, since I know she won't want to attend, I make my own plans. I leave her alone at night. I check in with her by text: are you home, have you eaten. I tell her I love her. I tell her good night. I appease my parental guilt by imagining my words and the glow of the cell phone screen enveloping her like the hugs I used to give her at bedtime.

Consistency and routine are what parents of young children often provide their kids. Lately I binge and purge. I am everywhere and nowhere. I am present and absent.

But I am committed. I am trying to be honest with her about my values and my choices and my desires and my own internal conflicts as a model for living an authentic life. Because despite this new phase of parenting, I actually believe I am a better person and so, by default, a better parent than I used to be.

However, many of my adult friends might disagree, especially after a dinner party I attended during which I professed that the two things I now want to teach my children are that people should have kids as young as possible and people should resist getting a job for as long as possible.

My friend shushed everybody and said, "Hold on. Let me see if I've heard you correctly."

There was this dramatic, pregnant pause around the table as everyone seemed to stop what they were doing to listen to my friend summarize my moment of parental proselytizing.

He continued, "You tell your kids to get pregnant and to not get a job. That's your advice?"

He waited. Everyone looked at me. Aghast. Mouths agape.

I replied, "Well, when you phrase it that way, it does sound a little . . . extreme."

"You think?" he laughed and the table went back to drinking and talking. I was momentarily relieved to not be on the spot anymore. I could see in my mind my daughter looking at me with those eyes, whispering to me, "What were you thinking, *Rad Dad*?" (italics to highlight the intense sarcasm captured in the enunciation of "Rad Dad" by a sixteen-year-old).

But I stand by what I said because I think I have a point.

I have for years believed that if we supported parents—especially teen and other young parents—if we looked to them as powerful, inspiring people rather than as irresponsible and having ruined their lives, as so many view them, we would create a radically more loving and supportive society. Think what it would mean if we celebrated young parents: we'd see more child friendly communities and events and spaces; there'd be less shame, judgment, and ridicule; and perhaps we'd even be forced to reconsider what we define as success. Older parents are crucial, of course, but they might need a little less emotional and social support.

As a young father, I had to struggle against so many things including my own community of young activists. I remember how isolating it was, how crushing it felt to be seen always as if I had made a horrible mistake. I often wonder what I would have been like if I had support from those around me, instead of having to justify my actions and choices. Perhaps I could have done so many more things with my time and energy.

Which leads me to my next bit of parental wisdom: don't get a job. I don't mean do nothing. I mean work to do what you love, what inspires immediately, rather than what will give you a paycheck or respect. For example, I could have worked to end deforestation, fought police brutality in my community, created art, or written bad poetry then rather than now. Instead, I worked my little ass off to spite everyone around me, to show them they were wrong about me, about young parents.

So today I realized that everyone, including myself, was telling my son to get a job because it looked as if he was simply working to cover his basic needs and then, heaven forbid, he was spending the majority of his free time enjoying himself, trusting his desires, following his heart, partying a bit too much for sure, but loving life, really living. Maybe we're all just jealous. Telling him to get a nine-to-five job, or a job that would curtail his ability to do the things that gave him joy, would be the worst possible suggestion I could give him.

So my Binge Parenting Mantra, my bit of worldly advice that I offer my son and my daughters and my friends and the world at large is this: have kids when you want them and resist getting a job that prevents you from doing what you love.

Or, a bit more poetically, trust the struggle and don't knock the hustle.

Perhaps my parenting skills are slipping, perhaps I was a bit more involved when my kids were younger. But what they have taught me as they've grown, what my struggle has shown me, is that it's not always about being good. It's about being genuine, loving, humble. It's about being honest and supportive. It's about learning to listen, acknowledging mistakes, relying on others when you need to. It's about evolving and sometimes bingeing and sometimes purging. It's about showing up, about honoring who they are while honoring who I am.

Maybe that's the final stage of parenting. Let's call it the What The Hell Do I Know About Anything, But Here I Am Phase.

Because that's the truth.

Here I am.

Moving through This Space of Unknowns:
Pre-Dad Thoughts
cubbie rowland-storm

I am in the back of Trisha's dad's Isuzu, doing what I've been doing on road trips since I was seven years old: reading, writing, and snacking. I'm thirty-two now, though, and I finally almost have my driver's license. My dad isn't alive to be smoking pot in the front seat, and my girlfriend is pregnant, talking animatedly to her dad who is driving.

She's four months along now and all of the (nighttime) morning sickness is gone. Now, she gets heartburn if she eats the wrong thing at the wrong time, and she doesn't feel fantastic if she has not eaten enough. She's a very health-conscious vegetarian, so our road trip through the Southeast is complicated, but we're doing really well.

When Trisha's morning sickness set in, I got all feminist-angry, imagining some scary 1950s scenario in which millions of women who have had to cook for their husbands, while they were pregnant and feeling terrible. Even going to the grocery store made Trisha feel terrible, and the idea that I, or any man, had ever been able to just tell women to do something that made them feel that uncomfortable was nauseating in its own way to me.

At the same time, while I attempted to honor Trisha's limits during her pregnancy, I didn't want to assume they were there. Since we are two fairly independent people, I didn't want Trisha to ever feel like I didn't believe in her. Even while I raged internally at a societal system that would have insisted she cook during her pregnancy, I also couldn't be sure my insistence on keeping her comfortable while she carried our child was entirely feminist. Our chores in the house have always been about, "Well, I know you could do this on your own, but I will do it for us, because I want to help. I know you are doing other helpful things, and that's awesome." So this was the first time I had to look at what it was like to think, "Maybe for a while, you can't do this thing. That doesn't mean that I don't believe in you, but I will help you and do it for you."

In a few months, we will have our first child. We live in the Bay Area currently, an excellent place for a transguy and his girlfriend to live happily. But I'm looking at grad schools, and we are looking for a place that is less expensive to live with our baby. But frequently the less expensive the place, the more nerve-racking the idea of raising our baby is. For example, we can afford a big house with a yard in Athens, Georgia, but there are gun shop billboards as soon as you get out of downtown. What will our baby learn about our queer little family?

I've learned that anxiety is rarely productive. I don't want to call the things I fear into being with my fear of them. But the decisions of my impending fatherhood affect others more than any of my decisions ever have. I'm a teacher, so I definitely know what it's like to be the adult in the room, but it's been really nice to go home and be my usual goofy bookworm self. I know that's going to change, but clearly I don't know how.

And as queers in the twenty-first century, the idea of chosen family is something we are very familiar with. Fortunately, we've experienced love and acceptance from our families of origin, enough that part of what's motivating our potential move is the desire to be closer to them. But we've got our little family of dear friends, and we will be leaving them just when the need for support systems may be the strongest.

It's so exciting and terrifying to be sitting in this space of unknowns. The next year is going to be filled with changes and decisions, and part of me just wishes to skip on to the end of it so we know what happens. Which school will I choose? Who will our baby be? How will we afford any of this? But I think, despite the anxiety that I have to admit is there, the year will be full of fun adventures, even as we miss out on sleep and make big, important decisions.

It's Funny: What Brought Us Together?
Annakai and Rob Geshlider

You want to visit your aunt and her mother. You haven't seen them in a year. You call, you make a plan. You decide you want your ma to be there too, in order to unite as many of this family as possible. But your Ma can't come till tomorrow. You call Aunt to cancel and ask if she and her mother can meet the next day. Aunt says:

Oh, I was preparing lunch because I thought you were coming today! I'm busy tomorrow.

Now, lifelessly hang up phone. You = utter-bummed. Major mistake. Think: *Why did I have to try and rearrange? Why didn't I accept the plan as it was?* You decide to drive to their house anyway, because when will you get a chance next?

You rush to cut flowers in the yard and bend their stems on the way out. Some break against your ribs. You buy manju before driving over the bridge and smush it into the backseat, hoping it won't slide onto the floor.

When you get there, you call Aunt again. She says: *Sorry, we can't see you today.* Oh frick. Did you upset her? Will she ever want to hang again? You sit by the creek at the foot of their house and eat the manju and try to cry. You wonder: *Is this my family?* You crave to be let in their door. At this point, you just want to see them to say you've seen them. You wouldn't mind if it was only for a minute.

You attach yourself to a redwood stump and gouge the saran wrapped manju in your hands. Eating the gift, enact twisted revenge. Turns out the manju is extremely stale. The glutinous rice outside is hard and cracking and the red bean filling is crumbly and dry. Think: *Maybe it's good I didn't visit, or else they would've ingested this sawdust.* Must've been made yesterday, the day you'd originally planned to visit. Think: *If I'd bought it yesterday and hadn't canceled and given it to them then, maybe it would still be fresh. Maybe we'd be savoring together. Maybe they'd be telling stories. Maybe we'd have Grown Closer.* Your mind can crank tirelessly, bloating with FOMO as you imagine the lives you could have lived. But here you are, living this one. Grind the angry balls of your feet into the moist leaf litter.

You tell Pa about the incident. How Your Own Relatives wouldn't let you in! He listens close and patient, then tells you about balance, by traveling back to 1968:

I am five. I am an observer in my own family. Like being perpetually in the audience. My mom wants to be on stage all the time. Which is frustrating, because a conversation's a two-way thing instead, my mom just talks and tells. Rarely gives anyone else room to speak. I don't think she consciously does this. Does that make sense? As we get older, there's more interpersonal stuff. Like fireworks. Constant verbal sparring and competition. Between me and my brothers, it's survival of the fittest. There was never, never, never a group hug.

We war for resources. We are countries fighting for oil, aka: brothers fighting over love.

Since everyone is talking, I become an observer. This is what I am taught to experience.

Your Pa speaks thoughtfully. He's mentioned some of these words before, but never all at once. The once-tidbits just became some united whirl, each story tying into the next. Pa continues: *Like my family, I also feel like an outsider in my school community. We are the only Jewish family in our neighborhood, and one of three among the thousands of students at my school. I have four close friends. We are by no means outcasts, but we are definitely different from the rest. Their families are African-American, Mexican, Chinese. There are hardly any other African-American, Mexican, and Chinese students in sight. We naturally gravitate towards each other. And thus, my first alternative family is born. This substitute family works for me. With my pals, I feel totally natural. We're on the same wavelength—which you don't feel with everybody.*

It's funny—what brought us together?

You wonder what brings you and Aunt together. Still feel sour from the phone call earlier. Why do you want to visit in the first place?

You share with Pa how you felt bummed 'n' snubbed. He says, *Maybe that's how Aunt felt when you called and canceled.*

He shares with you about balance.

Your Pa says, *Nobody really studies how to create a family. In no school that I went to did I take a course on families, and what they offer.*

Plans can backfire when you try to create the perfect one. When you try minutiae-meddling to arrange just what you want. You want to tattoo into your head:

You can't force anything.

You can't force anything.

One year later, you call again.

You visit.

You never say how you sat in the park and ate the manju alone.

Aunt never says how she sat in her kitchen after you canceled, eating lunch alone.

This time, no more store-bought shit. You bring ginger carrot cake and avocados. You hand them over as you step in the door. Starting with a gift.

This time, you eat the lunch Aunt prepares. You eat the same cabbage and mushrooms and bean sprouts and pork and cake and drink the same tea. Post-nourish, they tell you stories. Together, you touch their faces in the pictures from 1964.

You think, *Score! I'm hearing the long-awaited stories!*

You think, *Here I am, at last!*

You think,

Be gentle.

You can't force anything.

The Big Lie
Jeremy Adam Smith

From time to time my ten-year-old asks me what superpower I'd like to have. I always say the ability to multiply myself. That way, I tell him, I could do everything I need to do—volunteer at his school, clean the house, see my friends. And I could even have all the jobs I've ever wanted, just to see if I could actually succeed as, for example, a paranormal investigator.

But of course I'm not telling him the whole truth, which is that I'd also like to see what my life would be like if he'd never been born. Or if I had left his mother earlier in my life, instead of later. I don't share these thoughts with him for reasons that should be obvious to people who are not sociopaths.

These are my secret identities. We all have them, which might be one of the reasons why superheroes fascinate us. When the cowardly and compromised Clark Kent takes off the suit and tie, he stands revealed as his true self—Kal El, Kryptonian orphan and champion of truth, justice, and the American Way. The trouble, of course, is that it freaks out Lois Lane to discover that her coworker at the *Daily Planet* is essentially a mask.

Our secret selves hurt the people who love us, because (I believe) anything we can't see can become a threat. Behind every father lurks a shadowy stranger who might lash out in anger or go out for a pack of cigarettes and never come back. As children grow, they too begin to split, becoming strangers to the people who raised them. That's why Peter Parker must "protect" Aunt May from Spider-Man—or rather, from anxieties like Doctor Octopus and the Green Goblin. As all great superhero myths recognize, the superhero often creates the super villain, just as the good Victorian Dr. Jekyll creates the lascivious Mr. Hyde.

In this sense, all parents are superheroes. All parents are Dr. Jekylls. We want our children to feel safe, and so many of us create a lie, and that lie is essentially a power fantasy—an illusion of omnipotence and faithfulness that cannot survive contact with the daily grind. In sleepless nights we brew potions we hope will save us from the interdependence and expectations created by that lie.

This splitting isn't unique to the dyad of parents and children, of course. We all have multiple roles to play in the world; we all have our fantasies. We split as we grow—as the roles we must play multiply, so do secret selves, which can become inner ideals. For most people, the brew gives rise to inner comic books that are, at worst, a diversion, or even something to strive for. When those fantasies we hide erupt into real life—if we succeed in healing that fracture between inner and outer—the results can seem catastrophic to spouses, lovers, children, friends, coworkers. To the people we love, we can look very much like Mr. Hyde.

I think, sometimes, we have to find the courage to frighten the people around us, even our children, who must learn that you can't have a Dr. Jekyll without a Mr. Hyde—or a Spider-Man without a Green Goblin. There's bad in the world, and bad inside each one of us. The persistence of secret identities is a fact that we must simply accept in ourselves and in others. That acceptance is what will open the door to forgiveness, as I hope my son will one day forgive me for not being the father I have created for him.

"Nothing I Have Experienced as an Adult Has Been as Hard as Being Thirteen." Interview with Young Adult Author Frances Hardinge

Editor's note: I know, I know. You're thinking "Frances who?" Trust me, you may not know her now, but read the interview. You'll soon be getting copies of *The Lost Conspiracy* for the young adults (and young adult lit lovers) in your life.

One of the things I enjoyed so much about the book is that the people and situations are really complex; there is no overly simplified good or bad side, and that forces the reader to think outside the box about difficult issues such as racism, colonialism, and class systems. Your characters face these issues and have to come to their own conclusions and make their own choices. Can you talk a little about how you worked to create this space in your book?

I like to explore issues rather than just jumping up and down on my soap box. As a species, we tend to divide into tribes or factions for mutual support and surround ourselves with people who hold the same views as we do. When we're only talking to people who agree with us, it's easy to assume that our own opinion is the only natural, obvious, and sensible one and that anybody who holds a different view must be stupid, morally defective, or acting in bad faith.

In reality, people are complex. They sometimes do terrible things, both as individuals and en masse, but usually for complicated reasons and not just because they are evil, malicious, or hopelessly dim. Even people who might otherwise be smart, kind or honorable sometimes hold deep-seated prejudices which make them a part of a larger problem. Prejudice is fed by malice and vested interest but also thrives on miscommunication, misinformation, habits of thought, inherited conflicts, and fear.

Humans aren't at our best when we're afraid. Fear has a way of stripping us of compassion and conscience at important moments, and where there is difference there is nearly always fear. Often it only takes one negative incident to convince people that their fears were justified all along.

When writing, I always try to make sure that all my characters are real and rounded, rather than straw men that totter on with indefensible views so that I can tear them apart. Even when a character holds views very different from mine, I always want them to be able to justify their own opinions to themselves. I want the reader to understand how they reached their perspective.

The character of Minchard Prox, for example, starts the book as a not-unsympathetic character. He's a fussy young bureaucrat and a bit of a worrier, but relatively kind and well-meaning. I knot a thread of reader sympathy onto him as early as possible, so that when events pull him down a very dark path the reader will be dragged along with him and forced to understand why he makes the choices he makes.

My heroines belong to the Indigenous Lace tribe, an ostracized underclass on Gullstruck. I took pains to make sure they weren't simply portrayed as poignant "victims," however. They're not safe underdogs who can be comfortably pitied. They're adaptable, resilient, and secretive, with a tradition of revenge and a distant history of human sacrifice. I wanted to make it clear why other islanders might find them unnerving and alienating, whilst still showing the discrimination against them as unjust and dangerous.

So often the voices of young adults are ridiculed or ignored; hardly ever are they listened to. When you speak to young people who read your books, what are some of the things they ask you or say to you that surprise you?

I quite agree that young people are frequently patronized, underestimated, and ignored. I always try to avoid doing this, and don't believe in "dumbing down" my books. (Occasionally I've been told that my books are too complex, but only ever by adults. The younger readers appear to cope just fine.)

Sherman Alexie writes, and I paraphrase, "the best kids' books are written in blood," as a metaphor of the violence so many children witness or experience or are confronted with. Your book was hard to read at times because of the moments of violence both physical and emotional. Was this a choice? Were you worried about people's reactions?

This was very much a deliberate choice. I knew from an early stage that the book would feature a high body count. There is a particular chapter a quarter of the way into the book which is meant to be shocking. I was a little worried about adult reactions, but I was fairly confident that younger readers would take it in stride.

Some adults seem to believe that children and young adults exist in a cocoon, blissfully unaware of the harsh realities of the world. In my own case, nothing I have experienced as an adult has been as hard as being a thirteen-year-old. I remember it vividly, and I have no intention of pretending that my younger readers live in some sort of cloud castle floating safely above the real world.

Children and young adults deal with incredibly difficult situations every day. Even the friendlier schools can be jungles. Some young people are unofficial carers for siblings or even parents. Some suffer intense psychological and physical bullying. Some scramble daily through the minefield of difficult home lives. Most have very little choice as to who they spend their time with, so peer pressure is a terrifying force. Some live in areas where violence and danger are commonplace.

They're not blind or oblivious. They're usually very much aware of the problems and conflicts in their immediate surroundings, and in the wider world. More often than not, they don't want to be patronized and "protected" from information about the big picture. They want to understand it.

The Lost Conspiracy *is about so many things—traditions, family, strength—but it is also an effective and engaging analogy of so many colonial contexts in our own world. The main character is a young Indigenous woman. Unfortunately, there really is a dearth of books that deal with those issues with these kinds of characters. How did you decide to address race in your book without directly linking to any one contemporary cultural context?*

The Lost Conspiracy *was inspired by a year-long trip around the world that I took with my boyfriend. Whenever I visit somewhere new, I always try to find out about its history, so that I can understand what I see around me. We passed through Central America, the Caribbean, New Zealand, Australia, and Southeast Asia. Over and over again we heard different versions of the colonial story and saw the countries that it had shaped.

From the start I knew that I wanted to set it in a wholly invented nation, not a thinly disguised version of a specific real-world country. There were several reasons. I wanted to explore the concepts of colonialism in a general sense, rather than seeming to comment on a particular nation or culture. I wanted to weave in my own fantastical elements, which was easier with a setting I had created. Most important of all, I was aware that speaking for a specific real world culture to which I did not belong might well be presumptuous, and easy to get wrong.

The perpetual smile of the Lace tribe was originally inspired by the "Thai smile." In Thailand it's customary and polite to smile a good deal, more than you would in most European countries. I was struck by the misunderstandings created by this small difference in social convention. "You can't trust them," a Danish woman once told me. "A lot of the time, they're smiling at you but they don't mean it." I also had conversations with Thai locals who were wondering why so many (unsmiling) European visitors were in such a bad mood all the time. I used the "Lace smile" to illustrate the way that, with different upbringings and expectations, people's "instinctive" reactions to each other can start to play tricks on them.

I also wanted the colonialist Caval caste to be a mix of influences—I didn't want them to look like just another bunch of thinly disguised Europeans. That was one of the reasons for giving them their own bizarre form of ancestor worship, rather than a suspiciously Western-looking church. I didn't want either the colonists or the Indigenous culture to be too comfortable or familiar. I wanted the reader to be able to understand why each might find the other a bit weird, alien, and disconcerting.

I also decided against writing a "first contact" tale, describing a collision between two pristine cultures. I wanted to set my story many generations later, after all the waters had been muddied, and bitter battles had been fought and misremembered—after everybody's identities had smudged and slipped, and knowledge had been gained and lost, and nobody quite knew who they were anymore.

What would you like the young folks who read your books to walk away with?

Question everything you've been told. Read, search, learn, and dare to think the unthinkable. Don't let anybody tell you what to think . . . and that includes me.

A Clutch of Flowers: Celebrating My Love for My Daughter, One Bouquet at a Time
Jonathan Shipley

She sat in the back seat. Her mom—my soon-to-be ex-wife—was at the wheel. I was standing in the driveway. She must have known something momentous was happening. She knew, even at her young age, that the orbits of our lives were going to spin off, with trajectories similar to how they had been, but not the same. Never the same. She asked her mom to roll down the window.

"Daddy," she said.

"Yeah, sweetheart?" I said, getting as close to her as I could. I knew it'd be some time before I saw her again. Knew that I'd have to be alone with my thoughts in that empty house. Knew I'd come home from work the next night to cold rooms, to quiet and solitude. No laughing kid. No fun music playing. No smells of fresh-baked cookies and shampoo in her hair.

"I want you to have this," she said as she handed me a little stalk of lavender. "When you miss me you can smell it and then you'll think of me."

"I will," I said, taking a sniff. "Hey, it works!"

She smiled. "I know. I love you," she said matter-of-factly. And like that, the window was rolled up, the car crunched down our gravel driveway and cruised up the hill, turned left and out of sight. Gone. I had never felt worse in my entire life. Yet I had never felt more loved.

Me and the kiddo would always find ourselves with flowers in our hands. Every day when I got home from work to my wife, exhausted by taking care of our child all day long, my kid and I would go out. We didn't have to go far, just a walk around the neighborhood. She loved exploring the world right outside our front door and I was all too happy to oblige her.

We'd toddle along the road, coming back to the house with fistfuls of dandelions. Those are always the first bouquets made in a young life, aren't they? A bunch of cheery, modest flowers (by some definition, weeds, really) arranged in a shaving mug in the bathroom until they droop and wilt away. Soon, we graduated to daisies and daffodils, errant and scattered, growing in clumps in our Gold Beach neighborhood. "This daisy's as big as my face!" She'd squeal. "This daffodil is daffy!" We'd quack like ducks.

Later, we made flower gathering a game, a challenge. "We have to make a bouquet with nothing but yellow flowers." We'd pluck California poppies, goldenrod, butterfly weed. (Apologies to our neighbors for our surreptitious clippings. Flower thieves, we were.) We'd go home, slide open the back door. "Mom! We have something for you!" Our kid would hide the bouquet behind her back as if her mom didn't know what we had brought home. "Ta da!" Flowers! We owned only a couple of vases. Most all the kiddo's flowers were found in cups and mugs, old sippy cups and kitchen bowls.

When she got to be a tireless walker we'd go further afield. Sometimes up to the Point, an undeveloped piece of property owned by a gravel company where we found a mammoth lilac bush. We'd pick it clean. She'd get so many stems she couldn't hold them all, obscured by brilliant purples. Our house would be perfumed for days on end by those stems. We'd go to the forests nearby, pick holly branches, wild huckleberry, and rhododendron sometimes. We'd go to pastures and meadows and pluck apple blossoms, pretty grasses, water lilies from the pond if we could reach them. A bounty of color, shape, size, and smell enlivened our home. Perhaps she knew, subconsciously, how drab the house was without them.

There are countless divorce stories. No need to evoke them here. "We grew apart" is an old adage but it's apt as far as it goes. What we missed from each other, a connection, we found in our daughter. Love—pure, unadorned, simple and complex, raw, honest, unconditional. Again, this is nothing out of the ordinary, a parent's unending love for a child. The kiddo became my life, consuming all else. I gave to her and her alone my utter devotion. Did it strain my relationship with my wife, who had a similar devotion to our child? Undoubtedly. It's what happens, sometimes. Our child is loved though. That's for certain. An enduring, overpowering love.

The neighbors would see me and my daughter most every day, rain or shine. They'd spot us with a clutch of wild roses from the empty lot across the street, maybe a stray tulip or two liberated from The Point, or perhaps some cherry blossoms from that tree that hangs over the old founders' cemetery on top of the hill. "That's sure a pretty bouquet," they'd say. "Almost as pretty as you," they'd say. My girl would smile. "Would you like some from our garden?" The kiddo's face would light up. The neighbors would pick gorgeous dahlias from their plots, sumptuous roses, elegant poppies. "Your vase will like these, won't they?" My kid would smile and say, "Thank you." We'd trundle home and do our best to find places for all of them. If all the cups were taken, we'd use the plastic bucket she'd take to the beach down the big hill.

We still collect flowers. Now, a few years later, my daughter is in third grade. I'm writing this in her room. Nearby, amidst her Harry Potter books and hamster paraphernalia, is a flowering miniature orange tree she asked for at Christmas, a flower fairy figurine sits on her desk, mini pink daisies from the neighborhood park fill a little dessert dish, and lilies picked near the stairway we use to walk to school peek out from her bathroom.

She's with her mom right now. It's the schedule, the Parenting Plan. It's how things are. I'll never be able to see her every day like I did when I was married. I'm not able to tuck her into bed every night and wish her the sweetest of dreams. A lot of nights, I have her though. Lots of days. Many walks together home from school, picking flowers along the way—columbine and coral bells, wisteria and bleeding hearts.

It's not hard to see how much love there is here now—just look and see what's in the nearest vase. Lupine, camass, hollyhock . . . And if I'm here, and she's not, and the glasses are empty of buds and the vases are absent of flowers, I just pull out the little box in my closet—the one with the little lavender sprig in it that she gave me so long ago—and I take a deep breath.

The Modern Family:
When the Personal Becomes the Political
Bronwyn Davies Glover

In our family, we are a queer, cisgendered, female birth parent communally sharing a home and equal amounts of the parenting with a queer, transgender male ex-partner co-parent and their three-year-old, gender-unassigned gayby. Sounds pretty modern when I think about it. Sounds like something out of which documentaries are made.

But this isn't exactly what I had set out to do. Nor what I intended to become.

I did expect much from the politic of parenting once I entered the wild journey of the gay donor search, DIY home insemination, the radically queer choice of welcoming a child into the world free from gender assignment and the bumpy rides of attachment parenting and extended breastfeeding.

Really, much of what I expected has happened. And is happening. My little gayby uses overarticulate language about gender and identity and has an extraordinarily mature ability to move fluidly along the spectrum outside of anyone's binary assumptions. My body is still breastfeeding and co-sleeping, almost four years into parenting a sole child. Our flamingly gay donor is a close friend in our lives, whom our child refers to comfortably when retelling the precious story of just how intentionally they were made.

What I didn't expect and may never fully comprehend, is how those politics of my role as a parent are not nearly as personal, as challenging, as revolutionary as is the sudden reality in which I live.

My partner and I are ending our relationship as lovers. Partners for nearly a decade and a half, through residencies and emigrations, through gender and identity transitions, through squatter poverty and *very* planned parenthood, we suddenly find ourselves transitioning through the greatest change of all—our roles as traditional life and love partners.

I suddenly see myself moving through choices that feel like the only ones to make as my soul grieves the loss of my partner, my other. I move through choices that sit easily inside my skin as we both work tirelessly and consciously hold on to to our ideals that love is truly what makes a family and that regardless of relationship movement, we share love for one another and massive, incomparable love for our child. So we choose to live in the same house and move into separate bedrooms. We choose to continue sharing money equally through only one bank account. We choose to speak openly about the new people we bring into our individual lives as lovers. We choose to spend weekends on special family adventures with our tiny one. And, most importantly, we choose to use positive language about this unrecognizable change in our child's life so they may feel empowered and proud when communicating the dynamics of their household to their preschooler community.

This is the modern family.

This is choosing people and choosing love and choosing to continue believing in community, communality, and true revolutionary restoration.

And it is exceptionally hard. There are moments when my ribs ache for a norm I never knew I would say goodbye to. There are moments my heart holds so still in my chest, I forget beyond all political practice what it means to move intentionally through my day, and attempt to remember what it means just to breathe. When the communicating, the analysis, the hard ever-so-hard work of unschooling the mainstream narrative of what makes a family, the politics of the parenting in which we engage and the ache of witnessing us let go of our codependent togetherness bubbles up and overwhelms. I find myself in a stuck, screaming, eye-stinging moment of wondering if we shouldn't just do what everyone else does. Get separate houses. Get separate bank accounts. Share our child's time. Pay money according to parental roles. Grieve and grow apart.

We weren't modern in the ways we came together, we were queer. We weren't trying to create a new kind of family, we were simply wanting to create our own. We weren't co-parents sharing revolutionary moments of making a family with multiple partners or sharing polyamorous relationships, finding gay donors with whom to share equal parenting rights or adding more than two names to the birth certificate. Outside of chosen politics and identity labels, for all intents and purposes, much of our living aligned us with the normative: two parents, married and living monogamously together with a child, sharing finances.

And because of this and all things that have followed in my life, I now have to wonder: how many of us have struggled as far as our wombs would let us to try to keep intimate the family we've worked to create in the homes that we share? How many of us have worked tirelessly to stay open, to find avenues, tiny paths that might lead us to a map that could remake how our family might possibly stay living together? Sharing together? Being together? Perhaps the work I do is the work many of us have done and when some of us succeed, others within our community recognize the health and necessity in making choices that allow for things like separate bank accounts, separate houses, sharing time with our shared children as we move away from one another in all the ways our hearts grow apart.

I know that I can't anticipate what might happen as my life keeps moving. I know that I must hold on to what I feel and how my beliefs empower my choices as a parent, very recent ex-partner and committed co-parent in the tiny home I share with my tiny family. I know that much communication is required of me, above and beyond any way that I have communicated previously. And I know that all the ways I hold any politic of mine dear will be shifted and angled into views I've not yet seen. And it will require the widest of eyes late into the most exhausting of nights.

But if the revolution truly does start at home, then my lounge room is the rallying field. And my hallways are the route we take. And my bedroom is the meeting place that will implement our action. And if this revolution is to be successful in its ability to dismantle mainstream narratives, build individual capacity and restore community, then my home is my activism. My family is my cause.

My parenting is political because I am shaping what it means to love and be loved in a revolutionary context for my child. And I am modeling what it means to consensually participate in a chosen family space, free from obligation and expectation and built solely through the hard ever-so-hard work of open communication and restorative justice principles.

"*Are you guys good friends, Bronnie?*"

My tiny one's dark, three-year-old eyes are like a truth serum when they look up at me.

"*Yes, sweetheart. We care very much about each other. And we love you.*"

"*But do you love each other too?*"

"*Yes, we do. We have loved each other for a very long time and we live in the same house so we can parent you as a family.*"

"*Cause we are a family?*"

"*Yes, darling, we are a family. We used to be partners like some of your friends' parents. And we used to sleep in the same room. Now we are partners in our love for you.*"

"*Such good friends that you are always gonna be my parents?*"

"*Always and forever,*" I answer.

I don't know if I would know how to think about living communally with the person I am breaking up with if I wasn't privileged enough to identify on the more radical left of the queer community. I don't know that it would have presented itself as a possibility. I may have taken a breath, sighed the excruciating loss of my soulmate, and agonized over what days I would get to hold my child and what days I would be missing them. But because of a politic that sits outside of parenting and inside of a beautifully othered community I am so very lucky to be a part of, I am privileged enough to look at our situation with wider eyes. I am able to see how converting our backyard shed into another bedroom is an exciting venture that involves each one of our three-person family and invites many a deep conversation about the changes, the movements, and the faces of real partnership for both the adults and the child.

And I am able to see what it means to be a part of intentional love.

Which is what we are doing. We are being intentional. We are choosing the hard ever-so-hard as a way of committing to unschooling our mainstream narrative about what creates and maintains an acceptable, successful family unit. Even when it hurts so hard my heart is still and my brain has to remember to tell my lungs to breathe. Even when the dynamics are so new that we fumble and drop the ball we are delicately carrying. Even when the analysis keeps us up at night trimming its edges, questioning its girth. And especially, most especially, when our tiny one wakes in the morning and can find us both within minutes, a smile on their tiny, perfect face, for sunrise cuddles and intentional love.

This is our modern family. And our revolution starts at home.

PART 3

Bellybutton

Of all the body parts, the bellybutton is the most comforting; it's primal, an origins story; it's the actual place you were fed before you could feed yourself, a bodily reminder of your connection to your mother, of your dependency on another person. Every time I see a bellybutton, I look into the person's eyes, imagine the baby they once were, imagine exactly where they came from: a mother's womb.

Blood

Anytime I got a bloody nose as a young boy, I would let it bleed, let the blood run into my mouth, turn my teeth red, drip down my chin, savor the strange metallic taste, the oily consistency, the way it would dry on my skin. "Blood," my father always threatened, "blood is what matters, blood is what makes you who you are." He'd hug me deep, whisper like a warning, "You are my blood," squeezing me till I hurt, "you my blood." In the mirror, alone I'd repeat, "my blood, my blood," over and over until the words lost meaning.

WHO WE ARE

Not *the* Real Dad, Not *a* Real Dad
Amy Abugo Ongiri

I unexpectedly became a parent at forty-seven. I say unexpectedly, but we had actually been preparing for weeks and trying for years. After years of failed attempts at fertility treatment, our financial resources were exhausted, so conventional adoption was out of the question. We made the decision to look into foster care as a possible means toward parenting. We must have looked like strong candidates or the county was really desperate, because they rushed our application and after a month and a half of intensive training we found ourselves with two little boys in our care. They were just two and seven years old. We had wanted girls, but the need was greatest for African American boys. Being African American myself, I knew that we wanted black kids, but since we were queer women we assumed that they would be girls. In the rural Midwestern county where we lived, there weren't that many black kids in the system, so we didn't want to miss our chance. Also, when the social worker described their struggles with racism in school and how they had been in multiple placements in a very short period of time, we knew they needed us as much as we needed them.

I was ready for a lot of the challenges of foster care but like all parenting I wasn't ready for everything. I wasn't ready for the shift in perspective that having a two-year-old boy in your life would bring. He literally saw things from a different angle than I did. Once when I was putting him in the car, he pulled away from and wiggled past me and began for a second to run at full speed. In my panic as I snatched him back I screamed emphatically at him at him, "What are you doing?" even though I know full well that this is a question that no two-year-old is prepared to ever answer. He responded equally emphatically, "Birdie!" We both stood there in a parking lot for a full five minutes to watch a bird that I'm sure that I wouldn't have otherwise even known was there. Whether it was a leaf stuck to your shoe with a particularly interesting pattern or a nearby squirrel, he was so good at drawing your appreciative attention to little bits of nature that you wouldn't have noticed. The older boy and I had interests that were so similar that spending time together was just fun. We'd shoot hoops together, listen to music, go for a walk in the woods, hang out in what my partner called "big-boy time."

The only problem with big-boy time and all the other time that I shared with the boys was that I was not a boy, big or otherwise. The hardest part of the experience of foster care was experiencing my gender difference through the lives of these two little boys, who hadn't necessarily even asked make family with us. As a masculine-of-center butch dyke, I had long ago learned to not only to accept but to love my gender difference. I loved the look of myself in men's clothes. I loved embracing the masculine as well as feminine parts of personality. I loved the dynamic between butches and femmes. I loved being a gender outlaw. I had also long ago learned to accept the discomfort that my gender could invoke in others. What I was not used to was having that discomfort visited on two little kids in my care.

The kids, like most kids, pretty much accepted me without question. They seemed to really appreciate any attention and care that I gave them from working on phonics to teaching them to skateboard. We rarely have conflict. The truth is that I took to parenting like a duck to water. I even gladly traded in my prized customized low-rider for a minivan. My instinct to protect and care for these two little guys who had already been through so much was so great that it surprised me. When I picked up the toddler at daycare and he ran excitedly to me and screamed "Daddy" I inwardly cringed out of the fear that daycare workers would report me to social workers as an inappropriate role model. When other parents at school gave us the cold shoulder, I feared the negative effect it might have on the kid's ability to make friends.

Foster parents are literally co-parenting with the state and are justifiably under more scrutiny than other kinds of parents. Many people involved in foster care in my county were conservative Christians, and I worried all the time that my gender and our queerness as a couple would impact our ability to protect and nurture these two little guys whom we had grown to love so much.

Foster care is meant to be a temporary arrangement. We know it is our job to love, nurture and protect these kids just as long as we have them. I worried that our time with these little boys would be cut short because of my status as a gender outlaw.

As a foster parent, I am not *the* real dad. As a woman, I am not *a* real dad. Nevertheless, fatherhood means everything to me and I know by these kids love for me that I am good at it. I've waited a long time for this and I have chosen it. I know by my success at it that that it has also chosen me. When these kids leave my care they will know how to ride a bike and skateboard, how to read and set a table, how to dress themselves and meditate. Most importantly, they will know that I love them. I can only hope that one day they will come to think of my gender difference as much of gift as I do.

Invisible Dad
Mike Araujo

I'm answering e-mails, sitting on a bench, just kind of keeping an eye on things, trying to figure out what we're going to do for dinner. My son is happily playing on the slide. We always walk to the playground and don't really notice the other parents. We are in our own world. Xavier has just sort of figured out walk-running; he is the proudest year-old boy there is. It's endless fun.

Occasionally we go to a different park or just wander around; change is good, right? I like to think I'm friendly and approachable, yet at those other parks no one talks to me. In fact, I get stares and moms (it's always moms) will walk right up to me, avoid eye contact, and take their kids away; it's a really aggressive way of ignoring someone.

I am never sure about how this makes me feel, but I know I feel something. I don't really talk about this with my partner, not that she doesn't notice. It is difficult to talk about since I don't think I've ever discussed this publicly.

In my life I've always had to work with a more than a little swagger. It is a way for me to ignore what gets said or the jokes and conversations that end as soon as I walk up to my union brothers and sisters. There is this kind of lazy prejudice, as if their racism is a constant background noise. In reality it's exhausting, or at least it exhausts me.

But at the playground, I am just another faceless, nameless black man, an object of fear and derision. I feel fairly well equipped to deal with almost anything, yet in that moment when the playmate gets snatched away, I am a shuffling, shucking wreck. I fall over myself to explain who I am and what I'm doing there with my children; for god's sake I'm at a playground with my children. What the fuck else would I be doing?

I never really thought about the specific feelings it brings up because ultimately it is so humiliating. That is a feeling I am not used to. I build walls and structures to insulate myself from humiliation. I sit opposite CEOs and negotiate for workers as an aggressive equal. In a lot of ways I find myself happily in my middle age with my hands on some power, yet it has a codicil that casts a pall over everything.

In addressing issues of racism in my workplace, I talk to many people about behaviors and attitudes that are a habit, how the person with the bias really loses, and how to support the dignity of the person experiencing the bias.

At the playground, I find myself questioning this whole premise. There is a shame that is so hard to articulate. Are these moms going home and crying over their makeup tables about how they continue a tradition of oppression and how they wish that they could get themselves out of this cycle of hate? No, I suspect that they are completely oblivious to this.

I feel helpless and I am actually embarrassed to talk about this with my friends and Kris in any real way. Mostly I say "that's fucked up" and shrug it off. I guess I don't simply shrug it off. I take it home and I take it to work and I think I take it out on my kids. I take it out on my wife. I can't say exactly how; I just feel that I do.

How is a person supposed to deal with this constant battle and not completely lose their mind? Part of the helplessness I feel is that I don't have an answer. I don't want Xavier and Ella to know about this stuff, but I also know they can tell how tense and impatient I get when I'm on the playground and there aren't any other people of color there. I don't have any answers for this or any real concrete self-reflection, I just have these feelings and had to let them out. I want to be heard. I want to be seen.

All Things Big and Small—
Race, Gender, and Ferguson
Craig Elliott

When we were blessed with two healthy beautiful babies, our world went instantly from big to small. Learning to love and care for a human being was overwhelming, and while we were learning that we had most of what we needed to do a good job inside of us, it was also very, very hard. The prospect of parenting unfolding, often mere seconds ahead of what our children needed at that moment, was daunting.

As the kids became older, and their parenting needs were less intense in the immediate, and as we surrendered to the chaos and lack of control that comes with parenting, we felt we could once again look at the larger world around us. Our roles were about keeping them safe, helping them learn to live in community, and teaching them the skills to navigate this complex world.

Sometimes, especially in the higher socioeconomic community in which we live, I felt like the role of protecting kids was to keep them in "the bubble," never letting them experience the larger world, never letting them handle something difficult or painful, never letting them become their own people.

There is a lot of social pressure for parents to keep kids in bubbles. It is an illusion and a trap to think that we can do this—that we can control life around us so as to influence how our kids experience it. Certainly, this idea, this illusion, is a product of a society built upon Western, capitalist ideals of individualism, ownership, and wealth; it is also a defining norm of whiteness, masculinity, and upper-class values in our country. Being white, male, and of economic means allows for the illusion that life is controllable.

If we, as parents, stay in our micro spaces, we will miss the macro responsibility we have to equip our children with the tools of love, respect, and community, of social responsibility and activism, and to help them join us as social change agents.

I really thought I had all of that figured out. But then Michael Brown was murdered in Ferguson.

Maybe it was the cumulative effect of the killings of young black men at the hands of white men that woke me up; maybe it was the particular circumstances of Michael's life coupled with the fear I have of an aggressive police force that resonated with me; maybe it was none of that, and I really couldn't ignore it any longer.

Parenting isn't just about love. Feminist parenting isn't just about raising young men to respect women as people, not objects, but to also respect and love themselves so they can create relationships and a social order that allows for their full expression within the gender spectrum. Conscious parenting isn't just actively working to eliminate gender violence in ourselves, our kids, and the world around us. Socially just parenting isn't just about critically examining whiteness so that young men understand how whiteness permeates our collective social order and thus shift how they think and act.

I realize that parenting frameworks are incomplete, for at least two reasons: first, merely "not replicating" racism and sexism is not enough to eliminate them—our boys need to be active in eliminating racism and sexism and helping us define a new model; second, treating whiteness and masculinity as separate elements allows boys and men to make shifts "for others" rather than for themselves. It also misses how gender and race work at the intersection.

An article I wrote with my friend Eric Mata explored the intersection of whiteness, masculinity, and class, and how all of that played out in Michael Brown's murder at the hands (and gun) of Darren Wilson. What was clear to us is that our cultural version of masculinity sets boys and men up for collision courses where they duel for domination. We know, and it is reinforced by popular media and storytelling, there can only be one masculine winner. And that winner, more often than not, is white.

I worry about my boys growing up to be white male aggressors, not just treating women and girls as objects to be dominated, but treating boys and men of color as objects to be dominated as well. The values that have driven our parenting—love, respect, and social responsibility—will lead our boys to be good conscious people, but they won't help them navigate, unpack and shift the unconscious biases built into our cultural norms. As Howard Zinn beautifully illustrated, being good white men in a collectively racist, sexist, homophobic, and classist society won't eliminate oppression from our lives.

I am further reminded how our society shames men and boys when they operate outside the conventional behaviors of masculinity. It is similar for whiteness as well. Shame keeps us dominating, and abusing, and killing. Shame keeps us hurting ourselves and others.

We need something stronger than shame to guide us forward.

Helping create loving kind boys who know how to use their words instead of their fists is part of it. Developing a consciousness in ourselves and in our kids is part of it as well. These actions are on the individual level, however, and we need to also work systematically. Leveraging love and awareness to actively and vocally challenge hegemonic masculinity and whiteness when they are operating around us is an important part of it as well. And so is resisting privilege when we haven't done anything to receive it (other than being white or male).

Most importantly for preventing more Fergusons (and Oaklands, Sanfords, Detroits, Jacksonvilles, Charlottes, etc.) is for more white men to have conversations—with our kids around—to discuss how our whiteness, our masculinity, and class exist in our lives, and what we want to do to change it for all people. We need to have more conversations about what scares us. We need more conversations about what prevents us from intervening to prevent injustice and oppression. What I know for sure is that the only way out is through.

In talking with my kids about what was happening in Ferguson, I shared my own sadness, anger, deep frustration, as well as my hope that our societies can be better. I talked about my expectations of myself, of what it means to be a white man in our society, and how important it is to intervene when we witness injustice. I shared my desire that all boys and girls, and kids of all genders, be able to grow up with the safety, love, and opportunities that they have. Lastly, we explored things we could do in our neighborhoods to make a difference. It was difficult at times because I didn't always know what to say, didn't necessarily have the words to convey my feelings, or knew what we could do. It was hard because it required me to be vulnerable.

This is our role as family leaders—to create mini-communities of love, respect, and justice, and refuse to allow shame to exist in these communities. We role model vulnerability in the path forward, and we act courageously for good. We then allow our mini-communities of love to ripple outward into the families around us, into our schools and places of worship, and towns, cities, states, and ultimately our country.

Writing that piece with Eric was moving for me, and it helped me better analyze and examine my own experience with the intersection of whiteness, masculinity, and class—and how they are driving how I am co-raising my two boys.

I think about how Eric and I ended our article, and it seems appropriate to replicate that call to action here as well:

> As we continue to examine our roles of fathers, understanding our roles in passing on social expectations to our children, the spoken and unspoken cultural narratives of race, gender, and class are at play. Our role is to be conscious of and clear in our values (love, community, and justice), and act to create environments for our children to act in alignment with these values. Doing so allows us to create those other choices, and help our children navigate a new world that they are also creating (Elliott and Mata, "On Mike Brown, Darren Wilson and the Deadly Intersection of Race and Masculinity," October 14, 2014).

We aren't here just to equip our kids with the skills to navigate injustice, hate, and oppression and to act in resistance. We are here to help them create that new world built on love, hope, justice, and respect.

Kindergarten Angst
Eleanor Wohlfeiler

In April, we got our kindergarten assignment letter from the Oakland Unified School District. Our son was assigned to our neighborhood school, Sankofa Academy, though it is a mile and a half and five major intersections from our house. We knew nobody from our neighborhood or preschool or any other part of our life who was also headed there, and this is the town I grew up in, where I can't go to a café, farmer's market, or playground without seeing someone familiar.

We looked at twelve schools in two years, most of them Oakland public schools, a handful of charter schools, private schools, and a Berkeley school. Sankofa is a mere four blocks from Peralta Elementary, an award-winning Oakland favorite, known for its PTA-funded arts program and its strong community. The houses directly across the street from and in the surrounding blocks of Sankofa are zoned for Peralta.

As our neighborhood school, Sankofa is neither in our neighborhood nor the school of the children in its neighborhood. OUSD prioritizes neighborhoods for school assignment but not all neighborhoods have schools. Golden Gate Elementary, two blocks from our house, closed several years ago. Santa Fe, our next closest school, was closed in 2011.

Our OUSD guide tells us Peralta is 50 percent white and Sankofa is 5 percent white. Peralta had an Academic Performance Index score last year of 942 to Sankofa's 728. Peralta lost its Title One funding for schools serving low-income populations a few years ago. Sankofa currently receives the funding.

Several white neighbors have said they would not consider Sankofa. We have heard parents at "good" public schools tell us our kids will be fine wherever they end up, though they aren't interested in those less ideal schools for their own kids, and don't name what could be valuable at a school that does not test well or have supplemental funding from well-educated parents. In 2014 in Oakland, California, this surprises me, as we all engage in a critique of harmful reliance on standardized testing and at least pretend to hope that money is not the only thing that makes the world go 'round.

We were attracted to the energy at Sankofa, to the teacher we saw when we visited, and we were, with much awkward uncertainty, eager to see how the experience would unfold for our son and our family where we didn't look like most people. We have tried to stay open to the inappropriateness and limitation of our decision. Are we taking someone else's spot? How would Sankofa change if more people like us attended? Are we bringing something positive? What kind of idealists are we? How is that connected to our place of privilege?

It is only from that place of privilege that we don't have to worry about our son, who comes home speaking differently than we speak, because I imagine that when he is looking for a job he can use the same kind of English we do for an interview. It is only from our place of privilege that we feel comfortable "trying" Sankofa, under the unspoken, or at least quietly spoken, assumption that if we threw a big enough fit downtown, we could get our son into a "better" school.

We both have bachelor's degrees from good universities. We can afford to live on one income. We do, however, sleep in one bedroom, our car is as old as I am, and in our nine years together this is the first one that we have not shared with housemates. We live and eat richly. Very richly. My son reported after the first day of school that some of the kids were eating hot lunch out of a plastic bag. This was remarkable to him because we have banned hot plastic in our home. He has told me that some of the food he sees is not organic, as if that were exotic. Do the kids at Peralta eat exclusively organic food? At Sankofa, he has been given jelly beans as a reward for good behavior in the classroom. The parenting books we have read do not support rewards, let alone high fructose corn syrup rewards. We are learning over and over again that being parents means explaining, over and over again, that people do things differently, and that the way our family does things is important for our family, and maybe only our family. Now I can't explain that it is not healthy to eat out of hot plastic. I don't know exactly what to say instead. Is now the time to explain how much organic food costs? And how we afford it? And why we buy it? And what we are buying into?

There are so many things I wish didn't exist so I wouldn't have to explain them to my kids. When we were in the middle of an obsession with lollipops, thanks to *The Little Engine That Could*, we finally relented and agreed our kids could try one. Then we took them a few miles away to a corner store, so that they might not immediately realize that lollipops are also available on our corner. We can avoid and delay certain conversations with our kids, but our job is to help them develop their own moral compass—not in a vacuum but in relationship with the wondrously tempting, disappointing, and chaotic world that is all around them.

And however curated the environment we choose for our kids, the challenge of explaining and experiencing being different will always come up. My son, with his long, blond hair and his proclivity for a certain pink sweatshirt and his unfamiliar, gender nonspecific name gets asked at school daily if he is a boy or a girl. (On Thursday the boy who asked him had a large, sparkling stud in his ear and a streak of purple on his sneakers.) At the small, private preschool he attended he had the same questions and confusion. As society teaches kids to categorize, it is our job to teach them not to trust the categories, and to recognize that the categories have a powerful effect. Are we fools to think we will have a better opportunity to do this at a school where there is so much obvious "difference?"

School can be a small but necessary part of a child's day, or full-time child care, or a superlative place to cultivate extraordinary talents. For now, we are happy at Sankofa because our son is happy at Sankofa. He has friends, he is comfortable in his six daily hours as a minority (which in some ways accentuates his privilege), and we are challenged to engage in our own growth. We also have anxiety. We know a lot of people who love other schools, which is enticing, and a lot of people who wouldn't consider what we are doing, which is scary. When it came time to fill out Oakland's "Options Form" last winter, we debated and agonized and ultimately listed Peralta as our first choice, with reservations about actually going there. We figured if we didn't get in we would be reassigned to Sankofa, which would be fine, but we wanted the choice.

So when the letter arrived letting us know that we were, indeed, reassigned to Sankofa, I was surprised to find myself very upset. As my ultimate admission of privilege, maybe I was upset because I didn't like that we asked for something and didn't get it.

It is poignant but not surprising that through Sankofa we are slowly meeting neighbors we might never have known. I wonder, and hate that I wonder, how many of my friends are gathered on the Peralta playground where I am not. At Sankofa, we have been offered hand-me-downs for our younger children, and the doors are held open for me so I can thunder in with my stroller at pick-up. I help in our son's classroom and all the kids know my name and offer exceptionally adorable hugs. There are teachers we are excited about and this year there is music class once a week. The parents who are trying to form a PTA have insights and experiences that will be tremendous resources to the community once it gets off the ground. We have not had play-dates, or coffee after drop-off, and I have not yet met the posse of best-friend parents that I envision we might have at another school. But as we leave school every day, a dozen kids yell goodbye to my son. We heard that last year was the first year Sankofa had a waiting list.

Through My Grandfather's Eyes
Scott Hoshida

I was the first: the first grandchild, the first grandson, and, in my grandfather's eyes, the next person responsible for passing his name, my name, our name into the infinite future, into the abyss of eternity. And how? By having sons, of course. This is how things work if you come from old-school Japan. He did not want our name to die on his watch, and from a young age he impressed upon me that it was not only my duty to do this but my privilege. To carry the name was an honor. I feared that I would not be worthy.

The power of this right can be summed up in this small story: As a child, I told him during our New Year's Day feast that rather than serve both red and white sashimi, he should only serve the red one, the tuna. He would imitate my young voice: "Grandpa," he'd say, his voice an octave higher, "I don't like the white one." From that New Year's Day forward, he would only buy tuna for the entire family, no matter what anyone else said. It was his first grandson's wish, and that meant that all else would fall in line. I do not remember ever saying this, of course, but the retelling of this story has become a ritual of New Year's Day. For all of its problems, it has become family lore that everyone can repeat and tell on their own, but it doesn't sound right unless Grandpa is the one doing the telling. "How old was he?" my aunt might tease, and he would say, "four, no three years old." "Don't you mean two?" someone else would say, and he might shrug, "yeah, two."

Age is not what matters, but what it means: I am the privileged grandson. These privileges were extended to innumerable domains, and I enjoyed the spoils of such authority—unlimited Pepsi and salami before dinner, a choice of restaurants for my birthday (always a steakhouse), and first dibs on the sashimi on New Year's Day. Of course, such privilege did not last because such old-school cronyism was just plain unfair. The old boys' club had to shut down.

My sister was born and then two cousins, neither boys, and as the disparities between them and me became apparent, the women of my family, my aunties and my mother, fought him every step of the way. During most dinners, he would broach the subject and then quickly receive a quick volley of eye rolls and sidelong glances of annoyance. "You know, if I let the Hoshida name die on my watch," he might start off, and before he could finish, if he was lucky, someone might change the subject, but more often the room would grow silent. In our family, uncomfortable silences form like pits of quicksand. The more you thrash about, trying to talk your way through the awkward pauses and nods, the more frantic you get, the more desperate to cop a laugh, to field a question. I've seen strangers get sucked into this pit; recovery is slow. So, thankfully, he acquiesced, at least a little bit. He seemed to get it, and he began to give out equal amounts of money for our birthdays. But still he would make statements that started with, "My number one grandson," or "There's nothing better than having a grandson," and though he wouldn't put up a fight if we disagreed with him or insisted that he stop, it was clear that such an old dog would not learn new tricks.

As he grew older, the pace of his obsession did not let up, and while he was still healthy despite smoking regularly, it widened a space between all of us. In adolescence and my twenties, I could only match his insistent belief in these old traditions with my own inward ambivalence toward fatherhood and family. No children, I told my partners. I didn't want to pass this curse along to them, boy or girl. For the rest of my family, his unwavering focus on sons, grandsons, and great-grandsons made him an ingrate. Even though he sat at the head of the table, it was his wife, our grandma, who was the true host and center of our family. She would fly between the kitchen and table, stopping to nibble a bite or sip a Seven-and-Seven, cooking, serving, and cleaning while we sat and listened to him. It was not him, not me, and not our name that brought us together, but it was Grandma. Her memory quickly deteriorated while I was away at college, and at one point when she no longer recognized me, only flirting with me again and again as her memory saw fit, I realized that I had taken too long to properly thank her. Around this time, I slowly became resentful of him, the traditions to which he clung, and the loss of a relationship that I had once treasured.

• • •

But things change.

After a series of events that marked my entrance into middle age—marriage, steady work, nose hairs—I found myself driving to his house in Lincoln to announce that inside Susan's belly was growing the next generation of the Hoshida family.

In preparation for this momentous occasion, Susan made me promise that I would have a heart-to-heart with him to ensure that he would love this child no matter its sex, and I whole-heartedly agreed. It felt that for once, I could be straight with him. So, after the initial announcement to the rest of my family, I took my grandfather aside. He had grown much older. He replaced his cigarettes with oxygen tubes that were plugged into his nose and which criss-crossed the floor behind him to a machine the same size as his mini-fridge. He no longer slept in his bedroom, but on the couch in the living room so he could fall asleep while watching television. "Grandpa," I told him, "you have to love this child whether it's a girl a boy." He nodded. "All you need to do is to hope that it's a healthy baby." And he nodded again, yes, yes. A healthy baby, yes, and I felt like maybe this issue of being the number one grandson, his insistence on passing the names down only through boys, had been resolved. And I admit that I felt a little proud that maybe we had changed this for good. But those were the naive feelings of a father-to-be. Of course, the next day my sister reported that Grandpa had cornered her and told her: first, he would wait to die until she got married; and second, that it would be nice if the baby turned out to be a boy. What did I expect?

When Twyla emerged from her mother after forty hours of labor, in a stubborn and spiteful kind of way, I was too tired to care much about what my grandfather thought about whether his name had been passed down according to his rules. Before her birth, I had been quite sure that my son or daughter would feel that they should honor their family in their own way, not merely through the birthing of offspring or the passing down of names. I had thought this through, and I didn't want my child to have to think through these things as I did. But as we filled out the name form for the county, I wanted her to carry the name. I cannot explain the urge. We discussed whether to hyphenate or join our names, but we eventually agreed that hyphenation seemed too 1990s and creating a completely new name on the fly was complicated, and so when Susan, fatigued and happy, said okay, we decided on her last name: Hoshida.

I wondered if that was enough.

•••

This year, 2011, was our last in my grandfather's house for oshogatsu, and it was Twyla's second New Year with our family. I had hoped that we would continue meeting there until she was three or four, maybe even five, so she could remember, but she will not.

She will not remember his house on New Year's day, and no amount of explaining and writing will do it justice. She won't be able to smell the stale remembrance of cigarettes and fried grease that lingered in the long blue and green shag carpet. We won't be able to replicate the stuffy eighty-degree heat blowing out of the vents in the living room, and she will not wonder if using a brown paper bag as a grease cover for the fried chicken, like Grandma did, might cause a fire that will burn down the house. She will not remember pictures of our dead placed in the obutsudan just next to my grandfather's chair at the head of the dining room table. Nor will she remember the flimsy deck of cards Grandpa played with for one year only replacing the deck each New Year's day. The layered Jell-O, the five-dollar poker, the stories of my uncle showing up on my parents' porch piss drunk, the story of why we only eat the red sashimi, she will not remember these stories turned into incantations, these recipes turned into rituals, she will not be able to touch these memories with her hands, turn them over and smell them. I know she will not remember because I, too, do not remember.

I do not remember my great-grandmother, Kayo, because I was too young to form a lasting memory of her. A single photo documents that we both lived at the same time: me in her lap, and she in her chair. She was so old and I was so young, I sometimes think that between us we added up to one full person. When I see this image of us, without a recording of her voice or a video of her movement, I almost do not believe that she is real.

Maybe this is what he is fighting: the inevitability of his disappearance from earth. I am not sure that I blame him. Death is a mystery and for that reason scary, and no matter the spirit or story or myth we use, we must make sense of it. Why not a name? A name must be pronounced and recognized, fumbled over and explained; it unsuspectingly fastens memories and stories to its user. It lives. It is pondered. A name can live for a long as there are tongues and memories, passed on and on, person-to-person, while a person who carries that name cannot. And perhaps, this is what he has always wanted: someone to remember him. Or rather, someone who promises not to forget. To hell with his rules.

Recently, we moved Grandpa into a full-time care facility, and I brought Twyla to cheer him up. For the first hour, she refused to get close. She shook her head back-and-forth, no, no, no, like only a one-year-old can do. She cannot hide her fears or her desires, but eventually, after using cereal to bait her closer and closer, I was able to take pictures of her standing on his bed, slightly afraid but willing enough to give him a small, high-five, and him smiling.

I will remember you, I think to myself, and so will she.

Migration Is Beautiful: One Father's Journey
Plinio Hernandez

My mother arrived in the United States on a medical visa with my four-month-old sister in 1984 because my sister needed a major heart operation that would take place at Children's Hospital in Oakland. I arrived with my father a year later, at the age of six, and for the next three years I learned English, played baseball, ate burgers, collected G.I. Joes, dreamed of becoming a police officer, made friends with kids from India and Vietnam as well as African American and Mexican American/Chicano kids in North Oakland.

I learned to become an American.

But in 1988, my family was returning from a summer vacation in El Salvador and made a layover in Los Angeles that soon changed my perspective. As soon as we reached customs, I could tell by the angry tone of the Immigration Naturalization Service (INS) agents that something was wrong. We were sent into a secure room in the airport and questioned for hours. My dad was continually asked how he was able to attain our family visas and he recalls, in one of our many conversations about the matter, that there was no Spanish-speaking agent working. He with his broken English at the time and the agents with their broken Spanish tried to come to an understanding, but it did not happen.

The agents began to accuse my father of illegally obtained visas. "How much did you pay for the visas?" the INS agents kept asking. If you tell the truth we will let your family go. He was hand-cuffed and we were ushered away into another holding cell in the airport, hours later we were in an INS van with other detained kids and their guardians. It was the middle of a summer day in Los Angeles. The van had no windows in the back, no air conditioning, and a glass separated the agents from us. The two INS agents had their windows rolled down as they drove around LA, got food to eat for themselves and seemed to wait for hours in different parking lots, all the while the van was over a hundred degrees. Children were fanned by their mothers and kept asking the INS agents for air or water. One child fainted. Another threw up. Eventually, we arrived in what seemed a large two-story apartment building converted into a family detention center that housed immigrant children and their guardians.

We were placed in a room with bunk beds. Already there were a Chinese lady and her grandchild who was my sister's age. For the weeks that followed, my sister and the little girl played like best friends, seemingly unbothered by our situation. When the lady and her grandchild left, she gave my sister a pair of red Chinese slippers that my mother has saved to this day. My mother recalls that I had a depressed aura. I was eight years old and was conscious of what was happening. I remember crying, being sad and angry, and asking to go back to El Salvador, "They don't want us here, let's go back to El Salvador!"

I no longer wanted to be a police officer. I didn't even want to stay in the United States any longer. But my mother explained we have to stay because my sister still needed treatment. For the following weeks, we would go back and forth to court and my sister and I would sit outside the courtroom because we were minors. I would catch glimpses of my dad through the court door window as he was being brought in handcuffed. This was a confusing and saddening scene to me because to me, like most boys who are eight years old, my dad was larger than life, seemingly a superhero and seeing my hero handcuffed and visibly humiliated was a horrible experience for me.

In late June 2014, images began to surface of overcrowded condition in some immigration centers in Texas, Arizona, and California with a large amount of unaccompanied minors almost all from Central American countries. Today, I write about my experience in an INS detention center because I think about those children currently in detention centers and their anxieties, fears, and personal stories. I am currently writing this in our family's apartment, in an affluent part of the city of Berkeley, while my daughter plays with her bilingual books and a dollhouse I built her. My son is on the floor a few feet away from her learning and trying desperately to crawl. It's one of the first rainy days this fall in the

Bay Area and I lit a fire in our chimney early in the morning to have a nice cozy family Saturday.

This image is totally different that many of those children are experiencing right now and this makes me think about what will be the story that one of those children will be telling a few decades from now? Will they be writing something like this about their young counterparts that have made their way up to the United States?

My family experience was a little over twenty-five years ago. I obtained my US citizenship about six years ago and now—as a father of two, whose children were born in the United States with rights that the children in those detention centers do not have, and neither did I—I reflect on the past and feel sadness as a father and a person who lived a similar situation.

My artwork is based on my experience of migration as a way for self-healing and as an attempt to never forget. It centers on my personal family experience of immigration to the United States and a few years ago, before my children were born, someone asked me who my audience as an artist was. I responded that my audience was my unborn children and grandchildren. This idea is in the hope that my art can act as an important family archive as well as documentation of this very real and sad experience of leaving one's birth country in search of a better place. When my children are my age, with a family of their own, they can reflect on my work and say: this is what dad experienced, let's never forget.

ADVICE

Raising a Feminist
Madison Young

When I found out that I was pregnant, I knew I was birthing a revolution—a change deep inside myself that would alter my world forever. I knew that if I was going to be a parent, I would parent as a feminist. Parenting was political, the ultimate radical relationship. A foundational relationship of firsts.

As parents, we are a child's first experience in their developing and experiencing love and intimacy. We hold space and guide our little ones as they develop a relationship to their bodies and to the bodies close to them. With an emotional coach by their side, they learn how to articulate and express their feelings, what they want and how to gift affection using their words. They learn the meaning of "no" and the importance of consent.

Until I was really in the thick of parenting, I had no idea how all of these concepts and my feminist practices would come into play in the real world of parenting. But in the grand fashion of DIY, I am learning by doing, learning by connecting, by communicating, by listening and creating space for authentic expression of self.

Em is what you call a spirited child. Chock full of emotions and creative visions (I didn't get the quiet, chill Buddha baby), I got a unique child that challenges me in every way. A kid that came out kicking and screaming with a "we are here" personality that doesn't go unseen or unheard. I don't think that I really could have expected anything less.

Here are some of the radical lessons I've learned along the way and some of the challenges and successes they have been met with in my adventures of raising a feminist.

Gender Expression
I gave my child the name Emma, naming them after the radical feminist anarchist, Emma Goldman, whose fiery words had

inspired me in my work as an artist and activist. By the time my child was two years old they were expressing a desire to identify as neither girl nor boy. Their name shifted and changed from Emma to Emmerson to Em to Femme. Their gender and pronouns bounced from "he" to "she" to "they," ebbing and flowing as their vocabulary and expression of gender widened and became more complex.

This was not unusual for me. As a queer mama I made sure to have a full library of gender-diverse books for Em. I mindfully avoided gendering the characters in fairy tales or the people around us. For example if we saw a person walking down the sidewalk I wouldn't use their perceived gender to be an identifier but would reference someone like, "Do you see that person across the street in the bright yellow raincoat? I wonder if they think it will rain." I taught Em not to make assumptions about people's pronouns or genders and to ask what someone's preferred pronoun was.

I would check in with Em on a daily basis: "Hey Darlin', what's your preferred name and pronoun today?" and Em would inform me of their choices and that was that.

Kids at the playground would ask, "Hey! Hey! Is that a boy or a girl?" I would respond with, "You will have to ask them." "Hey! Hey! Are you a boy or a girl?" the kid would ask Em. "I'm not a boy or a girl, I'm just a kid," was generally Em's response.

Sometimes the kids on the playground would be frustrated by this response. "Don't they know if they are a boy or a girl? They can't be both. They don't get to choose," I've heard them say. But Em was choosing and letting us know and we listened.

Consent

"I wanna hug dolly. Em hug dolly," Em demanded at one and a half.

"Ask the dolly if the dolly wants a hug," I suggest.

"Dolly hug?" Em asks reaching out for dolly.

I pick up the dolly and respond, "I don't feel like a hug, but I'd love a big kiss."

"Big kiss!" Em claps her hands happy with the type of intimacy that her and dolly have negotiated.

Em is two and chasing a cat. I call Em over to me and have them sit on my lap. "Em, do you think the cat wants touch right now?"

"I don't know," they mumble looking at their shoes. "What is the cat doing with its body?" I ask. "Playing tag." Em smiles.

"Cats can't consent to touch with words, so we need to listen to their body language. If you present your hand when you're still and calm with your body, and the cat comes over and rubs up against your hand, then it is saying yes to some gentle touch. If it runs away, it is saying, 'Space, please.'"

Em is four years old. "I want ticka bugs!"

"Okay. Here they come. Ticka bugs are coming!" I say as I tickle Em's belly and ribs.

They roll around on their mattress laughing and wriggling under my touch. "Stop. Stop," they say breathlessly in a burst of laughter, and my hands stop immediately and return to my own body.

"Stop means stop," I say, reminding Em of our safe word.

"Whenever we say stop it's always important to stop our bodies right away, right?" I confirm making sure that I can see their eyes, so that I know Em is focused and listening.

"Right!" Em says, "Now go!" Em exclaims with robust enthusiasm. I continue our tickling game and then Em asks, "Can I tickling you, Mama?"

"Yep. But only on my belly not on my feet, okay?" I say, stating my desired tickle touch for our physical play.

"Okay, dude-a-rama!" Em yelps in excitement as they leap into tickling.

"Stop, stop," I laugh.

Em stops their hands. "Stop means stop."

"Go!" I say, and our physical display of affection and connection continues as we respect one another's words and limits.

We go to a park, to the mall, at the market and a person that will be standing beside us, looks at Em and smiles, then pets Em's head. There is nothing that Em despises more and every time it is met with a deep belly roar, a grumble often followed with a loud voice screaming in whatever public space we are in: "I did not give consent!"

We are currently working on gentler ways of communicating unwanted touch from strangers such as, "I don't like it when you touch my head. Please stop." But I do think that Em's current response is closer to what their namesake Emma Goldman would belt out.

Body Acceptance and Body Love

Em loves to run around naked. Em is a spirited child. Did I mention that already? This spirited kid is always warm even when others are chilly and Em is also really sensitive to textures and materials so running around in the buff as much as possible is Em's thing.

Em loves their body and loves to play the drums with their round belly. They will spend an hour making belly prints or using their entire body to paint using finger paints. We let Em know that clothes are for protecting our body, when we feel cold keeping us warm, and keeping dirt and bacteria out of our orifices and mucous membranes. When Em wants to run around naked, I just instate a rule that they need to put a towel down to protect their body.

Body Knowledge: "Head, Shoulders, Uterus and Vulva, Uterus and Vulva" my two-year-old and I sing as we identify those parts of our body. Growing up I didn't have a word for my genitals; my mother who works in the medical profession wouldn't give my vulva or anus a name. My genitals were referred to as "down there" and "unmentionables" and your "you know what." But the problem was I didn't know what and it was really disempowering. This lack of knowledge fueled my tiny body with a lot of shame and fear around my body parts. My parent's body shame reinforced a really unstable relationship with my own body. And it took years to reclaim and smash that stigma.

Much of that absence of foundational education, fueled my career in sex education and inspired me as an artist to further the conversation of body awareness. A primary goal of my artistic practice became to obliterate the stigma surrounding sex. In doing so, I believe we have the ability to advocate for a healthy relationship with our own bodies and in navigating healthy sexual relationships with others.

So how do I counter that as a mom? Em receives the knowledge that they seek as a curious four-year-old child. Em has names for their body parts and learns more about their own body as they continue to develop and ask more detailed questions and I provide age appropriate answers.

We use language like vulva and anus to describe our anatomy, and Em knows the ins and outs of menstruation. Em can answer questions like, What is menstruation? Why do some people menstruate? When do some people menstruate? What does menstrual blood look like? In fact I think Em knows more about menstruation than I did when I first started to menstruate when I was twelve years old. Em understands that every month my body releases an egg and the egg's journey from the ovaries to the fallopian tubes to the uterus and out the tiny hole of the cervix and comes out of the vagina along with some shedding of the walls of the uterus.

Em has a coloring book of vaginas and decorates diagram handouts of the uterus with purple glitter and watercolor paints. We have animated puppet shows on the topic of body awareness with our plush toy egg, sperm, and our gender queer vulva puppet, Val the Vulva.

We discuss what is and isn't healthy for our bodies—not what is right and what is wrong. We do talk about what is gentle and not gentle. We have frequent talks about the importance of consent, body agency, and ways to communicate with others about the type of affection we would like to gift.

Em knows that no one has a right to touch any part of their body without consent. Em knows that although it is okay to explore the touch of their own body and what feels good to them, until both people are grown-ups, it is inappropriate for any gifting or receiving of touch around mucous membranes. This includes kids sticking their fingers in each other's noses or in someone else's mouth. Em understands what our mucous membranes are and gets that those are areas of our body that have bacteria that is unique to our body and that we don't want to share that bacteria with others.

If Em chooses to explore touch of their mucous membrane areas in private areas like the bedroom or bathroom, that is totally okay. We just ask for "privacy please" and wash our hands afterward.

I keep a box of nitrile gloves by the bedside table and Em noticed these are the same type of gloves at the doctor's office and dentist's office. When asked why I had "doctor gloves" in the bedroom, I was able to explain that they acted as a barrier for bodies when entering a mucous membrane area. A few months later Em located a condom—still in the package—and enquired about it. I took a breath and was able to make what could have been an awkward situation totally normal and take the power and stigma out of a condom conversation. Because we have already had conversations about bodies, mucous membranes, and barriers, I was able to explain that the condom is a barrier for mommy's non-sharing vulva toys or a grown-up penis or a hand that might come in contact with a mucous membrane. Body knowledge is power.

• • •

There is no "wrong" section of the toy store: I love my father, I do. But we have different ideas around gender roles. When we went back to Ohio this past Christmas, to visit the family, Grandpa wanted to take Em shopping for toys. Em started loading up the cart first with a doll and then they headed towards the yellow Tonka dump trucks. Em had it on their Christmas list along with a space ship and a matchbox race car set.

As Em sprinted toward the trucks and race cars Em's heart sank as Grandpa said, "I think you're headed to the wrong section of the toy store, young lady." Em's mouth hung open and they stared at Grandpa with the truck in hand. I dove in toward Em. There are no wrong sections to the toy store, Grandpa. These toys are for everyone.

Sharing the Mic

As an artist, author, and filmmaker, I travel and tour frequently for work and sometimes I'm able to include Em on those tours. It's both an exhausting and rewarding experience to tour with my little one. There is not really any down time when you're touring with a kid. When you're not "working," you're "on" as a parent.

Em has been traveling internationally with me for tours since they were a baby so they adapt fairly well while on tour, which often involves new sitters, new foods, trains, planes, boats, and long days. It's work and a lot of transitions for a kid.

Em knows when I'm working on my writing or an art exhibit and will say that they have work to do too. Em will fill up multiple journals and sketchbooks with pen and ink drawings of how they see the world as we are traveling. When we came across an anarchist library, during a recent tour in Sydney, Australia, Em was eager to explore the library, as was I.

Em assertively went to the counter where a man covered in tattoos and dressed in all black was staring at his computer. "Scuse me! Scuse me!" Em shouted.

The gentleman looked down and found Em looking up at him. He was a bit surprised. "Yes?" he asked.

"Where's your kids' section?" Em asked.

"Hmm. We don't have a kids' section but I have a few things you might like." He brought a cardboard box down from a high shelf, and Em's eyes widened as they spotted a guitar.

Em plucked the guitar from the box and immediately jumped into the window seat in front of the store full of punks and anarchists. I smiled. It was my turn to sit back and let Em have the mic.

Em looked out at the small audience. "Would you like to hear something light or something dark?" Em asked them.

"Play some Slayer, kid!" a young teenager shouted with laughter.

Em looked up, shooting her a glare, and responded with "I'll just play something that is light and dark."

I tapped the young lady on the shoulder and whispered with a smile. "They only play originals."

Em proceeded to play for a good fifteen minutes, which is a pretty impressive set of original material for a four-year-old! I was thoroughly impressed.

Hopping That Train: Advice to Scared Fathers
Nathan Torp

It saddens me that this is the final issue of *Rad Dad*. It's been a much-needed torch in the darkness for me over the years. I remember when I first heard about the zine back in 2006. My girlfriend at the time had been visiting the Bay Area and brought home a flyer calling for submissions. It only took me eight years to get around to writing this, but I'm so glad I finally did.

But I'm not a writer. I've been a lot of things in my life, photographer, carpenter, youth leader, father, co-parent, lover, fighter, friend, community builder, radio pirate, thief, beggar, fool . . . but never a writer. The words are just always hard to find. I've always sought the words of others for solace and comfort. But now I feel it's my responsibility to contribute to the conversation about what it is to be a father, a political radical, and socially conscious human, to return some of that comfort and solace to the world.

I was nineteen when I found out I was going to be a father. I've never been so scared in my life. My girlfriend and I had spent the last two years hitchhiking around North America. We were crossing the Canadian border on our way to a G8 protest in Halifax when we realized she was pregnant. I was petrified; I had no idea how we were going to raise a child. We had a little less than $200 to our names, an empty tank of gas, and a battered old Volvo full of dirty clothes and torn books. We fought and drove across Canada for the next two weeks. We returned home to the small southern city where we had both grown up. This was 2002, the whole world seemed to be marching off to war. We were scared and angry and dumb enough to believe we could change everything. And if we failed we would raise a child who wouldn't. We rode trains west to Oregon to the EarthFirst Rendezvous. We fought some more as we made our way to see our friends in Santa Cruz and about halfway there, I walked away.

I caught a ride and left her standing on the side of the free-way. I'm not proud of this; in fact, it's probably the worst thing I've ever done. But I was scared. I was so terrified of the future, of my ability to raise a child in a world that seemed to be careening toward annihilation. My parents had me when they were nineteen and twenty. We were poor for most of my childhood. My parents never made it beyond the small Indiana town they had grown up in. I didn't know much about the world then, but I knew for certain that I didn't want to spend the rest of my life in that town, working a dead end job. Having a child seemed like a sure fire way to end up stuck there though, to just repeat the same cycle my parents had. When I walked away from her on that on-ramp in Oregon, I knew I would be back. I knew I didn't have it in me to just walk away. I knew it was against everything I believed in but in that moment, every instinct was telling me to run and run fast. We traveled separately through California, blew off some steam, and reunited for the trip home.

We made it through the pregnancy and the first ten months. But it was pretty obvious that we didn't make good partners. We could be great parents, just not together. The transition wasn't easy. There were times when we had very different ideas about how we wanted our son raised. There were times when our own personal goals didn't coincide. We made compromises where we could and learned to accept each other's opinions, however begrudgingly. Our lives and beliefs matured and changed and we adapted to new circumstances as they came up. We learned to see value in what each of us provided for our son.

She got married and had another son. I moved into a collective house and started college. A million curves and twist and bumps in the road laid ahead but over the next ten years we navigated them the best we could. We moved to Michigan so her husband could attend grad school. I dropped out of college and started a photography business. The economy collapsed and my business fell apart. I moved to Detroit and surrounded myself with an amazing community of activists and artists, farmers and musicians. A few years later we returned home to Kentucky. My son is now eleven years old; his mother is getting divorced as I am getting married. He has two wonderful siblings who I spend a lot of time with. The four of his parents (myself, my fiancé, his mother, and his stepfather) are all part of the same community and all support-ive of each other. This is the condensed version of our lives. There were a thousand triumphs and tragedies, successes and failures, missteps and stumbles that have lead us to where we are now. But I wanted to give you a little context.

See, I think most of us have realized that the traditional nuclear family is a sham. It's an oppressive patriarchal structure that, while it works for some people, doesn't work for everyone. We, however, have very few alternatives ever presented to us. There are single mothers and single fathers and married couples. Those are your options, choose one. But there are so many other ways to create "family," to support one another and support the children in our lives. I think my son is incredibly fortunate to have a whole army of adults that love and care for him, that have taught him and held him. He has this huge network of people, some of whom he doesn't even remember, who at the drop of a hat will do whatever they can to help him succeed. Many of my friends are just now entering into this crazy world of parenting, becoming fathers and mothers. Often one of them will look at me and my son and our life and ask, "So how do you do this?" Typically I just shrug and say. "You make it up as you go along and trust that you're doing a good job even when you think you're not." I feel like this is not great advice and in all reality it's not advice I'd like to give. Below is a short list of some of the things I've learned in the last decade of being a father that have helped me along the way.

— Treat your children as conscientious, intelligent humans that deserve the same respect and consideration you would give to adults.
— Learn how to walk away when you're angry.
— Learn to apologize to your children when you're wrong.
— Whenever possible, let your kids negotiate their rules and limitations. They are far more likely to respect those limits if they feel like they had some agency in creating them.
— Stop baby talking to your kids when they stop being babies. It's patronizing. (This one's a personal pet peeve.)
— Worry less. Communicate more.
— Don't hide yourself from your kids.

— Don't worry about what other people think about you as a parent. Especially nonparents.
— BUILD COMMUNITY.
— Parenting, like all relationships, is a collaborative effort. Teach your kids to participate in that relationship.
— Trust yourself.
— Trust your kids.
— Read parenting books with a big grain of salt.
— Expose your kids to as much awesome stuff as you can find: books, music, movies, plays, art, people . . . whatever you're excited about.
— Find a way to make a stable income. Raising kids is hard, raising kids with no money is really, really, really hard. (I'm still struggling with this one. Fucking capitalism!)
— Take time for yourself.
— Don't be too hard on yourself.
— Censoring and sheltering your kids from things that are scary or difficult does them a disservice. Use those opportunities to create dialogue.
— My parenting mantra: "Know Better, Learn Faster."
— Listen to your kids' ideas and solutions to problems. You'll be surprised by how often they are better than yours.
— Find a mentor.

I hope some of this helps.

If these words have somehow crossed your path and you're a young scared father-to-be, I hope they provide you some comfort and solace. The trail is never clear and the forest often dark but seek out the paths cut by other papas and mamas before you.

I know you're scared.

I know you have no idea how you're going to do this.

I know you think you can't. But you can and you will. It will be hard and you will struggle. But you'll learn and everyday it will get easier. You can't do it alone; find yourself a supportive and healthy community and if you can't find one start building one. Trust yourself and forgive yourself when you think you've screwed up. (Trust me, you'll think that a lot.) It will never be perfect; it will never be easy. One thing that always helps me is to remember that we're not trying to raise a kid who will be successful in the world we live in.

We're trying to raise a kid who will be successful in creating a better one. We're not trying to raise an engineer or a banker or a lawyer (though it's fine if they become any of those things . . . except the banker). We're trying to raise a caring, conscientious human who recognizes the atrocities of the world as it is and has the tools and resources to confront them. Thus far I think we've done a good job. If you find some resonance in these words or find yourself needing advice and solidarity, feel free to e-mail me at nathantorp@gmail.com

Keeping a Poo Journal and Other Bits of Advice from One Parent to Another
Simon Knaphus

I try really hard not to give unsolicited advice to new and expecting parents, so a call for submissions asking for advice is a fun opportunity. Here are some things that either I wish I would have heard (or listened to) in those early days or that ended up working well for me:

> Let your little one do stuff that makes you nervous (especially in the woods and at the playground). They are going to anyway. This will help them discover their own sense of what is and isn't safe based on an awareness of their own abilities and comfort. It also sets you up as an ally of exploration rather than a naysayer.

> Keep a poo journal of everything that you have cleaned poo from. I am at the tail end of the poo-cleaning part of parenting, but I wish I had a list. It would be hilarious.

> Don't buy stuff until you know you really need it. Money is time.

> Keep a journal generally. This is always in the next ten things to do on my list, and so far it hasn't happened.

> Teach kids of all genders that boys are not to hit girls, and teach them that this important rule comes out of a very problematic history between men and women and is based on harmful stereotypes about women and weakness, but that, nonetheless, we still live in a social context in which the problematic history is still very much alive, and in which the way that we are socialized makes it more harmful for a boy to hit a girl than for a boy to hit a boy or for a girl to hit a girl.

Teach your kid the word "patriarchy." Let it come from you, not just the women in their life.

Teach your kid that not everyone is a boy or a girl. (And in the not-hitting rule above, it is especially important not to hit people who are neither boys nor girls because they get treated badly all the time.)

Teach your kid to be an ally, and how standing up for someone is different than just not teasing them.

Snuggle that little bambino with all you've got.

You might end up being a single parent for one reason or another. This will not ruin your kid's life if you don't let it ruin yours. For real.

Love your friends and family with reckless abandon.

Don't worry too much about other parents, including your own.

Treat yourself with kindness and compassion.

Let your kid watch you mess up, stop, repair, apologize, and learn from your mistakes. Then they can say, "I learned it from watching you, Dad. I learned it from watching you."

Be vulnerable, reject shame.

Eat food that is yummy and nutritious.

Learn to do new things and share them with your kid.

Talk to your baby like they are intelligent and care about what you have to say. They are. They will. They do.

Start helping your kid use the toilet before they are old enough to form the opinion that your will is to be resisted. This happens alarmingly soon after the first birthday.

Be yourself.

OOOOOoooo boy, you're going to mess up so bad sometimes. It's rough. Every parent really really fails every once in awhile. It doesn't mean you are bad. People who think they don't mess up are lying to themselves and missing out on opportunities to learn.

You will be amazing beyond what you ever thought you could be. Joy and love and wonder await you. Have fun!

Balls and Eyes; or,
How to Talk with Your Kids about Anarchism
Tomas Moniz

Talking with your kids about anarchism despite the vilification and ridicule it gets in the mainstream media (if it gets any attention at all) should be a no-brainer. If you don't, no one else will. This is, of course, easier said than done. It's like those moments when we must address other complicated and complex issues like, say, sexism or racism or capitalism. With those issues, admittedly much more intense and important, you just kinda plunge forward and talk honestly about it—none of this faux-parenting belief that you should wait until your children are older. Poor parents can't put off talking with their kids about what they can and can't afford, queer or trans parents can't avoid addressing issues of discrimination, and parents of color don't wait to prepare their kids for how to deal with racism.

Now in no way do I equate talking about anarchism with the importance of addressing those other issues, but I do see a similarity in being honest about a subject that is for the most part silenced or misrepresented.

However, if, as I believe, radical families are necessary for truly creating a revolutionary society, for supporting the multigenerational movements to come, then it's talking that's important, the questioning, the challenging, even if it's complicated, contradictory, or flawed.

The Cops
Let me just say that my biggest detractor about anarchist praxis is my youngest daughter. She refuses to even say the word correctly, sputtering out an-ar-car-chist like it makes no sense to even say properly.

Anyways, I'm listening to Boots Riley's album called *Street Sweeper Social Club* and there's this catchy tune called "Clap for the Killers." It says, "give it up for the gangstas." So I'm standing there, singing it and chopping onions.

Enter my daughter with her little posse of twelve-year-old friends, "Um, Dad, why would you clap for killers?"

I pause. Four pairs of cocked eyebrows and eyeballs staring at me. Clearly I need to think about how to answer this.

"Well, I think it's metaphorical."

Mistake. Metaphorical language and twelve-year-olds don't really mix.

They look at me like I'm speaking Finnish.

I run and get the lyrics, but they already have lost interest, and I feel like I've just failed some important opportunity.

A few minutes later though, I find them out in the backyard, so I explain to them about how the line in the song is about appreciating what some people do that the government deems criminal, or that sometimes will get you arrested by the cops.

Sensing a weak point in my argument, my daughter retorts: "Not all cops are bad, Dad. You know they stop crime, sometimes."

I look at all four of them, a picture of the typical diversity in the Bay Area, a bunch of mixed race kids.

Here is the moment to both honor what they are saying yet try to fight some of the mythology they are inundated with, that is fed to them nonstop at schools, in the movies and for so many in their own houses.

They do fight crime, I admit. Not all cops are bad people, but sadly sometimes they are the criminals. Who gets policed is sometimes about how much money you have or how dark your skin is.

We are all silent for a second.

My daughter nods her head and says, like the cop that killed Oscar Grant.

She may in fact still disagree with me about anarchism and clapping for killers, but at least she is willing to talk about it.

Voting

My other daughter tends to be a little more willing to see the possibilities in anarchist living.

Dad, are you gonna vote this year? She is looking at me. We've talked in the past about wishing there was a book on anarchism geared for teens because in her high school classes on politics, everyone loves to ridicule the newbie anarchists in the classroom. She tries to help out but doesn't quite know what to say.

So back to voting.

I want to offer some badass slogan about how their ballot boxes will never hold our dreams, or whoever they elect, we are ungovernable, but there she is staring at me, waiting. Nothing challenges anarchist ideals like parental guilt.

"Well, do you really think it matters or makes a difference?" I ask her, trying to flip the script to get her to talk and let me off the hook.

"Yes, I do."

And she waits, and this is where theory falls away. She wants real, honest conversation.

I confess, it angers me that it's a choice I feel I have to make because if I don't something bad will happen. Why should I have to do something out of fear, you know. It really fucking sucks.

She shakes her head a little in agreement; she reaches her hand to my shoulder like she's reassuring me and says, it's kinda like doing homework. It sucks but you gotta do it. So you should still vote.

Natural Consequences

One area that anarchism and parenting connect is the notion of natural consequences. It's of course much easier when they're older, but yes, you can be an anarchist and say no to your children. Yes, you can be an anarchist if you refuse to let your child run through a restaurant or a grocery store; boundaries and limits do not an authoritarian make.

So the idea is transparency. As they get older, you discuss the consequences. This is all well and good while they actually listen to you. However, be prepared for the dreaded moment when your child says: "Hmm, okay, so if I hang out with my friends and decide not to come home, you're telling me that I'll be grounded for a week?"

"Yes," I say, feeling slightly arrogant in my position of doling out natural consequences, until my son responds.

"All right then."

"What?" I stammer, not sure what he means. "You'll be grounded," I repeat.

"I know," he says. "I love you and I'll see you tomorrow." He proceeds to hug me and walks out the door.

"Wait," I say stunned and feeling like I have been outwitted. As he leaves, I wonder if this is the consequence of parenting: learning to let go.

Empowerment

But for all the laughs and the conundrums that come with trying to parent in radical or anarchist ways, there are the rewards.

My son choosing to follow his heart rather than his wallet as he enters young adulthood.

My oldest daughter silk-screening shirt after shirt at her high school's walkout, the excitement and belief that so much is possible spread across her face afterwards like a smile.

Or this.

I worry about safety now, not the don't-choke-on-broccoli safety but, as a father of teenaged young women, about sexual violence or harassment.

I want to live in a world where my sixteen-year-old daughter can take the AC transit to her home in south Berkeley without fear; and I don't want to instill that fear in them.

Self-defense and self-determination have always been an important anarchist principle, one not lost on my daughters. They've taken a few self-defense classes; they have strong powerful women as role models in their lives, and we talk about how to protect themselves.

So when my daughter asks to take the bus home one early Friday evening, I respond, "Well, okay, but what do you do if you feel uncomfortable in a situation?"

"Balls and eyes," she yells, almost making me drop the phone and cover my own balls and eyes.

I gather myself and say, "Well, I was thinking you should raise your voice and ask other adults for help first."

"Hell no," she says, "someone mess with me it's balls and eyes."

As I wrote this, I realized I failed. Perhaps none of this is about anarchist parenting per se. But I discovered that for me, anarchist parenting doesn't follow a model, doesn't fit nicely into an approach; perhaps, like all good anarchist endeavors, it's a bit nebulous, a bit fluid, but underlying it all is an attention to the relationships we create, to living authentically and honestly; perhaps it's a little like a line from the novel *Letters of Insurgents*, and I paraphrase, in the end what are we left with when all the instruments are rotten? We are left with ourselves and each other.

I like that. What's left is us, you and I, the families we create . . .

List 3: How to Talk to Kids
Jessie Susannah

So here's the deal: Kids aren't "like" tiny human beings. They *are* tiny human beings. (Okay, sort of like tiny drunk human beings. Or in the case of my particular kid, like a fratboy on mushrooms.) So you know that whole thing where when you interact with other human beings you (hopefully) try to act right? You should do that with kids too!

If you don't have experience doing it, interacting with kids can be stressful. Like what are you supposed to say or not say? Are you supposed to change your voice tone? What if you don't know what Thomas the Train is? Here are some highly opinionated tips to help ya and to pass on to the kidless allies in your life.

Children's liberation!
I'm dead ass serious. Respect kids, don't treat them as objects. Trust them as the authority on their own experience. Take their experience, needs, and opinions seriously. Don't laugh at them, talk about them like they're not there, or say everything they say and do is cute. Don't use your intelligence or privilege to manipulate them.

Trust yourself and be your best self
You completely have the capacity to work with other adults to protect kids and create a healthy environment for them and with them. Kids need to feel safe, have their boundaries respected, and feel seen and protected by the adults around them. Kids need you to be an adult. Shit, I do, too.

"We begin by listening"
(a powerful and always relevant principle of the Allied Media Projects Network)
Listen to how kids talk. Listen to how this particular kid talks. Use words that they use, that are relevant to them. Listen with more

than your ears. Pay attention to what the kid in question notices, what they look at, what their body language is saying. Think about what might be going on for this kid in this moment. See where you connect and relate and start from there.

Model bodily consent

You can do something awesome that will help end rape culture. Really actually. You can help kids (aka tiny people) learn that they get to make choices about how and by whom their bodies are touched and that they should ask before they touch other people's bodies. Kids are cute and sweet. They are more openly loving than most adults. Please do not exploit that openness. Physical affection from a child (or anyone) should be a freely given symbol of their loving familiar relationship and feelings towards you. *Ask* and obtain permission before hugging, tickling, touching, picking up, or kissing a child, including a baby. If a kid says no, respect that boundary absolutely without question. Do not make a game out of asking if you can tickle a kid and then doing it anyway when they say no. If a kid, especially a boychild, wants to jump on you, or play physically, ask them to check in with you about how it makes your body feel and whether you want to or not.

Be friendly and be genuine

Kids do not understand sarcasm or cultural reference points. Kids don't know or care where you got your stank-ass attitude from. Kids *do* know if you're talking to them in a hella fake tone of voice. Be real, be present, and be nice.

Remember how to play

Be silly, sweet, and creative. Get wacky and psychedelic. If you don't do a lot of playing in your day-to-day and it's hard to remember how, enter through an activity that you feel comfortable with: draw something, beatbox, show a piece of your jewelry and explain what you like about it, tell them the name of a plant. Show off a trick. Do that thing where it looks like your finger's getting cut in half. Unlike the rest of us, kids really do think it's cool that you can juggle.

Say yes

When kids invite you to do something they are offering you an opportunity for intimacy and friendship. It's a precious gift. Instead of spending a few minutes explaining why you aren't available, just get into it and play for five or ten minutes. If you are short on time, create play with a time limit, like, "I'll set my phone alarm for seven minutes and we can play Legos. It will be short but we can play more another time," or "Let's play three rounds of hide-and-seek and then i need to go."

Bring your politics with you

Kids are absorbing everything. Think about how your words might reflect and form ideas. Corporate marketing to kids is very real. If you are anti-corporate, don't name-drop characters, etc. If you are a feminist (and if you're not, can you work that out? thx.), don't start conversations with (especially girl) kids about their appearance or their outfit. Ask them a question about what book or animals they like, for example. Don't believe in the gender binary? Ask the child or parent if there is a preferred pronoun and don't make assumptions based on outfit color "clues." Be thoughtful of how you talk about police, bosses, soldiers, etc. Some cool (alternate word) choices can be "search" instead of "hunt," "friend" instead of "boy" or "girl," "organizer" instead of "boss." Think about how you use the words "bad" and "good," especially to describe people. It's actually kind of cool and fun to do.

Kids are spiritual teachers

They push you to do that ultimate piece of growing up: to think outside of yourself. Allow them to teach you compassion, patience, and mindfulness, and gain perspective on the formation of your own psyche, how you got to be how you are now. Allow them to gently show you how to truly become your best self: a self who owns your own stuff; who has good boundaries; who has the capacity to respectfully and genuinely interact with people who have different needs and skills than you do; a person who shows up and is present.

PART 4

broken circles

i used to hate round things my dad telling me make a fist circular & solid punching me to show how hard a closed hand could be made us eggs sunday mornings regardless of our chants for omelets or a scramble he always served them fried & flat & round he had circle tattoos on his hands that didn't connect broken he called them told me they were a mistake voice locked & tight

how to heal a broken man   how to close the circle
how not to break

my lover laughed at my story said the opposite was true the world works in broken & imperfect circles like arms hugging a baby's toothless smile the way a dog spins around & around before sleeping the word moon sung by nick drake the soft & rounded edges of the adobe home

my grandmother was born in   the fat & plump sopaipillas my tia makes

one morning my son gathered blue eggs from our new chickens we marveled at their warmth feathers still stuck to shell cradling them in the half circles of our palms like precious things

father you are wrong   everything connects
nothing is broken

Rad Family Dos and Don'ts

A little bit of parenting wisdom earned from our mistakes. Now's the time to pass them on. If you have other examples, send them in . . .

Do ride bikes with your seven-year-old child. Don't put said child on handle bars without helmet and bike them to school.

Do take your six-year-old girl on trail runs in the hills. Don't forget to tell her to avoid the cow patties.

Don't keep your kids' teeth around the house after the tooth fairy has come and gone. Do tell your son the tooth fairy must have dropped it on her way out if he finds his tooth in your desk drawer.

Do toss a cloth diaper over your infant boy's penis while he's lying on the changing table, unless you want to see how high his pee fountain is.

Don't play "airplane" with your baby above your head while you lie on the sofa if he has just nursed, unless you enjoy being regurgitated on.

Don't bribe your teen daughters *not* to have sex.

Don't tell your kids that the cute twenty-four-year-old they caught you sneaking into/out of your room is gay and therefore "just there to cuddle."

Do rock your colicky baby to sleep using the football hold and the music of NoMeansNo. It works.

COMMUNITY AND ALLIES

Writing Our Own Manual:
Persistence, Community and Disability Parenting
Krista Lee Hanson

My partner Burke was out of town on the day of the end-of-school-year picnic, so I took my son there myself. It felt important to be there, in part because he might enjoy playing with his kindergarten friends, but just as much because we were still working to claim all-school spaces as ours, too. Lucas has a severe muscle disease that makes his experience of the world very unique. I wish I could have left home confident the organizers had thought about Lucas in planning this event, but we know better than that from experience.

I pushed Lucas's chair up the ramp to the playground, and we started looking for his friends. Two girls from his class ran up, waving and cooing their sweet "Hi Lucas!" They grabbed his hands—which he can barely move to grab back—and we took off looking for the person blowing bubbles. I pushed Lucas's chair off the blacktop and onto the school's field; it was rough going. Parents and kids came over to talk to Lucas, meaning well, but no one could hear him because of the blaring music, so they talked to me instead. I passed their questions about summer plans back to Lucas, prompting him to tell them about the dinosaur camp he was excited about. But I couldn't even hear him, and his body was uncomfortable from the bouncing over clods of grass. When I got my ear up close enough to his mouth, I heard him telling me he wanted to go home. We had been at the party for five minutes.

I understood why he wanted to leave, but Burke and I both take pride in forcing access for Lucas out of situations that look inaccessible. And it took a lot to get there—arranging child care for his baby sister, motivating myself to do this when I was tired, plus all the other planning it takes for us to leave the house each day, including remembering things like clean diapers, a fully charged ventilator and suction machine, blenderized food plus feeding tubes, and a stocked emergency-supply bag that we must keep with him at all times in case his airway becomes blocked. So I persisted.

• • •

We chose Lucas's elementary school because it brought together many things we wanted: public education, an alternative school with a stated interest in social justice and environmentalism, and a "medically fragile" program, meaning there would be staff and kids in the building who might be able to relate to Lucas's experience. Although disability law states that children should be placed in the school closest to them that best serves their needs, Lucas doesn't fit into any of the school district's categories for disability, which assumes a simple low-to-high functioning spectrum. Lucas was born with a severe neuromuscular disease, so he has needed significant help with the most basic tasks, such as breathing and moving, since the day he was born. In school he is an advanced reader, but he needs assistance with lifting papers to where he can see them and writing down answers. If you ask him how he's different than his classmates, he'll (correctly) tell you he knows more about dinosaurs than them.

So we had to work hard to get Lucas placed at this school, and were relieved when we finally got the paperwork in the mail confirming our choice. We were even more relieved when we then met with the special-ed teachers and staff, who quickly figured out that Lucas was awesome. But when we left the special-ed room to go visit the "regular" kindergarten classrooms, kids came up to us in the hall to point us back to where we were coming from. "Special ed is back there," they said. I explained to surprised fourth graders that Lucas would be going to kindergarten like the other five-year-olds.

So a year later, out on that playground we were trying to claim as ours, too, Lucas and I stuck with the picnic for a full forty-five minutes, Lucas barely patient as I tried to include him in conversations that he didn't have the energy to participate in. He wanted to play with his friends, who under other circumstances would have included him, but running around a field was beyond the limits of his wheelchair and weak body.

We were finally heading out when a parent I didn't recognize came over to say hi. She told me that her daughter was older, and that she spent her whole day in a special-ed classroom. "How did you know to ask for Lucas to be placed in a regular classroom?" she asked. I hadn't ever thought about it. We just knew it was right for Lucas, and in the moment I couldn't quite form an answer. I muttered something about never asking permission, just assuming and pushing ahead. But I didn't want her to feel bad about not knowing something that legally should have been presented to her as an option over and over again. So we said goodbye and Lucas and I finally went home. But her question has stuck with me. How did we know? No kid comes with a handbook, but when your kid is born with a disability—physical, cognitive, sensory, behavioral, or all of the above—you really are writing your own manual as you go.

. . .

I often think Lucas was lucky to be born into a progressive and radical family and political community. It has meant that we know how to organize and fight, and it has meant our friends have loved Lucas completely since the day he was born.

Burke and I met in El Salvador as organizers and leaders in CISPES, the Committee in Solidarity with the People of El Salvador. We led trainings on the history of neoliberalism and imperialism, led political campaigns, and mentored new organizers. In our work we regularly talked about power and oppression, though in hindsight we barely paid lip service to disability and ableism because it wasn't part of our lives then.

I remember when I was pregnant, noticing the parents who wore their babies strapped to their chests at meetings and political demonstrations. "That's what we'll be like, bringing up a baby in the movement," I thought. We joked that our baby's first direct action was when we joined a group that shut down the intersection in front of the White House the day Obama hosted Colombian President Uribe. I was six months pregnant, so I didn't lock down in the middle of the road, but I played a key support role from the curb to make the action possible. We were proud parents-to-be, not letting pregnancy stop us from full participation in radical politics.

Then our world changed. Lucas was born, two months early, floppy, bruised, and barely breathing. Our first year with Lucas we spent hunkered down, first in the neonatal intensive care unit (NICU), then at home, doing our best to learn how to parent a ventilator-dependent baby. This meant learning how to pick up a body attached to so many tubes and wires, then learning to recognize the signs of respiratory distress and move quickly to manually clear his airway (using a home suction machine) so he could keep breathing. Or, if that didn't work quickly enough, using resuscitative breathing to bring a gray-blue baby back to pink. It was a heartbreaking, adrenaline-packed time, so we barely had time to look up and remember the "political" parents we thought we would be.

But of course radical politics is bigger than showing up for the media-grabbing direct actions. We grieved not being the family we had imagined, but we also dug in our heels and declared to the world that we would love and support our child in whatever ways we could. We started a blog where we wrote passionately about how we were ready to learn from Lucas and be transformed into the parents that he needed. We had strong convictions—like loving everyone not despite but because of their gifts and limitations; allowing ourselves to be forged and transformed—that came from our liberation politics. We had learned about radical, deep solidarity. Now we were turning those lessons into loving a baby who was very different than the baby we expected, who existed in a body very different from ours.

And we turned our organizing skills into parenting skills. Just getting Lucas home from the NICU, three months after he was born, was a feat of incredible advocacy. We had to learn how to navigate hospital bureaucracy, private and state insurance policies, local law and federal law, and the maze of disability power brokers in Washington, DC, where we lived when Lucas was born. The fighting and learning about his needs and rights hasn't slowed since then. So I think the shorter answer to how we knew to insist that Lucas be placed in a mainstream classroom is that Burke and I had been schooled by organizers and activists for a decade before he was born. We had studied the history of liberation movements in the U.S. and around the world, and we knew that, as Frederick Douglass said, "power concedes nothing without a demand." And even though we had a lot to learn about disability specifically, our general training in organizing meant we knew what questions to ask, how to relate to power, and how to execute a strategy—when to push harder and when to switch gears.

• • •

It is important to note, and worth a second essay, that we come to the struggle for access and inclusion with a lot of privilege as white, cisgendered, middle-class, and wealthy folks. Poor families dealing with disability, and families of color, immigrant families, and families who do not speak English as a first language have to deal with so many more barriers than we do. I often spend a week trying to get a doctor on the phone, and I have a very flexible schedule. Even then, Burke and I still get overwhelmed trying to figure out the byzantine system of preapprovals for necessary tests and medical gear. Recently we had to sign a release stating we would pay $30,000 for a power wheelchair if our insurance declined to pay for it, since our insurance suddenly stopped offering preapprovals for medically necessary equipment or treatments. I am sure that parents with blue-collar jobs, without the flexibility to make daytime phone calls or extra cash in the bank, must have to work so much harder to navigate this world.

Lucas was born not just into a family with organizing skills, but also a lefty community that was open to loving him exactly has he is, and to letting themselves be transformed. I remember the first big political event we attended with Lucas, a bi-annual CISPES activist training gathering we call "summer camp." The summer Lucas turned one, the camp took place on a farm in rural Virginia, more than an hour from where we lived in Washington, DC. The prospect of leaving our home—with all our medical supplies, emergency gear, and backup emergency gear all in place—was a huge undertaking. But we decided it was worth the work (and inherent risk of forgetting something important) to reconnect with the people and issues near to our hearts.

I remember arriving after everyone else and finding that they had saved the best room in the main farmhouse for us. We later took Lucas out to lie in the grass while we listened to open-air workshops. Today, we're used to Lucas's suction gear bringing loud noise into quiet places, but at that time it still felt awkward. But instead of being uncomfortable, I felt like even our interrupting noise was welcome in that space. The organizers included time in the agenda for a discussion of disability justice—a first for CISPES. Lucas also weaved his weak but eager fingers through the grass and put twigs in his mouth for the first time at that summer camp. And, most importantly, he was surrounded by admiring people who wanted him to be there.

• • •

Lucas has a lot to offer people who are willing and patient. Our community has learned how to make spaces and events accessible. But when I hear our friends talk about how knowing Lucas has changed them, I think it is something deeper they've been willing to learn, too. Lucas has taught us complex lessons about what it is to be fully human. His severe physical limitations make him look so extremely weak and vulnerable and dependent, yet his spirit shines with peace and joy and good humor most of the time. But you can only learn these things if you're willing to slow down, hunker down to look Lucas in the eye, and listen closely to his slurred speech. Our friends and community have been almost eager to open themselves up to these lessons.

Of course our experience isn't representative of everyone—and I don't mean to let the left off the hook for our continued perpetuation of ableism. Many disabled folks with chemical sensitivities have asked that meetings and events be fragrance-free, yet their requests are often ignored as though this and other less-visible disabilities aren't real. Most marches are planned by youthful, nondisabled folks, so they move so quickly that we end up nearly left behind, struggling to keep up at the back—sometimes closer to the police escort than the marchers—along with the other chair users, people with other kinds of mobility limitations, families with young kids, and elders.

Nonetheless, we continue to experience a real sense of welcome for Lucas in social justice circles. Since we moved to Seattle, we've connected with an antiracist parent collective, a local environmental justice group, and a radical philanthropic organization. At different times, the leaders of each of these groups have reached out and asked us what they can do to make an event be more accessible in general, and specifically what we need to be able to attend. What if the administration at Lucas's school cared about disability, access, and a culture of inclusion enough to prioritize that in the planning of all-school events? What if parents of children with disabilities could trust that in meetings about their child's individual education needs, everyone at the school was prioritizing inclusion? What if the renovation of any public building or park included consultation with people with disabilities so that the space might be designed to welcome everyone? What if there were enough public resources available for people with disabilities to have all their basic needs met so that they could be full members of their communities, instead of struggling to get by day-to-day?

Burke and I still do everything we can to make the world appear welcoming and accessible to Lucas, but as he grows he will be able to see beyond our efforts. We won't be able to lift him and his chair anymore to help him access otherwise inaccessible spaces. He will notice ways in which the world throws up barriers, or looks through him instead of at him. I wish we could always shelter him from pain, including the pain of facing discrimination and exclusion, but of course that isn't possible for any parent. So we go with second-best: we fight to make the world more welcoming and accessible to people with disabilities in all the ways we can, and we surround Lucas with our loving, radical community.

How to Parent on a Night Like This
Carvell Wallace

My son is home from school. He stays in bed while I take his little sister to her fourth-grade class. He watches about eight hours of television. I have to work. We watch *Skyfall* together in the morning. The violence is a little beyond what I would normally allow, but something about a father and son watching a spy thriller together . . . I can't resist. A Final Showdown at the Scottish Manor. Helicopters and explosions. Cars with semiautomatics in the headlights. Sawed-off shotguns.

I pick my daughter up at 3:30 while he stays at home. I take her to the grocery. We talk about persimmons and how to tell if they're ripe. She asks me how I decide which chicken to buy. I explain about air-chilled, and free-range, and grain-fed, and hormone-free. I realize that I don't actually understand "air-chilled." I send her clear across the store to go find peanut oil. She does. I am impressed.

In the car, she asks about her brother. I tell her he's home alone. She is quiet for a few more minutes. Then she tells a story of the time her mother went to the store and left them home alone. And they heard a sound. An explosion of a kind. And her older brother started panicking, telling her it was gunshots, telling her to close the blinds and hide on the floor. And how she became terrified and FaceTimed Mommy from her iPad. And Mommy tried to calm her down, but eventually came right home, leaving a cart filled with groceries in the aisle.

Helicopters are already circling downtown.

She tells me that she now knows that they were overreacting. That it was probably fireworks. It didn't sound like real gunshots. She's heard real gunshots. They happened one afternoon while she was playing on the schoolyard. The teachers told them to run inside and they didn't even have to line up. That's how she knew it was serious.

We come back home and the kids are reunited. Rare is the day that one has school and the other doesn't. They are so used to being together in the same cars on the same schedule, even at different schools, that when they see each other, there is awkwardness. They want to check in. If they were adults, they might say, "How was your day?" and "I missed you!" But they are not adults. So they argue about who is the worst teacher at the elementary school, and then reminisce about funny episodes of sitcoms that they've watched. She quizzes him on his menu, keen to make sure that he didn't get an ice cream or a cookie on his day off. She's always keeping track of things like this. Everything must be even.

The grand jury decision is expected to be read at 8 p.m. CST.

She begins her homework. He watches vaguely racist and sexist YouTube videos.

I make her a snack of plain yogurt and granola.

Rumors are starting to spread that there will be no indictment.

I already know there will be no indictment. I've been a black man in America for a long time.

The house is quiet, everyone engrossed in their screens. I am agitated. Scrolling social media, lead in the pit of my stomach.

We've been here before. As a family.

We are black people in Oakland. We talk about race a lot. We talk about gender a lot. We discuss transphobia and homophobia a lot. We discuss capitalism and civil rights a lot. We've heard helicopters and chants and seen the streets burn. We've been to protests. We've held signs and played drums. We've had our car broken into and our heart-covered backpack and pink size-3 trench coat stolen from the front seat on the first night of Occupy. We've driven past armies of cops in riot gear in our minivan. We've been here before. We are black people in Oakland.

I send them to the corner store, so they can get outside and I can have some quiet. Three dollars each. I wonder if they'll be attacked walking down the street. Black people sometimes get attacked when white people are scared of the reality of race.

Darren Wilson is not charged, and it makes me wonder if someone is going to attack my black children.

I decide to make tacos al pastor. I'm keeping it simple this week because Thanksgiving is a few days away and there's going to be a shitload of cooking for that. I already have some frozen pork that I made months ago. I heat up the meat and tortillas. I am not very woo woo at all, but the one thing I know is that when I cook while agitated the food does not taste good. I try to calm down but I can't. I brought my phone and Twitter feed into the kitchen. Scrolling with my pinky, leaving cumin residue on my screen.

They return with Rollos and 7 Up.

People are now live tweeting the speech. Apparently it's taking forever. "What's next, an interpretive dance?" a particularly funny tweet asks. The tortillas burn. I throw them out. Start again.

I consider playing the press conference on the living-room TV. But my daughter warned me about that. She warned me when she told me how frightened she was of the firecracker that may have been a gun. What will the TV show my nine-year-old before she goes to sleep? I decided to let them stay lost in Netflix.

The food is . . . meh. Pork is overcooked. Salad dressing too vinegar-y. Beans underdone. But the rice turns out great. When all else fails I can always make amazing Spanish rice. Nevertheless, they finish every last bite and ask for more.

I retire upstairs while they do the post-dinner chores.

I want to put my phone down but I can't. Every moment without it feels terrifying. I read more on Twitter. Protesters have taken to the street. They've closed down 580. The freeway. I'm happy for them. Friends are uploading videos. I've been to enough protests in Oakland. I know this will be relatively harmless. A few white kids with masks will try and break shit. The police will not be stupid and everyone will go home relatively unscathed. It just has that feel.

It's hard to continue. I wish it was my kids bedtime. I wish the dishes were done. I wish the house was clean. I wish America wasn't racist. I wish Mike Brown was in police custody. I wish Darren Wilson admitted guilt. I wish America admitted guilt.

I post on Facebook "How do you parent on a night like this?" People respond with advice about how to talk to kids about race. Well-meaning, but missing the point. I don't mean what do you say. I mean how do you go on.

How do you go on?

How do you make lunch for tomorrow and sweep and handle bath time?

How do you parent with a permanently broken heart?

I text their mother. "Hi," I say. She responds. But I stop. She is white. I don't actually want to talk to any white people right now. I love her, though. She is an exceedingly kind, strong, and loving person. And I make a note to tell her then next time I see her.

My son is being a dick. He keeps messing with his sister. He keeps not following directions. He keeps jumping around the house like a . . . well, like an eleven-year-old boy. My patience is wearing thin. I want to yell at him. Will you calm the fuck down? Do you know what the fuck is happening out there? But I don't. Because he will know way sooner than I want.

Mike Brown kept messing with people.

Mike Brown kept jumping around.

Mike Brown kept not following directions.

But when I tell him to brush his teeth and he bullshits for another ten minutes. I finally lose it.

"Hey!" I yell. The room grows intensely quiet. "Get your shit together."

I can see behind his eyes as he calculates how to respond. Another joke? An angry backlash? He does neither. He looks hurt. He fixes me with a sad stare, milking it just a bit, and then mopes upstairs. When he is five steps away, I call him back. He makes a joke of not wanting to get closer to me. "Come here," I say. He moves an inch. "No, *here*." He moves another. "*Here!*" We do our little routine a few times more. We watch a lot of comedy together.

When he is close enough to touch, I reach out and hold him to me like I've maybe never held anyone to me in my entire life. I feel his warmth. The narrowness of his bones. The quick beat of his little heart. I bury my face awkwardly in the back of his neck. I choke back tears. I don't want tears now.

"Dad. Are you all right?" He knows this is the next funny thing to say.

"I love you" is all I can manage.

I stop before it gets any weirder for him. "I love you too, Dad. You're a great dad." And I can tell he means it.

Later they are both in my bed, in jammies, wet and clean from showers, blankets pulled to their chins. I read them two chapters from E.L. Konigsburg's *From the Mixed-up Files of Mrs. Basil E. Frankweiler*. They are fixated. They laugh hysterically at parts. They sit quietly rapt at others. Good food, good hugs, and good writing. For a second, I think I may have solved all the world's problems.

She falls asleep after a time, curled like a conch shell in the vastness of my bed. He, as per usual, won't quit. He begs me to continue. I tell him that it's not fair to her. He is disappointed but understanding. He turns off the lamp next to my bed and nestles himself in my blankets, not even pretending that he's going to his own room, not even pretending that it matters where I sleep.

I read Darren Wilson's grand jury testimony by the light of my phone.

Two hours later, I'm prepared to try and face the darkness and quiet of night.

I look at them both lying in my bed. They are unbelievably gorgeous children.

The thing about sleeping kids is that, in that moment, you can express your love for them in its complete fullness. I stare at them for a long time and memorize their faces. I allow these faces to be etched into my soul for all of eternity. I do this because I'm afraid I will lose them. I do this because I know I will lose them.

I may have even said, "I hope you don't ever grow up." But now, one day later, I'm not sure if I did.

Losing My Shit
Dani Burlison

Not too long ago, I lost my shit. It wasn't the first time and I assume it won't be the last. It happens sometimes—maybe every few years—when the extra challenging aspects of life like single parenting, unraveling from toxic relationships with family members or lovers, losing loved ones to cancer, suicide, or freak accidents, financial stress and car problems come to a head. I have often found myself walking a tightrope between balance and complete emotional and physical collapse, tiptoeing on the brink of the abyss.

For many years, I'd do one of two things when I started losing my shit. I'd either dive into the depths of depression, wrapping its dark, musty cloud around me like a wet wool blanket, or spin recklessly into a fit of anxiety so intense that it would hurt to breathe.

During my last shit-losing fiasco, I leaned heavily toward depression.

At first, I felt embarrassed for returning to the dark side. Relatively speaking, things are pretty fantastic in my life at the moment. My teen daughters are wonderful, fun, compassionate humans. I no longer venture into unhealthy, emotionally abusive relationships. I love my job. I spend my time teaching, writing, and being outdoors. I recently took a lovely vacation. I am surrounded by wonderful people. *What the fuck is my problem*, I sometimes ask myself. Trying to comprehend and address the varied catastrophic events that seem to come in waves, causing the world to career into upheaval and sometimes struggling to make ends meet and dealing with health issues, often leave me feeling exhausted, defeated. I know I am one of those overly sensitive people who is cursed with recurring residual mental health issues, so as strong as I know I can be at times, there are moments when I can feel myself getting worn out and frayed around the edges. Luckily at times like these, I have a community to fall back on. They are there to fill in the blanks, allowing me to unravel when necessary so I don't end up cracking and breaking for good.

Still, with children around, everything is more complicated. And oddly enough, raising teenagers brings a certain peculiar type of parental isolation. Long gone are weekend morning coffee dates with fellow moms, the kids stacking blocks at our feet while we whisper-vent about messy houses, recurring health issues, relationship woes, and financial problems. For me personally, the parent-bonding activities I once so enjoyed when my kids were small and portable have fallen by the wayside, regardless of the complexities and stresses that come with parenting older kids. Having teens with growing independence and increased loads of homework and social engagements, I'm often home alone with my thoughts which can be rough if depression sets in. Sometimes I reminisce and think it was easier to deal with when my kids were tiny and kept me busy with activities and I was living in the moment with them, down on the floor with piles of crayons and books and half-finished art projects.

There are no black-and-white simple solutions to the complexities that arise in regards to addressing mental health issues when you're also a parent. Instead, with depression and a multitude of other factors, families live in a perpetual existence of varying shades of gray. The guilt that arises with the onset of depression only feeds the shadows, increasing their weight. Talking to kids about depression and reaching out for support while in the trenches is a difficult yet necessary endeavor.

It's hard. We want to protect our little and not-so-little babies from the darkness that accompanies depression. We want them to move forward without fear and depression can be a scary-as-shit thing to confront. Without a community that understands and values honesty even when it isn't wrapped tightly in a pretty sparkly bow, I'm not sure how I would do it.

When my kids were younger, there were times when we stood in line at food banks after scrounging for change to buy gas to get us there. We lived in our car for a few months. We lost a family member to suicide. I survived and left an especially toxic relationship. On a few occasions, we came home to water or electricity that had been shut off due to nonpayment. We went without a working car for two years (easy in a big city, maybe, but not where we live).

One of my children and I have dealt with chronic illness. Any of these factors alone, added to the daily stresses of parenting while already on shaky mental ground can be and was a lot to deal with. This is where community support is crucial, even if just in the form of a sympathetic ear.

The last time things fell to ruin, I made some phone calls, mostly to other parents who had experienced various levels of mental health issues. I checked my pride at the door and reached out, something every parent finds themselves doing from time to time, regardless of their circumstances. I was seriously considering checking into a mental health facility and hated myself for considering what I felt would be abandonment of my daughters. In one afternoon—with the help of my community—I had offers of rides, dishwashing, a meal delivery, child care, and errand-running so I could recoup with some much-needed down time. Most importantly, I was reminded that I will never, ever be alone no matter how heavy life's burdens become.

Too often, parents (especially single parents) live in isolation. Working long hours, carting kids to and from school and various activities and squeezing in time to address basic needs like household chores, paying bills, and collecting food from stores and gardens leaves little time for relationships outside of the immediate family. Without these relationships, I'd end up feeling completely alone when issues arise. To many what is most important but rarely available, is the daily support that parents sometimes miss when wrapped up in the grueling task of raising munchkins. Simple things like phone calls during a mental health crisis, a roll of toilet paper, a cup of tea from a neighbor, or a ride for the kids when the gas tank has run dry, can restore the ability to move through the day with relative ease and can maybe even deliver a night of decent sleep. The ability to breathe without panic or exhaustion can mean the difference between quality time with the kiddos or a complete meltdown and in my experience, self-loathing.

My kids and I are fortunate to have narrowly avoided major catastrophes.

Though life changes and people come and go, my community remains present and whole-heartedly committed to being my/our extended family. My kids have a vast pool of adults to rely on in emergencies (or simply when they need a quick break from me) who swoop in, offering examples of what is possible when people are committed to changing the world by working together.

As for me, I continue to teeter, though the past few years have brought my feet to some steadier ground. I may very well lose my shit and regain my balance again any day now. It might happen over and over again. Regardless of the levels of my general emotional well-being, being a parent is a tough, unpredictable job. I'm lucky to have a community of copilots assisting me.

Some Tips for Community-Based Mental Health Support That Have Saved Me:

1   Find at least three other parents who you can call in mental health emergencies (I say *at least* three here because we all know how busy life gets and if number one on your list isn't free to talk, move on down the list). Make yourself available, too, but always have and respect boundaries.

2   If your kids are young, start an informal child care co-op. This means, taking your friend's kids for two hours one day and handing yours over to the friend for two hours another day. Spend those two hours doing something nice for *yourself*. Take a bath, a nap (I can't stress the importance of sleep enough here), go to a movie, peruse the local bookstore, have sex/masturbate, write a story, draw a picture of a cute barista, whatever makes you feel good.

3   Start or join an online parenting community. I was one of the very fortunate moms who reaped an insane amount of benefits from being a part of the *Hip Mama* community back in the day and I'm telling you: It saved my life. Venting, laughing, meeting up for political protests/rallies, sharing recipes, making "real life" friends, solidarity around breastfeeding and "alternative" lifestyles, tips on washing cloth diapers, swapping clothes through the mail. (I still have a tent someone sent me from Canada. I've taken it on trips all over the country and the world and I think about the mom who sent it to me every time I'm out on an adventure.) Virtual communities can be incredibly awesome.

4   Housecleaning parties! Gather a couple of moms/dads to-gether and clean each other's houses while the kids play. Spotless houses don't stay that way for very long (and are overrated in my opinion) but it is fun and helps the mental feng shui a bit to have a clean house—even if for just a few hours.

5   Community meals! All you have in the pantry is a bag of split peas and some rice? I bet your mama friend up the street has carrots and potatoes. Get together and make a meal to share with her family. There's nothing better than cooking and talk-ing and eating and sharing with someone else in the same boat. Do you have a local Food Not Bombs group nearby? I spent ten years hosting and cooking with Food Not Bombs and the parent allies I met became crucial to who I am as a mom.

6   Get to know your neighbors. Or at least *one* neighbor. Organize neighborhood block sales, utilize your community garden, offer help when you see someone struggling to get their groceries out of the car. Get to know their kids, have your kids get to know them. Bake them cookies. There is nothing like the peace of mind that comes when you feel safe and known in your neighborhood.

7   Self care. I know, it's so self-indulgent, but it is *so necessary* to be a good parent, person, member of society. Drink plenty of water. Cool it on the sugar. Eat your veggies. Go outside and spend time in nature. Take a long hot bath at least once a week. Learn about plant medicine and meditation and essen-tial oils and witchcraft and get together with other parents and discuss and share what you've learned. Go to therapy. Take medication if you need to. Get a lot of sleep. Surround yourself with people who support you supporting yourself in these ways.

Where Is Your Grown-Up?
Simon Knaphus

I make people uncomfortable. I guess I've known this for years now: awkward questions about my body, my identity, my relationship to my children; the way that people stumble over pronouns. I can't help but notice the discomfort in people during daily interactions. Usually these encounters feel like a normal part of my everyday life, but sometimes they leave me feeling exposed or frustrated, isolated, or invisible in all ways other than my trans-ness. I like it when my kids see me handle these situations matter-of-factly and with gentle humor, but when I stumble or let people make incorrect assumptions I am afraid they will learn to be uneasy or ashamed of who I am, and who we are as a family.

I don't want to make people uncomfortable—it's just not how I was raised. I'm uncomfortable in those situations too, and my kids end up feeling weird. I'm also not going to pretend to be something I'm not, namely a woman. I tried that and if the mess of making people uncomfortable is like a campsite full of mosquitoes, denying my gender is like having a body full of mosquitoes. Also, there really isn't anything wrong with being trans (aside from other people's issues). The fact that I was assigned female at birth and am now male carries no inherent value.

Most people I have uncomfortable gender moments with are kind, curious, and well-meaning. They are good people and they talk to me despite their discomfort. They want to know how to include me and my kids, and (consciously or not) they want information about me that will help them relate to me because our cultural framework for interacting with one another is very gendered. Over time, many people with no other transfolks in their lives have become obviously comfortable with me. Also, there are people who I have known for years who still have to perform mental gymnastics in order to form a sentence referring to me. To their credit, they still hang around. Usually the discomfort fades with time and understanding.

It is a real joy, and a rare treat, to meet someone who has already been through the initial hurdle of becoming trans-aware: someone who isn't flustered by my identity and welcomes and affirms my family. I think most people who aren't intentionally transphobic want to be welcoming, or at least want to be comfortable with trans people. Also, though trans people might not seem to be everywhere, it's not because we don't exist. Sometimes we stay hidden—the uncomfortable, dangerous, and exhausting work of being "out" can be too much. When we discover the absence of discomfort in a social situation, it can be like a breath of fresh air.

Very few people are 100 percent perfect gold-star trans allies. I know I'm not, and I'm a trans person with the audacity to write about trans inclusion. For example, I called myself a "tranny" for many years, unintentionally alienating and disrespecting trans women. For trans women, this word has been used too often in ways that are disrespectful, dangerous, and hurtful. I'm pretty embarrassed that I didn't understand this until so recently. The trans women in my world were undoubtedly telling me and it wasn't getting through. I am very thankful to the person who finally pointed me to an article that set me straight gently but firmly. The voices of trans women are often drowned out by the voices of trans men. Male privilege, misogyny, and unexamined biases and oppression are alive and kicking in the trans community. I want to learn how I can better be an ally, to trans women and to many others. I compiled what I believe are a few key ideas for welcoming trans families and I'm including a few of those ideas here.

Where's Your Grown-Up?

Not every kid has a mom or dad, but almost every kid has a grown-up of one kind or another. If you need a kid's grown-up, it is helpful to ask, "Where's your grown-up?" Questions like, "Where's your mommy?" sometimes work, sometimes are not useful ("Well, Mommy is at work but my uncle is right over there."), and sometimes are unintentionally hurtful (a kid without a mom might be sensitive about this, and all sorts of terrible things keep kids from their moms—incarceration, illness/death, geography, drama). When you ask a young person where their grown-up is, you get the information you need, spare some feelings, and create a welcoming environment for many different kinds of families.

Gender-Neutral Bathrooms Are Crucial

If you happen to be planning an event, or are in the position of choosing or designing a venue or other public space, please consider bathroom accessibility for everyone. Ideally, the gender-neutral bathroom should be as geographically convenient and un-yucky as other bathrooms. Make sure everyone knows that there is a gender-neutral bathroom, both so it can be used and also because it raises awareness about our need for relief! Any bathroom can be made gender-neutral by putting up an inclusive sign, even if it has many stalls and the sign is handwritten. Regardless of whether you find or make gender-neutral bathrooms, please notice where they are so you can easily answer the question, "Do you know if there is a gender-neutral bathroom around here?" Yesterday my kids and I were at a restaurant and my seven-year-old returned from the restroom very excited to tell me that the bathroom there was gender-neutral. He's a top-notch ally for this and so many other reasons.

Respectfully ask parents about things you don't know about—and refrain from asking things that are none of your business (like surgical status). When talking to kids, refrain from asking weird questions. If you hear someone else asking a kid weird questions please jump in as an ally. Weird questions are usually either none of the asker's business or things that should addressed to the adult. Jobs/income can be sensitive because trans people are unemployed at twice the rate as the rest of the population.

Wait and Listen

At some point, you may hear a grown-up talk about a child, saying "he's twelve." The terms you heard are probably preferred terms and it's probably okay for you to use them too, but always notice if you hear something inconsistent and (if it's your business) check in with the subject of the term to see what they prefer.

Also, please don't correct a kid when they identify someone as family, describe a member of their family, or describe themself. Sometimes we make guesses about a person, but we don't really know who they are until they tell us. When you say, "That's not your mommy" or "you're not a girl" you are probably wrong and you are definitely not being nice. (I hear kids do this all the time, and I hear grown-ups do it more than I like to think about. If you hear this argument happening, please politely insert yourself as an ally—chances are the kid on the receiving end could use some backup.)

"Children" and "Grown-ups"

Using gender nonspecific (and role nonspecific) language to address people as a group and as individuals leaves room for people to bring their own identities and relationships.

When someone calls me "she" or "your mommy" or addresses a group I'm in as "all the mommies," I have to either be silent and let my children see me take a step into the closet or I have to tell someone that they are wrong and make them feel all uncomfortable and then explain who I am and apologize for myself, taking the risk that they will be weird to me or, even worse, to my kid.

The "I'm actually his papa" conversation is hard for me, and I'm a big ol' grown-up in a big ol' grown-up world. Also, after ten years of having conversations about my trans-ness I've gotten pretty good at it. I can't imagine what it would feel like to be a five-year-old trying to navigate "I'm actually a girl" conversations, but I imagine it would be much more scary and that the closet would be very appealing. Unfortunately, people don't do very well in closets.

Being thoughtful and understanding toward trans people is a step toward all of us being more comfortable with each other.

The Step-Dad
Brian Whitman

Alice and I took a number of trips together during the eight years that we were a couple. Drove across state lines, flew to the east coast once or twice, and even took a slow-rolling train across the Midwest once, which was surprisingly romantic. Our previous trip together had been to Las Vegas, where I proposed to her in front of the Bellagio. We got married the next day. But our trip to Florida somehow seemed like the first vacation we'd ever taken together. Maybe because it was our first trip after being officially married, or maybe because her daughter, Katrina, was coming with us. It felt like a family trip, with me playing the role of the "man," the "husband," the "father." Carrying luggage to the car and making sure we got to the airport on time. It was a role I'd seen played in countless movies and television shows, and I was doing my best to live up to those standards.

I'd never exactly wanted a family. Well, when I was in high school and still a Christian, I guess back then I wanted a family. It seemed like what was supposed to happen. But once I left home and went away to college, my thoughts on everything started to change. For several years I dated around, experimented with different types of intimacy, and with different types of people, never really thinking I would ever end up as the family-man type. It was quite by accident that I fell in love with Alice, and very soon after that I began to think of Katrina as my own daughter.

Katrina was only three when we first met, with hair almost all the way to the floor. A tornado of a little girl, full of more energy than any of us knew what to do with. She ran around like a maniac, kicking and screaming, saying she hated everything, then the very next moment would be laughing and giggling, telling me she loved me. She was just like her mother.

Although I'd never planned on being a father figure, it was an easy thing to enjoy. I loved to help fix breakfast, or play silly made-up board games with Katrina. I'll never forget the first time I heard her read. We were on the way to her dad's house, me driving and Katrina in the passenger seat. She started reading billboards and names of businesses. I nearly drove off the road in shock. "You know how to read?" I exclaimed, and she just laughed. "Duh, I'm in school now," she told me. As fast as kids grow up, it happens even faster when there's a joint custody situation. You give them away for a weekend and they come back with all sorts of knowledge and experiences.

Over the years, Katrina had lots of names for me. Sometimes it was Billy. For a while it was dad, or "my other dad," and then eventually "step-dad." I attended her 12th birthday party earlier this year, held at the house of her real dad and his wife. I felt honored that they had invited me, even though Alice and I had just gotten our divorce. When all of Katrina's friends showed up, she took my hand and told them, "And in case anyone was wondering who this guy is, he's my step-dad." Then I could see her remembering the recent events and added, "Well, sort of. He's kind of like my step-dad. Well, he's just sort of like one of my really good grown-up friends."

Whether I was her friend or her dad was always a blurred line, a line just as blurred as the one that separates my childhood from my adulthood. I'm never quite sure myself, which it is or where I fit. A certain level of immaturity seems cute through your teens and twenties, but by the time you hit thirty, it's tougher to pull off. Katrina eventually settled on calling me her "BFFE," her best friend forever and ever, which seemed fine.

I'd been looking forward to this trip to Florida for some time. Not because it was Florida, a place I'd never been too interested in, but because it was a family trip. For me it was a chance to do something new. For Katrina it was a chance to stay in a hotel, swim in a pool, and maybe go to Sea World. But for Alice, it was a work trip. It wasn't a vacation at all.

We landed in Orlando around three in the afternoon. Alice was already stressed out and tired, trying to prepare for everything she had to do over the next few days, so I suggested that she chill out in the room while I took Katrina outside to the pool. A chance to soak up some real Florida sunshine. At this point, Alice and I had been married for about six months, and it was already looking like we'd be lucky to make it another six. Not long before this, I'd mishandled a situation that caused her to question why we were even together in the first place. It was not an uncommon mindset, for either of us. Our relationship could easily be stereotyped as "the two crazy artist types who fall in love." We've all seen that plot-line play out, right? When we fought, shit got broken. Windows, lamps, etc. Neighbors would complain. But when we loved . . . Well, same things, but in a good way. It was a passionate love affair, one that was at all times either burning hot or icy cold. Never an in-between, and always too powerful to walk away from.

It was tough to leave Alice in the hotel alone, because I knew the first thing she would do is call her new friend, John. She'd met John online, and had slowly built up a friendship that was now beginning to blossom into romance. The classic "husband" role I was beginning to develop wanted to put his foot down! Forbid her from ever talking to him again! But that's not who I really am. I'm a free-loving, free spirit, someone who is in general secure enough with himself to be okay with his lover having other love interests. Alice and I had been polyamorous at different points in our rela-tionship, and had each dated others over the years. Just not after being "married." It was hard to see her fall for someone while at the same time falling away from me, but I thought that my best shot was to give her space, while at the same time showing what a good father-figure I could be.

So, as soon as we checked into the hotel, I took Katrina out-side to the pool. The sun was high in the sky, and that little fish of a girl dove right into the water, while I laid down on one of those poolside recliners and promptly went to sleep. Now, if you can't guess where this story is going, let me reiterate a few points.

1   Florida, that place with the sunshine
2   Three o'clock in the afternoon
3   Guy who's sort of new to the parenting thing
4   Nap time

I slept for about two hours, waking up only long enough to roll over and go back to sleep. Katrina splashed around and had a great time. When the sun finally went down it had already done its damage, though I didn't realize it until I saw the look of shock, pure shock, on the face of Alice upon our return to the hotel room. Like the good mother that she was, she began inspecting her child, spinning her around and seeing which parts were red and which parts were *really* red. She said I looked terrible, so I stepped into the bathroom and immediately confirmed her conclusion. Then that horrible question.

"Didn't you put any sunblock on her?"

The whole time we were together, I could never bring myself to lie to her. Never felt right. Plus she was part psychic. Ever date someone who's psychic? It's tough. Can't get nothing by them. But lying in this situation would have been pointless anyway. My beet-red skin was answer enough. Sure, I knew enough to help my daughter out with math homework, but basic protection from the sun? I was clueless.

I spent the rest of our five days in Florida acting like I was fine, even though it hurt to put on clothing. I was rubbing aloe vera on myself every two hours, and the whole time all I could think was, "I bet John would have remembered the sunblock." Oh, the trappings of polyamorous relationships! Using imagined comparisons to reinforce the bad things we already feel about ourselves! One simple mistake and I felt like the worst dad in the world.

But nothing ever came of Alice and John. They met in real life and didn't have much in common. And the relationship I had with Alice ran out as well. We still talk on the phone from time to time, and have vowed to remain friends, vows that are more realistic than the ones Elvis had us repeat to each other that weekend in Vegas.

It would be easy to be bitter about the whole thing, but that's not who I am. Not how I am. I miss Alice, and I sure as hell miss Katrina. I rarely see either of them now. But I'm thankful. Thankful that for eight years I played a part in raising a human being, doing my best to teach her the things I think are important. By age four she knew the difference between soy milk, rice milk, and cow's milk. By age six she had a basic understanding of transgender issues. By age seven she declared she was vegetarian. Then back to omnivore. Then to pescatarian. She and I played video games, played soccer, went on bike rides. We watched all the Pippi Longstocking movies together. Went to the zoo, baked cookies together, all that sort of stuff. It's amazing to think about all that I tried to teach her in such a short time, but even more amazing to think of all that she taught me. I don't know that I'm exactly the "family-man" type, but thanks to that little girl, I definitely understand why someone would want to be. And for that, I'm eternally thankful. For a long time I thought getting married and having kids was just something people did when they ran out of ideas. And for a lot of our population, sadly, I'm sure that might be true. But that doesn't mean it's all bad. Whatever we choose to do in this life, if we do it *our own way*, and for our own reasons, then it can actually be really awesome. I'm glad I got married! (I'm also glad I got divorced!) And I'm definitely glad I was given the chance to help raise a child. I wouldn't change it for anything in the world.

Becoming Papa, Signing Contracts, and Telling Grandma

scott winn

I have never been a good liar. It both feels bad and people see right through me—a good trait I think. But lately when Mom called and said, "So, what's new?" I'd lie saying, "Not much." Meanwhile, my whole life was changing. It felt bad, but I was not ready to tell her, so I'd been avoiding her calls.

Eventually though, I told her there were big changes in my life, and I wanted to chat sometime when Dad wasn't home. This is typical, we figure stuff out before we tell Dad. Mom is always in the middle—a position she hates, and loves. We made our plans for the next Sunday afternoon after lunch during harvest so Dad would be back in the field. He wasn't, but now was the time.

"Well, Ma, there is something I have wanted my whole life, and I have spent the past two years focused on working to make it happen. And it is happening. In February I am having a little girl. You are going to be a grandma again." My eyes filled with tears. For years and years, I had imagined and wanted this moment of telling my mom I was going to be a father.

Now, telling your mom she is going to be a grandma is not always a cause for caution, but in this case, I was cautious. I was a forty-five-year-old single queer guy. If she ever thought I was going to have kids once I came out in my mid-twenties, I am sure she thought that ship had sailed. I had anyway.

There was silence. It seemed to last forever, though I am sure in less than half a minute I said, "Ma, are you excited?"

"I am smiling like a Cheshire cat!" she declared.

This was a good start, she was hanging out with Alice in Wonderland.

"Well, wait. How are you doing this?" she asked.

I had rehearsed my answer.

"Well, I am going to be co-parenting with a friend of mine. We are not in nor have we ever been in a romantic or physical relationship. What co-parenting means to us is that we are both going to be equal parents—we have a contract—and we will each be responsible for half of the expenses and half of the time. My friend is a transgender man—so he was born and raised as a girl, but in order to be happy he transitioned to become a man in his twenties. You have met friends of mine who were transgender when you were in Seattle, remember?"

"Yes, I do."

"Well, he is still able to have kids. He is pregnant. So we used his egg and my sperm and we are having a baby!"

Some more silence. Then some more.

"Well, Ma, do you have any questions?"

"Well, it sounds pretty simple. It sounds like he's pregnant!" she replied in the way my mom does—in a rather matter of fact tone—seemingly questioning what questions she could possibly have.

I was in awe at how quickly she seemed to just not see it all as that big of a deal. She has continued since then to use the correct pronouns virtually all the time, settling into the fact that a man was pregnant *with* her grandchild, and not really looking back or even caring (in a good way).

Then she went on to laugh and cry and get all excited and begin the process of inserting herself right in the middle, speaking her truth, as my Mama always does.

"Well, did you 'do' it?"

"No, Mom, we didn't." I was expecting this question. "We did an in-home insemination. So I masturbated in a sterile cup and left, and then he did the rest." The mention of masturbation seemed to end that line of questioning.

After we talked a bit more, she paused and laughed in a sorta "oh, shit!" kind of way. "Oh my, what are we going to tell your father?"

My pop is a rather set-in-his-ways kind of guy—a self-identified and proud redneck, a farmer with a kind, tender heart. He was never been the most excited about change—and twenty years after I came out as gay it seemed we were finally cool.

"Well, what do you think?"

"Oh, I need a week to think about it, let's keep it between us for now, okay?"

"Sounds good to me!" Family secrets are just part of being a family it seems. And, I was relieved to have more time, "We can talk more about it. We can decide if I should tell him or if you should." I had no desire to tell him, but also was trying to support her in not always being in the middle—a position I hated her in, and loved.

"Oh, I think I should tell him."

After talking details and due dates and all kinds of stuff Mom had a big idea. "What will we name her?" I wasn't sure why she thought "we" would, but . . . "I know, we can call her Marissa Kay! Missy for short!"

Coincidentally, Mom's name is Karen Kay Winn.

"We will talk about it, Mom. Thanks for the suggestion." There was no way in hell I was gonna call my kid Missy, I knew for sure. One, it was a bit too girly for the way I wanted to raise my kid. And two, my last girlfriend, two decades before, was named Missy. A great woman, but not a legacy I wanted to bring into my papahood. And, three, it wasn't my decision to make alone.

We talked for an hour and I was so happy after months and months of fear and dread about this conversation. My mom is amazing.

"You have made me so happy. I love you"

"I love you too, Ma."

We hung up.

An hour later the phone rang . . . it was Mom.

"Well, I am so excited I had to call someone, so I called Wanda." Wanda is her best friend. They are quite a pair. They get together and drink coffee and chain-smoke and laugh and cry and share it all. They were raised together since they were babies—with Wanda's grandparents taking care of my mom and her sister while my grandma worked her factory job making brooms. She was left by her husband to raise the kids alone when they were both under two. My grandma is one of my sheroes. Her name, Lois, became my daughter's middle name.

"We had an idea. We'll call her Wanda Kay!" There was the "we" again. I just laughed and said we would think about it. It would be an amazing legacy.

Mom called a few days later with another grand idea.

"Well, I have been thinking. I know what we will tell your father. We will say you two hired a woman to be a surrogate—and she will carry the baby, then you two will adopt it!" She seemed proud of herself, and a bit unsure.

"Mom, you seemed so cool about it all on Sunday, now you seem a bit concerned."

"Well, Scott. A man having a baby is a pretty big deal!" She declared seemingly utterly exacerbated by my lack of understanding of the situation. The reality of homophobia and transphobia had set in and the excitement of being a grandma was now tainted by the messiness of our society. I knew that feeling. It messed with me too.

"Well, Ma, I don't think that'll work. Our daughter is going to know exactly where she came from. We will tell her from the beginning, and support her in being proud and know how much she was wanted. We are not embarrassed about this at all, and have nothing to hide."

"No, you shouldn't be. You are right. Let me think some more."

Eventually, Mom had decided to tell the whole family. I would love to be a fly on the wall to hear what words and language she used. After weeks of no word, I put mom in the middle and told to her to have Dad call me, "It is just what a Dad does, he congratulates his son when he is going to be a father." The next day he called.

"Hey Scott, sorry I have not called," Dad said when I answered. "But I wanted to say how happy I am for you."

"Oh, thanks, Grandpa! Do you have any questions?" I asked.

"Well, I guess I do. So, this gal is gonna have a baby and then become a man?" He couldn't wrap his head around a man having a baby. I went into my rehearsed speech I had given Mom.

"Well, you all do things differently out there," he said after a pause. He was clearly not in a fighting mood. "I am just happy for you, Scott." I was so touched by his sweetness, my expectations were pretty low.

Now the family all knew. Grandma Karen was on board and doing her work to bring Grandpa along. My journey to becoming a papa just got a lot easier.

Making Commitments to Other People's Children: Building Intimacy with Parents and Kids
Kermit Playfoot

I am not a parent and am not planning to be in the near future. I have read and thought a lot about parenting though, because many of the people I am committed to are parents and children. It has been great getting to know other people's children, to be an adult friend in their community who can hold a hand, read a story, change a diaper, or provide child care for an afternoon. Often, I have done these things to support friends who are parents; but very quickly, I also develop independent relationships with their kids. Irrationally, I become committed to these creatures without knowing anything about the kind of people they will become.

In the last year and a half, at least half a dozen good friends have taken concrete steps towards having kids, gotten pregnant, or given birth, including my sister and two of my housemates. This has prompted me to think more about my own relationship to parenting and to come to a more concrete realization about the fact that I will probably not be a parent myself. Figuring out how to connect with children and support friends who are parents, however, has helped me know myself better, expand my understanding of the world and strengthen my feelings of connectedness to the intimate life of my community.

As a teenager and young adult, I didn't really know any young children or anyone I considered a peer who had children. About a year and a half after I moved to Berkeley, a nine-month-old baby and his mama moved into my collective house. Oliver was the first baby I knew as an adult. His direct eye contact and the way he felt emotions intensely and expressed them immediately were both appealing and a little bit scary. It took me a while to be relaxed hanging out with him, but once I did, it was great to be able to crawl around and laugh with him, to feel comfortable picking him up and giving him hugs.

In a way, building intimacy is simply the process of letting someone know and care about your experience of the world while you get to know and care about theirs. All of my friendships enrich my life in part because they allow me to understand the world from a different point of view. Becoming friends with Oliver while he lived with me taught me a lot about what it was like for him to be a baby and toddler, things I used to know but had forgotten and things I never knew.

It was also great getting to know Crystal, both as Oliver's mama, and as a fabulous friend and person in the world. Living a meaningful life is essentially about finding significant projects, connecting with people in powerful and intimate ways, and inhabiting our bodies as much as possible. For all of my friends who are parents, their kids are both one of their central projects and some of their most important intimate relationships. When two people are paired as intensely as a parent and young child, it can be difficult to figure out how to think of and get to know them separately. I strongly feel, however, that beyond doing actual child care and being friends to their kids, supporting parents means being willing to view them as whole people, as people who have many interests outside of their own children. It is important to hold and respect the individual humanity of parent and the child while at the same time acknowledging the importance of the bond they have with each other. To deny their separate identities would mean to see them more as archetypes than as real human beings struggling to live in the world, to create emotional distance rather than supportive intimacy.

I have managed to see more and less of Crystal and Oliver (who is now six and a half) at different moments since they moved out three years ago, but I remain committed to being someone who cares about what happens to them and a friend who can be called for support when needed. Last spring, I was able to have a regular afternoon play date with Oliver, which allowed us to reconnect with each other a bit. I enjoyed playing with him, negotiating what we were going to do together, asking him questions about his life, hearing him talk about his latest enthusiasms, listening to the way he made sense of his world and sharing the pieces of myself with him that seemed relevant or relatable.

Oliver is able to create stories and express his desires fairly well but gets frustrated when he is not able to do the things he wants to do. One of the challenges of being an anarchist who also has relationships with children is that I find myself sympathetic to the frustration Oliver has about not having control over his life, but I can't let him do whatever he wants when we hang out. I often have to establish explicit limits around how I want to be treated or what is a reasonable serving of ice cream, to make decisions about the structure of our play that are not really that negotiable, or are only negotiable within certain limits.

Figuring out ways to set rules and say no to kids while at the same time trying to respect their power and desires and avoid recreating relationships that echo the domination of the system is not a question of either honoring a child's autonomy or providing structural frameworks, but about trying to do both at the same time. Adults have generally figured out how to regulate their emotions, respect their own personal boundaries and those of the people around them. With my friends who are kids, I have to be aware of and responsible about the fact that they are still growing, still figuring out how to exist in the world, socially and emotionally. Treating children like I would treat an adult is as inappropriate as treating them as inferiors or people whose ideas and desires don't matter.

About a year ago, my sister gave birth to the first baby in our family in almost eighteen years. My niece Sophia is pretty great. I have experienced extreme physical joy playing with her, talking back and forth with her without using fully formed words, making her laugh and holding her hand when she was learning to walk, testing the limits of her own autonomy. I feel committed to being in her life in important ways, which will take effort because we live several thousand miles apart. Our connection has been formed primarily during two trips back east in the last year and I am not likely to see Sophia more frequently in the near future. I am motivated to find ways to maintain intimacy from a distance and make the time I do spend with her and her parents count.

I was talking to a friend the other day who mentioned that having his (proverbial) tubes tied had allowed him to be a lot more pro-child. I never really considered myself anti-child and I haven't had a vasectomy, but I do understand how letting go of the idea that I will have my own kids has allowed me to be more open emotionally with and willing to make some level of commitment to other people's children. As an uncle, housemate, or friend, I have to find ways to negotiate my own beliefs and personality with the way each of my young friends is being parented; to respect the decisions that my friends who are parents have made and be authentically myself. Because I am not trying to practice for my own parenthood when I interact with kids, I don't need to compare my commitment to my newborn housemate, my one-year-old niece, or my six-year-old friend to any sort of ideal parent-child relationship. I think this helps me to have a perspective that it might be harder to cultivate or maintain if I was expecting to be responsible for feeding, clothing, raising, and housing a child every day. Bringing this perspective to the collective life of my community hopefully helps to support everyone in it, including parents, children, and other people without kids.

Being an Ally to Parents and Kids
Sasha Vodnik

Ever since my mid-twenties, I've wanted to be a parent. The stars have never exactly aligned on that front for me, however. As a queer non-trans guy dating mostly other non-trans guys, the biology of my relationships has never lent itself to reproduction. And while I've explored a number of other avenues to becoming a parent, the guys I've gotten seriously involved with haven't wanted kids. Now I'm about to get hitched to a guy I love to pieces, and who's clear that he doesn't see himself as a dad. The decision to commit to my relationship with him was only possible because I first went through a process of re-envisioning what being a significant presence in the lives of kids could look like for me.

Today, I am an uncle of three awesome kids. Ever since leaving home in the Midwest, I've returned twice a year to visit my family. For two weeks every year, I get to spend time with my nieces and nephew. I've gotten to give them bottles and rock them to sleep as infants, help out with parties in their grade-school classrooms, watch them play softball, and take them to movies. I've gotten to hear about their friends, their struggles, and what really fires them up.

Back home in San Francisco, I also play a significant role in the life of an eight-year-old—the child of two friends, and now a friend of mine in her own right. I took her to school once a week for her first few years of school, and recently I've started spending an hour a week in her classroom. She and I have also kept a standing date to hang out for an afternoon one weekend a month, going to the park or the library or simply making crafts and drinking tea together.

My role in the lives of all these kids is part circumstance and part choice. And I think the choice piece of that, in particular, is a crucial part of the work for social justice that's fundamental to how I live my life.

235

Finding My Way

At age twenty-eight, I'd been interested in being a parent for a few years. I was single, and I decided that if I wasn't in a relationship by age thirty, I'd pursue single parenting. At thirty, in a relationship, I discovered my then-boyfriend didn't want to be a parent, and at thirty-one, newly single, I went through foster parent training and certification. Living in Virginia at the time, I was overwhelmed by visions of kids being taken away from queer parents—stories like that of Sharon Bottoms, a lesbian whose mother successfully sued to have Sharon's own biological children removed from her custody, arguing that, as gay sex was illegal in the state at the time, Sharon was a criminal and thus "an unfit parent."

While I didn't shy from the idea of that sort of fight, I couldn't stomach the idea of the life of a child I cared about being turned upside down because of it, and I ultimately opted not to be a foster parent.

A few years later, back in San Francisco, I went through foster parent certification again. At the end of the process, though, I was left with the merest hint of what single parenting might look like, and it shook my determination. I couldn't afford an apartment with an extra bedroom, as required by foster care regulations, and had no clear idea how I'd realistically balance a forty-hour-a-week job with caring for a child. I realized that millions of people—mostly working-class and poor women—do these very things, in the vast majority of cases making things work through force of will and a willingness to ask for help. I have deep respect and admiration for single parents but, for myself, I was unsure I could pull it off. And in the moments when I thought I could, I feared the sacrifices it might require of me.

So after years of moving forward based almost solely on determination, and then stopping short, I stepped back and took a look at my situation, along with my assumptions and my options.

I struggled with what it meant to be a "parent" versus what it meant to be "someone who helps out with kids." When I worked my way past some of my assumptions about the relative values of these roles, I was able to hear a little more clearly some things that people in my communities were telling me. One was that, just as I imagined that being a single parent could be a hercule-an task, in many cases it is, and single parents—and most other parents—could use breaks from time to time. I also heard that kids could use as wide a variety of safe role models as possible, meaning that getting to spend time with attentive adults who are looking out for them and who aren't their parents gives kids wider sets of emotional resources as well as expanded possibilities.

What I've Learned

I've been fortunate to see and hear about the experiences of close friends who I work with in movements for social justice and who are parents—the joys and challenges of being parents, along with the widespread difficulty of finding or even creating a continued place in the cultures of our movements as parents. I'm convinced that we can't afford single-generation movements and that we deserve multigenerational movements. For all of us who want to see a strong left, who want to take steps toward a more just world, I think we need to see ourselves as part of building and sustaining multigenerational community. Young adults shouldn't be isolated, trying to reinvent the wheel simply for lack of authentic relationships with movement elders, and none of us who are grown should leave our children to that fate. By prioritizing children—and elders—at the hearts of our movements, and by putting effort into maintaining that space and strengthening it, we can continue to knit these bonds of community and affinity and mutual aid that must be part of the foundations of strong, vibrant movements for justice.

I'm equally convinced that for all of us who aren't parents, there are roles for us in the lives of children. For anyone trying to figure out how to take the next step, here are some pieces of advice I've gotten from parents along with some things I've learned along the way:

You need to show up. Wanting to support kids and parents is an important first step, but on its own it isn't enough. You need to be prepared to make commitments, you need to be serious about them, and you need to follow through. If you forget some of your commitments to spending time with kids, or if you often cancel at the last minute, parents can't really depend on you, and kids, depending on their ages, will draw their own conclusions—generally not flattering ones. In addition, as with any two people getting to know each other, your actions are way more important in a kid's eyes than your intentions, however honorable.

Listen to children. Anybody can tell a kid what to do—and in case you don't remember, kids get a lot of that already. What all kids need is more listening. Whether you're going on an outing or playing a game, it can be as simple as asking what they want to do. Once you get to know specific kids better, you can ask about things that may be different on a given day, like a different mood or something they seem particularly proud of. Create space for kids to let you know who they are, and then create even more space for them to safely be who they are when they're with you.

Listen to parents. If you want to be an ally to parents, it doesn't work to come in with your own agenda. You need to be clear about what you can offer and what you can't, but you need to ask and listen to parents when it comes to what they want and need. Your role is to support parents in the complex web of responsibilities and roles that make up the layers of their lives. If you're listening, you'll hear them spell out for you where that web is weakest, where it seems to be fraying, where a little support from you would make a world of difference for them and their children.

Children have to come first. Being involved in a kid's life can be downright harmful if you're there only to score cred. I'd even argue that being an effective ally for parents and kids isn't going to work if you merely think it's important. I think it's important to be able to embrace the creative chaos that's one of the many ways that children enrich vibrant communities. For me, helping kids grow has by necessity been a process of getting outside my own head, even getting silly sometimes. It's also been serious practice at stepping outside my experience as a single nonparent—where the choices and goals are generally up to me—and learning to set my own stuff aside sometimes.

Bring your authentic self. Kids don't need some idealized model adult; they need you. By modeling who you are—whoever that is—you give kids the chance to experience what makes you you: your tastes, your cultural practices, your ways of expressing yourself. Kids aren't carbon copies of their parents, so more role models means more tools for them in being themselves.

Have fun! For me, being involved in kids' lives nudges me to take myself less seriously, give me honest feedback (little kids don't pull punches!), and gives me chances over and over to hear how kids see the world. As a bonus, I get to be part of stronger multigenerational movements that welcome the energy and experience and perspectives of both kids and parents.

The first time my nephew and older niece sent me a Father's Day card, I was so surprised and happy that I started crying. They still send cards every year (and I still get weepy)—caring gestures from strong, loving kids who are rapidly turning into strong, loving adults. It's a tangible moment every year that reminds me that parents aren't the only loving adults kids need in their lives, that there's room for all of us—indeed, that all of us are needed.

Building Family: A Conversation with Chris Crass

Editor's note: we're serious when we say that "rad dad" is an action, not a label. It takes work and commitment; it needs to be nurtured and supported. One of the best ways to do that is to lean on others, to find community, and to discover role models. To me, Chris has been a role model of activism and determination for years. When I learned he was also becoming a father, I immediately wanted to talk with him about how activism has informed his parenting but, more excitingly for me, how his parenting informs his activism.

The phrase "the revolution begins at home" gets tossed about in conversations about social change. As a new father, what does this mean to you now?

As a teenager, coming into radical politics and activism, revolution did begin at home, as I began forming my own sense of self and turned my parents' house into the gathering spot for our local youth activist group and community. My parents raised me to believe in equality and justice and to be community minded. Forming a collective that was part of the Love and Rage Revolutionary Anarchist Federation and then starting a Food Not Bombs was how I put that into practice. In those years, my parents created a supportive, encouraging home where my revolutionary ideas and actions began.

Soon after I moved out on my own, I got together with some more politically experienced friends and started up an anarchist/ Food Not Bombs collective house in San Francisco called Praxis House. The idea was that our home would be a space for us to live our values while also being a base for our activism resisting capitalism, white supremacy, patriarchy, and the state. We had a quote from bell hooks displayed on the wall as you walked in the front door. It read, "We can make homeplace that space where we return for renewal and self-recovery, where we can heal our wounds and become whole." Our walls were covered in movement posters, our bookshelves overflowed with left/radical newspapers and zines, images and slogans of empowered queer sexualities and feminist genders were everywhere, visitors from activist communities all over North America and Europe couch-surfed with us . . . These and our shared regular political work all served to help us feel connected to our vision and values and to a larger global movement of movements.

As a collective we shared household responsibilities, supported one another, struggled through interpersonal conflict and often over beer or coffee created space to think and reflect on our actions. We struggled with how to share responsibilities in good ways, how to communicate with one another in respectful ways, how to bring our liberation values into our romantic and intimate relationships, and home is where we explored our sexuality and gender. "The revolution begins at home" mostly meant that homeplace is, to quote bell hooks again, "a site of resistance" to struggle against systems of oppression and exploitation.

Then two of the longtime members of Praxis, Rahula and Jeff, decided to become parents and a beautiful little person named Natasha became part of the collective. As a house we agreed that we wanted to be a space that would be supportive of their new family. We talked about how having a baby in the house was going to change our dynamic from a constantly on-the-go activist house that held regular parties, meetings, and Food Not Bombs cookhouses into a home to build a family (blood and chosen) that would be an important part of little person's childhood. Revolution at home took on new meaning.

In what ways has becoming a parent allowed you to reflect on the ways your long history of activism in the past perhaps included parents in surprising ways and perhaps excluded them. Or to rephrase it: How has parenting made you a better activist?

The political concerns and priorities I had as a teenager were different than the ones I had in my late twenties and are significantly different than they are now as a dad about to turn forty. Today for me as an organizer, I think about how can we build a movement that is multigenerational, loving of all kinds of families, loving of kids and older folks, and open to the deep learning that can come through an expanded perspective that all these folks will bring.

We need political movements that have space for people who are at different places in their lives and that value the experience and perspectives they bring. Radicals who are parents and building family have a lot of important insights about how we can do this, but if family and parenting are thought of as something else, something other than activism, then it makes it hard for those insights to be optimized. The most significant way that this is changing and will change is by more and more parents bringing leadership to building the Left. And when I say "Left," I mean the broad, progressive, social justice Left that millions of people are currently part of and of which smaller, radical Left countercultural political scenes are just one part. One of the ways more parents and many other people with limited time and capacity can bring leadership to the Left is by thinking about the many different roles people can play and how more and more people can be involved. We need to always be asking ourselves, "How can we create more and more opportunities for people to be involved?" To me it's not a question of how to get people to care; the Occupy movement showed us that millions of people not only care but are willing to take action. What we need are organizations and efforts that have sustained opportunities for people to be involved, feel part of something bigger than themselves, and be nourished by the vision, values, and practices of a thriving, vibrant, healthy movement for liberation.

What's something new you learned about yourself after becoming a father?

I am humbled every day. I am humbled with how hard it is. I am humbled thinking about all the people around me whom I know and don't know, who are raising kids. I'm still a new dad. My son River is two, so I am still a newer member of the parent world. So when I see people with three or more kids, I just can't believe it. I want to give them a medal and say thank you for raising these kids.

I'm also a stay-at-home dad, so there has been many a day when I've got a kid who won't stop crying, laundry piled high, a kitchen filled with dirty dishes, the living room in chaos, groceries to be put away, and dinner to be made. In those moments, I don't question our ability to build a liberatory society in the midst; rather, I feel incredibly connected to the millions of other people who have gone through the same thing. I think about how much love, tenderness, and care people bring to their kids and families, much of it quietly and privately in their homes, and I think about this love as a powerful force for liberation values.

How has fathering renewed your commitment to social justice and change?

I feel even more deeply than ever before how much I want to make lasting changes in society so that our kids grow up with more role models, options, and resources to live antiracist, feminist, socialist, liberation values in every facet of life and have them grow up with political, economic, social, and cultural institutions practicing those values. It isn't that this is a new feeling, but now it lives in my body in a very emotional and spiritual way and is a source of power.

That said, I also experience this tension within me, the tension of wanting your kid to have all the best versus thinking collectively about our kids as a society. The false scarcity of capitalism and hierarchical authoritarianism tells us that there isn't enough for everyone and that other families and kids are a threat to your family and kids. One of the reasons I love going to demonstrations and political events with my son is that I want us to be around other families, other people in our communities as we work for shared goals of justice, dignity, and equality for all, whether we're at a union rally, an immigrant rights demonstration, helping organize the community mobilization for Trayvon Martin, or marching to end domestic violence and rape culture. I look for opportunities for River to be with other kids and adults who love him, as I want these spaces to be places where he experiences the joy and camaraderie of working for liberation.

The other major way my commitment has been renewed is within my family and how we think about building our family. My organizing has taught me that unless we have intentional commitments to practice our values, and build towards our values, the dominant values of white supremacy, patriarchy, capitalism, and authoritarianism will become the norm. My partner and I have been drawing on our organizing experience to think about how we want to build our family with visions of what we want, goals to help us move towards that vision, and structures/rituals/rhythms of life to support us to live our values and intentions. This goes back to the original question about revolution beginning at home, and that's how we feel about it. We don't think of this in a rigid, forcing the beautiful complexities of life into abstract cookie-cutter ideas; we think of this as one of the most important practices of praxis-based organizing we will ever experience. We are building our family, we are building the environment for our kid and other kids in our lives to have, hopefully, magical and healthy childhoods. We are building our family culture and homeplace that will be both a site of resistance to injustice and oppression in society, but also a site of liberation for play, learning, struggle, and joy to live the beauty of our lives in community with our family, friends, and comrades.

List 4:
A Ridiculously Simplified List of Things to Communicate to Your Child and Pitfalls to Avoid When Parenting

Things to communicate to your child:

Your body is your own and it does not have to conform to anyone's standards.

Your words matter. Always.

TV, movies, and video games are not real. Always question what you see, especially in regards to stereotypes.

Consent is always at play. Nobody is entitled to touch you nor are you entitled to touch anyone else.

Sometimes parents are wrong, and it is okay for you to tell us so.

Children of all ages have thoughts and feelings and those things matter. Listen to them.

Everyone has their own learning style. Go at your own pace. Remember that "school" may be only a tiny part of your education.

Don't be afraid to be better than your friends at a given activity. Your true friends want you to be the best.

You're in control of your life, but we are here to keep you safe until you're ready.

Pitfalls to parenting:

Denial is not parenting. Censorship is not parenting. Be vigilant in bringing up issues of race, class, and gender privilege. It's a myth that you are keeping them innocent by not addressing real world issues.

Not holding them accountable because you want to be their friend.

Don't just hug and kiss your girls. Hug and kiss your boys.

Show them you love them constantly, even when they mess up, with hugs, kisses, and listening. To quote J.K. Rowling, "We've all got both light and dark inside us. What matters is the part we choose to act on."

Don't think that your child is always innocent.

Being too stuck in a pattern or mode to ask for help from your community or other parents.

Not giving children the space to fall flat on their faces.

Not attending to them when they do fall flat on their faces.

Don't try to immediately extinguish your child's pain.

Don't halt your own curiosity by pretending to have all of the answers. Learn with your child.

Don't just teach, model. Model forgiveness, model love, model engagement and curiosity, model excitement and joy, model that it's okay to express sadness. It's not so much about *what* to communicate as about *how* to communicate.

Remember: You'll be raising an independent, thinking being who will question the hell out of you, challenge your assumptions, and need space to feel their impact on their surroundings. Be patient and have thick skin.

AFTERBIRTH—
CONCLUSION

Family Stories: A Reckoning, a Healing
Zora Moniz

So much comes down to healing. When we engage in confronting the issue of black and brown bodies being failed, jailed, and murdered. How do we heal? What does it mean to heal? This is a story about my life now, my memories, and ways to shape my life as it lives and unfolds and changes.

Healing for me is thinly slicing onions and caramelizing them in olive oil in my mother's kitchen.

My brother. Arched eyebrows perfect like they were tweezed, prettier than mine. A little scar cutting one in half, a memento from his time in Los Angeles, maybe he was seventeen.

I leave home and move to Los Angeles, too much black coffee and sometimes not enough. Cheap, cheap whiskey, liquid gold. Artificial light, more fake wood. Fake community, ephemeral space called dormitories. Monster GMO strawberries. What dark black earth were these pulled from? That was my first year at school. My second year I live wrapped in layers of calm blue. Leaving Westwood and seeing Los Angeles in different ways, the warehouses and gaudily named apartment buildings, the panaderías, and veiny highways. I taste privilege, shoveling poached eggs on Gruyere pizza into my mouth, I absorb chilled wine, feel the slimy beads of ice sweat on vodka tonics. Too much too much. I pick my own lavender. I start going into Bel Air and Brentwood. Sometimes there are no sidewalks. I steal fat lemons and jasmine, I forage their fallen, forgotten, will-be waste. Back to the first place I can really call home, my own. To the first people I really shared it with. The people who began to bring out the sides of me I don't want to see. The embarrassment, the jealousy, the guilt, the cockiness, the selfishness, the want, the include me please. I want to do everything right. Is there a right? Terrified, throbbing through blue with stark clear uncertainty. I am completely sure in my unsurety, I am lucky to know that everything will work itself out.

Where were you in those years I can't quite remember? My brother was gone. My family went away, left him behind in jail for being a stupid teenager. We all are. After being in for one hundred days, he went cross-country by car with my grandma and her boyfriend sucking on sweet ribs and collard greens. From Oakland to Brooklyn. He lived there for a year, surviving off frozen chicken breasts and street pizza. He was gone through my eighth grade to my sophomore year, I think. It is all filmy now.

Healing for me is sleeping in the gold and burnt orange room that is my father's, in our cube house that breathes in cold air, fragrant with night blooming street flowers.

My brother slicks back brown hair, peach fuzz on his lip, head tilted back, belt low on his hips, rough fingertips spray-paint stained.

I walk halfway down the stairs and peek into the bright living room. My brother tells my parents, his friend crying by his side, that they were turning the corner on Fairview and a boy pulls out a gun. Give me your shit. They were carrying a paper bag of Xbox games. Brother says, you won't shoot me, you're not gonna kill anyone. His friend hands him all the shit, and the boy runs away.

Healing for me is running. Quick. Kneecaps bouncing up and thighs defined and snapping back and forth. Up the hill. Arms glide in consistent arcs, dimpling shoulders when reaching the farthest point back before swinging forward. Again.

When we were going to Thailand and my brother didn't come home the night before our flight. I see my mom crying, maybe he is dead in a ditch somewhere?

The boy makes me sad. My brother's response is true. What harm congealed into this?

My friend Annakai and I went to an amazing art exhibition titled *Manifest Justice*. That felt like healing. It felt like square white space that was poured in with thick thought. Pain, anger, resignation, hope, passion. Every piece pricked at me. Some really struck me. One was the span of a smallish wall, mug shots lined carefully and symmetrically to cover the space, all different backgrounds, all staring into the camera, all on death row. All dead now. Their faces were abstracted with text. Words were repeated over and over again, printed consistently over their black and white faces. Their last words. You poke your nose closer and squint your eyes, trying to read. I am innocent. It says. This offender declined to make a last statement. It says. I'm an African warrior, born to breathe, and born to die. He says. They are taking the life of an innocent man. They say. I just love everybody, and that's it. I give my love to my family, who has kept me strong. I'm ready to come home. Mario Marquez, Execution #87.

None. Samuel Hawkins, Execution #92.

I will wait for you. Karla Tucker, Execution #145.

I know you can't hear me now but I know that it won't matter what I have to say, I want you to know that I did not kill your sister, if you want to know the truth, and you deserve to know the truth, hire your own investigators. Pedro Muniz, Execution #152.

Find peace in this. Javier Medina, Execution #277.

Parting words.

Who is this artist, exposing a painful truth? Amy Elkins is her name.

You look around and realize everyone else is doing the same, uncomfortably face to face with these prisoners. Their parting words printed like stamps on everyone's eyeballs. You can see it in theirs, glistening back, returning your stare. You turn and walk away slowly. It won't go away.

My dad was raised in Hawaii with his mother. I don't know so much about that. Three skinny bronze brothers, throwing soft yellow rotting mangoes and catching sand crabs.

So many years later, I am walking in these LA streets. It's a rare misty night, cars zoom by, and the air seems consuming and all expansive. I can look up and feel the immensity as sparkling dew floats down. *Manifest Justice* felt right, you think, yeah, your friend agrees. It feels like every fucking thing I've been studying in the real world.

Blood was lost when my grandfather was left in New Mexico. In some jail, some prison. Something. I remember meeting him for the first time many years later, but I was young. We drove into a Sonic because we had never been before. I got a grilled cheese and we all got excited about a curiously creamy cherry lime slushy topped with whipped cream.

Healing for me is my mom, soft skin and inky poppies twining up her arms. Tasting her fresh almond milk and butter beans.

I am still following the bloodstains backwards. They've mostly turned a rusty black. But at the end I find it is hot and still cradled strongly in veins of other family members. My great aunt smiles with teeth, tells me to try and cut the pig's stomach lining, that it is tougher than you might think. I try and cut into it all confident, beige and wrinkled and wet on the kitchen counter of a semi-permanent trailer.

Why do I feel more afraid when the police are around than when they aren't?

The next time I see my grandfather, it is his funeral. Itchy heat covers our faces.

Everyone touches him. My cousins and tias, reaching fingers to place them delicately on his forehead, it is really hard for me, I barely knew him, but he is blood. After the funeral it's my brother, sister, dad. No one knows what to say. My dad squeezes our shoulders and takes us to Sonic for the second time.

Healing for me is reading. Horror, fantasy, and science fiction. Poetry, a sentence I like, literature that takes over slowly, slyly saturating my vision with what it wants me to see, this is one of the most magical feelings. I slurp up every last word and taste it on my tongue.

A police car sits coolly in the middle of the gallery space, sunken and battered. Poppy-red tomato splatters leave seedy stains as cacti and palms reclaim its broken window squares and gnarled oiled exhaust pipes. Crumbly wet earth exposes itself smiling like it knows what it's doing.

Sometime my first year in LA, I am at some strange contemporary art after-party in downtown. A big brick warehouse on East Sixth Street, LA skid row. We stumble out all heeled boots and sweat-slicked long hair, warm flushed cheeks against yellow night. I wasn't drunk enough. We walk back to our cars neatly lined under the low moaning highway. Our windows have been smashed in, the whole row of cars. My purse, my books and journal. I was pissed off. I should've hidden it. something. My friend gets real mad. He's angry and full of spicy booze. He calls the police. I tell them not to. It's almost two in the morning, I am sad and want to go home. I tell him they won't do anything for us. He does anyway. We wait for forty minutes. Its 2:42 a.m. now. I grow more impatient and irritable. When they show up, the first thing the police officer says to us is, do you know where you are? You know you're on skid row, right? Yes, we fucking know we're on skid row at 3:14 in the morning. They do absolutely nothing. A black homeless man walks by in the middle of the street pushing a grocery cart wrapped around with intricately bundled trash bags. Hi there, he says, as we all turn at the wheels' scrabbly screech on the asphalt. We nod back. The officer looks down at his shabby notepad and whispers under his breath, there's your suspect, right there. My mouth opens and I can't even really believe what he said. That's racist classism bundled into one ignorant individual who has the power of the law on his side. It makes me angry and then scared that police like this exist. That maybe most police exist like this. Maybe police are set up to exist like this. We finally make our way home. 4:09. Spicy drunk friend hanging his sad angry head out the window. Suddenly LA seems very big again.

Healing for me is falling into art. When I really get into it, it draws itself. Charcoal or graphite shade round and break, soft shards of loose dust smudge. I get it all over me.

Another blurry memory. I was in sophomore year in high school. Smoking weed on a lazy summer Thursday with some good guy friends. We lit up our joint. I was wearing denim short shorts and a little T-shirt, swinging the skinny strap of my vintage purse over my shoulders, balancing on concrete slabs that formed benches into a semicircle amphitheater. The police show up out of nowhere. We all freeze. Three big white policemen. We put out the joint and I shiver in the presence of their masculine aura. They search our bags, ripping the lining out of my purse to see if I had any secrets in there. They take down our names. Ask what a girl like me was doing there with three boys. They are my friends I reply. He checks my back pockets. My back pockets, on my tiny tight jeans. Could I really be hiding something in there? No secrets. None at all.

I got a text from my brother today, saying he was sorry if he was ever mean. I think he likes what he's getting into now. I will see him this summer back in my hometown.

I am in the middle of a horrifyingly fragile time of my life. I am nineteen and terrified of turning twenty. Twenty, somehow, has become too old for me. I think, is this how I imagined I would be like when I was nineteen, is this what I imagined I would look like?

The boy with the gun. My brother Dylan. My grandpa Aragon. Where was healing for them? What is healing for you? How can we savor and instill spaces for healing into spaces where it is so often forgotten?

Nesting: A Redefinition Of
Tomas Moniz

Come
This is a give away poem . . .
When my hands are empty
I will be full.
—Chrystos

Lately, I have been obsessed with babies. It's a tad bit disturbing and definitely fosters some socially awkward moments because I usually avoid interacting with the parents and go right to the baby. To be honest, parents of young children usually bug me, but I know it's not about them. It's about me. I'm envious of their palpable radiance and exuberance at their child, something I realize I miss in my life. Or perhaps I'm simply jealous of how adorable all of the baby accouterments are for today's parents. Seriously, parenting products are so amazing now.

But any chance I get, I walk up to random babies and engage with them.

I practice all my Rad Family etiquette, which usually freaks out the parents even more. I want to avoid all of the words loaded with value judgments like handsome, beautiful, strong, adorable, cute, sweet, big, precious. The list goes on and on, full of adjectives that play into socialized gender conditioning.

So alas, *baby* is my go-to word.

In a distressingly higher octave than necessary, I coo, "Look at that baby! Such a wonderful baby. Baby, baby, baby. Look at those baby toes, those baby arms." This, of course, makes the parents more suspicious of me all up close and personal with their child. Usually even the baby has no idea what's happening and so reacts accordingly, by crying.

At which point I coo, "Look at those baby tears. Look at that baby face." I don't blame the parents; I would have reacted the same.

I want to reassure them by saying, "Don't worry, I'm Rad Dad," like I should be wearing a cap or something. Eventually, though, I am forced to converse with the parents or child care provider (who is usually even more suspicious of an older, slightly disheveled dude coming up to their charge). I admire their energy and enthusiasm, how they remind me of where I once was, of who I used to be: a hands-on, down-on-the-ground, constantly facilitating the world and my child kind of guy.

An everyday father.

A stark contrast to the kind of parenting I am engaged in now.

As they walk away, I understand where these feelings are coming from. The adults look so alive, happy, even if they clearly are exhausted and overwhelmed; there is a beauty to those early parenting years, a dedication, a purpose I have never discovered elsewhere. Today, I miss that. I feel like I came to the party too early and now that I am leaving it, everyone's showing up. With babies and hella cool strollers. Seriously, I needed a degree in physics to figure out how to close my double kid stroller that was something like eight feet long and about 150 pounds.

Yet when I recall the fifteen-minute struggle to collapse it so it could fit in the car, precariously perched over the car seats, I think of it fondly.

This is what people call "empty nest."

And it doesn't stop with babies either. I worry about the way society is generally so unwelcoming to kids and parents out in the world. When I see parents getting frustrated with their child because the child is having a fit or being . . . well, a child, I want to reassure the parents by yelling, "Don't stress out. It doesn't bother me."

It's even worse when I feel like they are acting that way because I am there, a seemingly childless lone man. The other evening at a sushi restaurant, a child had one of those stunningly powerful/comical meltdowns. He wanted to hold the fish swimming around in the decorative aquarium. Seems like a perfectly reasonable desire and, as a parent, I probably would have been tempted to hoist him up and encourage him to dangle his cute little palm into the water to see if he could catch one. But he was told no and so proceeded to voice his displeasure. Now, if it were a commercial, I'm sure the glass would have shattered as a result of his high-pitched squeal. It put my own high-pitched baby squeal to shame.

The parents were horrified. They looked at me, and I could see the father getting angrier, mumbling threats to the child out of embarrassment. Sadly, I remember doing the same kind of reprimanding to my kids, whispering under my breath to wait until we got home, an empty plea for them to just be quiet, to stop attracting so much attention.

So I shouted above the screaming, "My children did the same thing. I totally understand." I happily ate my vegan sushi while the kid continued to reach new levels of auditory heights. Soon enough things ended: the waiter brought out a plastic fish for the kid to hold, they finished their meal, and when the father paid their bill, he nodded to me. I nodded back.

Let me repeat: empty nest.

I know these are the musings—dare I say the romanticized ramblings—of a man who clearly no longer spends an inordinate amount of time with young kids. But maybe that's exactly the kind of work someone like me can do now: find ways to support those who are where I once was.

I dream of creating public understanding towards children having meltdowns; I want to foster a supportive attitude in the adults around them, who all smile in commiseration with the parents rather than give dirty looks or make the parents feel unwelcomed, or worse deficient, ineffective, bad.

I fantasize about being some parenting superhero who swoops in right when the parents are about to lose it and defuses the situation.

Parenting is hard. But it's honest work, work that challenges you to be your best self. Despite those oh-so-public (as well as the countless private) difficult moments, parenting gives purpose. You try and often fail, yet your kids forgive you. There is something to learn there. You are forced to balance prioritizing your children's needs with your own. You develop emotional muscles you never knew about. You break open and love in a way you will never love again.

And then, it happens. They leave. They fly away like you always wanted them to, like you knew they had to, and you are left with memories and calluses and a few scars to remind you of the parent you once were. But the world feels empty, albeit perhaps much quieter. But there is an absence, a longing. That nest feels mighty big.

I've asked parents who have transitioned from the various phases of parenting (see the last issue of *Rad Dad* for a detailed explanation) into empty nesting, an analogy that began with birth mothers as they nested just prior to delivery. I don't think there is a father or partner expression that is the equivalent. In parenting literature and mainstream culture, there's an absence of stories about fathers or non-birth parents dealing with either the nesting phase or the subsequent empty nest. When I researched empty nest, many articles used non-gendered language; however, most were clearly geared towards the birth mother focusing on the connection between nesting at birth to the emptying of that nest years later. In fact, the only book I know of that even alludes to the non-birth parent "nesting" is the classic yet so problematic *Horton Hatches the Egg*.

We need a new analogy perhaps, an equivalent one, because I know I need to hear the stories about everyday fathers or non-birth parents, those down-on-the-ground dads, those people who have spent years committed to the work of parenting who find themselves on the other side. Think of how these stories might challenge those rigid gender dichotomies that foster the assumption that if you didn't birth the child, you're somehow less invested, less involved, that you won't struggle with the child leaving. Think of how we might create a language of commiseration and support that extends beyond parenting. Actually, perhaps gender is beside the point as it almost always is; perhaps the question is more general.

How to discover who we have become post-birthing and babying and kid wrangling and teen supporting and young adult loving?

How to let go or parent from afar?

How to embrace who we have become?

I have no idea. But parenting has taught me over and over: I may not know, but I'm gonna find out. Like my kids discovering their own path, I will soon discover the writer and the person I've grown into over all these years: messy and loving and emotional and scarred and committed.

That feels like a good parallel: seeing the similarities in my kids' journey and my own, separate but adjacent, necessarily apart but close enough that we can cheer each other on.

So if you see me out in the world, ask me how I'm doing or what I've learned. Let's create a new way to talk about parenting and loving and letting go that includes all adults and genders and family structures. But I warn you: if you have a baby with you, I'm going to play with them first.

About the Contributors

Even though **Mike Araujo** was born in the Bronx, he considers Rhode Island to be the most beautiful place, because of its history, culture, landscape, and people. He is committed to working for workplace equity and justice. He is the son of a Head Start teacher and a janitor at Brown University. His father was also the first Cape Verdean lightweight championship contender in 1951. He is the proud father of Sarah, Xavier, and Eleanor, and the lucky husband of Kristina Brown. He looks forward to a more just and loving society.

Artnoose is a fierce punk rock single mom who operates a letterpress printshop in Berkeley, California. She has been letterpress printing the personal zine *Ker-bloom!* every other month since 1996. She lives in a longstanding Bay Area collective house with five adults, two kids, and two cats. She ate samosas during her forty-hour labor with her son.

D.A. Begay is a good combination of wit and sarcasm. She will do almost anything for the story. She loves being a Dada to her two kids almost as much as much as she loves being a human. She reads more than she sleeps. And she only sleeps to dream. She works to stay in the space between the rock and the hard place because that's where the best stories live. She has her mother's spirit and continues to walk in beauty. Oh, and she's really into the evolution of the spirit. Hers, specifically.

Carla Bergman is a producer, mom, writer, and activist. She is the codirector of EMMA Talks, a speaker series by women. Carla has joyful threads in many initiatives and projects near and far, with incredible artists, thinkers, and activists. She co-directed the film *Common Notions: Handbook Not Required*, was one of the editors of *Stay Solid: A Radical Handbook for Youth*, and is currently working on a book about joy.

Thi Bui (cover artist) was born in Vietnam three months before the end of the Vietnam War and immigrated to the United States with her family in 1978. She is currently finishing her graphic memoir, *The Best We Could Do* (Abrams, 2017). She is a founding teacher of Oakland International High School, the first public high school in California for recent immigrants and English learners. She also mentors students in the MFA in comics program at the California College of the Arts. She lives in Berkeley with her son, her husband, and her mother.

The seventh of nine children born into a large working-poor family in a rural Northern California farming community, **Dani Burlison** weaves humor, honesty, and a passion for social justice into her writing. She is obsessed with Leonard Cohen, holds an MA in culture, ecology, and sustainable community from New College of California, and lives in Sonoma County, California, with her two teen daughters.

Welch Canavan has lived in Washington, DC, and Braddock, PA, where he has been involved in political organizing, an intentional community, and DIY punk.

Jonas Cannon is an author/zinester from the Midwest. He published the underground hit novel *The Greatest Most Traveling Circus* in 2014, as well as the six-issue zine *Cheer the Eff Up*, a part-fiction, mostly true letter to his first child about punk, parenthood, and struggling with depression. He lives in Chicago with his wife and two sons.

Dawn Caprice is a genderfluid litterateur, single parent, artist, and consulting wizard. Zie resides at the intersection of twenty-first-century Cascadia and the rain-swept edge of possibility. Hir work, which involves old gods and the birth of new cultures, the alchemy of darkness and light, and the semiotics of mystery, is in process.

Airial Clark is a San Francisco Bay Area–based parenting coach and sexologist. After receiving a bachelor's degree in anthropology and English Literature at UC Berkeley, she was admitted to the human sexuality master's program at San Francisco State University. She completed research for her master's thesis on race, family structures, and alternative sexuality in 2012 while raising her two sons as a single parent. Airial is a contributing writer and content expert for media outlets including Plaid for Women, the *Good Vibrations Magazine*, *Shades Magazine*, *Oakland Local*. She has been interviewed as a parenting expert for Salon.com and the *San Francisco Bay Guardian* and featured as a guest on international radio programs such as *Sex Out Loud* with Tristan Taormino, *Sexploration with Monika*, and *Sexxx Talk Radio*. In collaboration with organizations including the Center for Sex and Culture (CSC) and the Center for Research and Education on Gender and Sexuality (CREGS), Airial has led workshops providing parents and caregivers tools they need to become the resident sexuality expert for their families.

Chris Crass writes and speaks widely on antiracist organizing, feminism for men, and creating healthy culture and leadership for progressive activism. His latest book, *Towards the "Other America": Anti-Racist Resources for White People Taking Action for Black Lives Matter*, is available as a free e-book at www.chalicepress.net/OtherAmerica and in paperback. His previous book, *Towards Collective Liberation: Anti-Racist Organizing, Feminist Praxis, and Movement Building Strategy*, was published by PM Press. He and his partner Jardana Peacock are raising two beautiful boys, River and August. You can learn more about his work at www.chriscrass.org.

Alicia Dornadic is a researcher and artist. She has conducted over one hundred interviews with people on the topics of health, transportation, technology, and daily life. She works with organizations and communities to solve design problems. Alicia curates exhibits, most recently *Strike Away*, a show of 450 altered matchbooks by 225 artists at Paxton Gate, San Francisco in 2015. Find more of her work at spikedpunchbowl.com and Instagram @adorndesign.

Philana Dollin likes to have fun while getting things done. She is a federal government employee by day and a fundraising performance troupe founder by spare time, some of which is at night. She is currently raising two children with her female partner in a multi-faith household. Firm believers of the notion that it takes a village to raise a child, their home is filled with family, friends, love, and light.

Craig Elliott is a social justice activist, a feminist, a father of two boys, a writer, and a teacher. He lives in the East Bay (Northern California) and is actively involved in his community. He has dedicated his life to creating more justice and love in the world.

Zach Ellis writes creative nonfiction and is a hospital concierge. He lives in Portland, OR. His memoir *Being* was published by Instant Future in 2015. His writing has appeared in *Nailed*, *Rad Dad*, *The Gravity of the Thing*, and *The Nervous Breakdown*.

Rachel Galindo is a formerly incarcerated mama.

Established in 1995, **The Annakai and Robert Geshlider Corporation** strives to be blunt yet kind. "Geshlider" might mean "gaslamp-lighter," but the corporation is not entirely sure. Either way, four of their ancestors were glove-makers. Daughter-Annakai gargles words for breakfast. Dad-Rob is currently developing prosthetic limbs for amputees.

Bronwyn Davies Glover is a cisgender, white, feminist, queer writer, performance artist, and parent whose writing has been published in *Mutha Magazine* and her works presented in Rhubarb: A Festival of Women, Summerworks Theatre Festival. She is co-founder of Trigger Festival and Dot & Dribble Productions and a proud RAD parent!

Danny Goot is a badass parent living in the Bay Area! And loves coffee.

Ariel Gore is an award-winning editor, memoirist, journalist, and fiction writer. She teaches online at literarykitchen.com.

Krista Lee Hanson lives in Seattle with her partner, Burke Stansbury, and their two amazing kids. Krista spends her time parenting, teaching yoga, organizing, and learning all she can about dinosaurs and disability and determination by hanging out with her kids.

Frances Hardinge is a writer who wears a black hat. Notoriously unphotographable, she is rumored to be made entirely out of velvet. Sources close to Frances who prefer not to be named suggest that she has an evil twin who wears white and is hatless. This cannot be confirmed.

Plinio Hernandez was born in El Salvador in 1979 and moved with his family to Oakland in 1985. He currently resides in Guadalajara, Mexico, with his wife and two children. Plinio holds an MFA from UC Berkeley and a BFA in photography from Otis College of Art and Design. He cofounded Pueblo Nuevo, an artspace in West Berkeley that ran from 2008 to 2012, and in 2012 he was a California Association of Museum Writing Fellow. Recently, Plinio has worked in small community museums managing, curating and teaching. In addition, Plinio has taught art at UC Berkeley, Berkeley High School, Kala Art Institute, and Root Division. Plinio's art practice centers on examining history, geography, and personal narratives of migration, identity, and memory that are materialized through elements of drawings, sculpture, collaborations, videos, and performance.

Scott Hoshida lives and works in the East Bay with his partner, two kids, and four chickens. He teaches in Berkeley and is completing a novel set in Occupation Japan.

Mindi J. We miss you. Contact us.

Simon Knaphus is a full-time homeschooling solo parent and activist lawyer. He gave birth to two fabulous kids and has been learning from them ever since.

Daniel Muro LaMere lives in Minneapolis, where he is a high school English teacher and occasional poet. At the time of this writing, he is days away from welcoming twins into the world, and maybe a little terrified. Read more at www.danielmurolamere.com.

Jennifer Lewis is the editor of *Red Light Lit*. She received her MFA in creative writing from San Francisco State University in May 2015. Her fiction has been published in *Midnight Breakfast*,

Transfer Magazine, *Fourteen Hills*, and *Sparkle and Blink*. In 2012, she was the recipient of the Leo Litwak award for creative nonfiction and for fiction in 2015.

Robert Liu-Trujillo is a father, husband, and lifelong artist. He has illustrated three picture books, one of which he also wrote, called *Furqan's First Flat Top*. Robert is part of a growing movement of independent storytellers and publishers in the Bay Area.

Ian MacKaye cofounded Dischord Records as a teenager in 1980 and went on to form the bands Minor Threat, Fugazi, and the Evens.

Tomas Moniz is the founder, editor, and writer for the award-winning project: *Rad Dad*. His novella *Bellies and Buffalos* is a tender, chaotic road trip about friendship, family, and Flamin' Hot Cheetos. He is cofounder and cohost of the rambunctious monthly reading series Saturday Night Special. He has taught writing at Berkeley City College for over ten years. He's been making zines since the late nineties, and his most current zine *addition / subtraction* is available, but you have to write him a postcard: PO Box 3555, Berkeley, CA, 94703.

Zora Moniz is an artist/writer/activist/creative/human currently living in Los Angeles studying world arts and cultures with food studies and urban planning minors at UCLA. She was born and raised in the Bay Area with her crazy, beautiful family and her writer father who, according to Zora, "kindly likes her various stages of writing enough to publish them."

Tasnim Nathoo is a writer based in Vancouver, BC. She was a contributor to the AK Press book *Stay Solid: A Radical Handbook for Youth* (check out her piece "How to Heal a Broken Heart in 10 Steps") and is currently working on several picture books and other projects related to feminism, radical parenting, and finding your destiny.

Amy Abugo Ongiri is a masculine-of-center lesbian author and educator who hopes her children can grow up to be strong and free. She wishes more radicals/queers/people of color would get involved in the foster care system.

Jesse D. Palmer, Esq., Fern's dad. Writes for Slingshot Collective. Works as an attorney and lives in a communal house in the Bay Area.

Kermit Playfoot is a friend, flatmate, uncle, and teacher who has been published in *Slingshot* and *Rad Dad*. These days, he is teaching English and building intimacy in Barcelona while trying to remain connected to assigned and chosen family on the east and west coasts. Some of his work can be found at kermitplayfoot. wordpress.com.

Roger Porter is a writer and educator from Oakland, CA, whose first book, *The Souls of Hood Folk*, is available at www.lulu.com. He has a degree in English from UC Berkeley and an MFA in creative writing from Mills College. He describes himself as an average everyday man from East Oakland who writes about average everyday hood life. He blogs at ghettosun.com.

Jonathan Shipley is a freelance writer and proud father of an astounding twelve-year-old girl. His writing has appeared in the *LA Times*, *Fine Books & Collections* Magazine, and many others. He's lost to his girl at Yahtzee 1.8 million times.

Jeremy Adam Smith is the author or coeditor of four books, including *Rad Dad*, *The Daddy Shift*, and *The Compassionate Instinct*. His coverage of racial and economic segregation in San Francisco schools has won numerous honors, most recently the Sigma Delta Chi Award for investigative reporting and a John Swett Award from the California Teachers Association. His articles and essays have appeared in the *San Francisco Chronicle*, *Utne Reader*, *The Nation*, *Mindful*, *Wired*, and many other periodicals, websites, and books. He edits the website of the UC Berkeley Greater Good Science Center.

Burke Stansbury is a community organizer who got involved in politics after spending time living in Mexico and Central America during college. He was the executive director of the Committee in Solidarity with the People of El Salvador (CISPES) for five years, and since 2010 has worked with the Center for Community

Change as a national field organizer. Burke lives in Seattle with his partner Krista and their two children, including six-year-old Lucas, who was born with a neuromuscular disease. The experience of parenting a child with a severe physical disability has had a profound impact on his life; along with Krista, he blogs about the wonders and challenges of being special needs parents.

cubbie rowland-storm is a dad, grad student, and educator. Each of these roles make him feel profoundly lucky, but even though he loves writing about children's literature and teaching a bunch of awesome kids, he wishes he could spend more time with his family. You can contact him at cublet@gmail.com.

Jessie Susannah is surfing the cosmic waves of this incarnation as a divorced Ima, a Jewish Priestess-in-Evolution, and a $Money Witch$. You can find out more at www.healyourfinances.com or on Instagram @money.witch

Shawn Taylor is a parent, husband, and writer whose writings have appeared in *Rad Dad*, Ebony.com, the *New York Times*, and various music and pop-culture magazines. He is a popular comic book/geek-culture blogger and is one of the founders of www.thenerdsofcolor.com and is a cofounder of the Black Comix Arts Festival, an annual comic book gathering that promotes literacy and critical thinking by introducing youth to comic books and mythology.

Nathan Torp is a badass parent living in the middle of the United States.

Sasha Vodnik is an uncle many times over. He lives in San Francisco.

Carvell Wallace is a father and a writer living in the Bay Area. If he had cats, he would name them Melancholy and Ennui.

Brian Whitman is a zinester in his mid-thirties, and for a brief but wonderful time in his life he did his best to help raise a child. He currently lives in New Mexico where he plays pinball, rides his bike, and eats at a place called Thai Vegan every week.

scott winn is raising his daughter as a solo, half-time parent that began as part of an intentional 50/50 co-parenting relationship. He has been active in movements for racial, gender and economic justice for several decades. He is currently active with the Coalition of Anti-Racist Whites and is a member of the board of the Western States Center. He has a blog called Papa Praxis: Parenting, Progeny and Politics at www.papapraxis.net. He loves pears and the color brown.

Eleanor Wohlfeiler was raised in Oakland, CA, where she is now raising her three kids and starting to imagine what is next.

Allison Wolfe is a Washington, DC–based singer, songwriter, and zine writer who has been the lead vocalist for several punk rock groups including Bratmobile and Partyline.

Madison Young is an author, artist, feminist pornographer, and mother. Young has presented on the topic of sexuality internationally, including at Yale University, Northwestern University, and University of Toronto. Young's writings have been published in *Subversive Motherhood*, *Daddy: A Memoir*, and *The Ultimate Guide to Sex through Pregnancy & Motherhood*. Young is featured in such media outlets as BravoTV, the *New York Times*, *Huffington Post*, and HBO. Madison Young lives and works in Berkeley, California.

PM Press was founded at the end of 2007 by a small collection of folks with decades of publishing, media, and organizing experience. PM Press co-conspirators have published and distributed hundreds of books, pamphlets, CDs, and DVDs. Members of the PM team have founded enduring book fairs, spearheaded victorious tenant organizing campaigns, and worked closely with bookstores, academic conferences, and even rock bands to deliver political and challenging ideas to all walks of life. We're old enough to know what we're doing and young enough to know what's at stake.

We seek to create radical and stimulating fiction and non-fiction books, pamphlets, T-shirts, visual and audio materials to entertain, educate and inspire you. We aim to distribute these through every available channel with every available technology—whether that means you are seeing anarchist classics at our bookfair stalls; reading our latest vegan cookbook at the café; downloading geeky fiction e-books; or digging new music and timely videos from our website.

PM Press is always on the lookout for talented and skilled volunteers, artists, activists and writers to work with. If you have a great idea for a project or can contribute in some way, please get in touch.

PM Press
PO Box 23912
Oakland CA 94623
510-658-3906
www.pmpress.org

These are indisputably momentous times—the financial system is melting down globally and the Empire is stumbling. Now more than ever there is a vital need for radical ideas.

In the nine years since its founding—and on a mere shoestring—PM Press has risen to the formidable challenge of publishing and distributing knowledge and entertainment for the struggles ahead. With over 300 releases to date, we have published an impressive and stimulating array of literature, art, music, politics, and culture. Using every available medium, we've succeeded in connecting those hungry for ideas and information to those putting them into practice.

Friends of PM allows you to directly help impact, amplify, and revitalize the discourse and actions of radical writers, filmmakers, and artists. It provides us with a stable foundation from which we can build upon our early successes and provides a much-needed subsidy for the materials that can't necessarily pay their own way. You can help make that happen—and receive every new title automatically delivered to your door once a month—by joining as a Friend of PM Press. And, we'll throw in a free T-shirt when you sign up.

Here are your options:

    $30 a month: Get all books and pamphlets plus 50% discount on all webstore purchases

    $40 a month: Get all PM Press releases (including CDs and DVDs) plus 50% discount on all webstore purchases

    $100 a month: Superstar—Everything plus PM merchandise, free downloads, and 50% discount on all webstore purchases

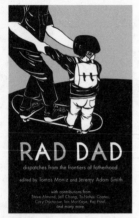

Rad Dad: Dispatches from the Frontiers of Fatherhood
Tomas Moniz and Jeremy Adam Smith
ISBN: 978-1-60486-481-6
$15.00

Rad Dad: Dispatches from the Frontiers of Fatherhood combines the best pieces from the award-winning zine *Rad Dad* and from the blog *Daddy Dialectic*, two kindred publications that have tried to explore parenting as political territory. Both of these projects have pushed the conversation around fathering beyond the safe, apolitical focus most books and websites stick to; they have not been complacent but have worked hard to create a diverse, multi-faceted space in which to grapple with the complexity of fathering.

Today more than ever, fatherhood demands constant improvisation, risk, and struggle. With grace and honesty and strength, *Rad Dad*'s writers tackle all the issues that other parenting guides are afraid to touch: the brutalities, beauties, and politics of the birth experience, the challenges of parenting on an equal basis with mothers, the tests faced by transgendered and gay fathers, the emotions of sperm donation, and parental confrontations with war, violence, racism, and incarceration. *Rad Dad* is for every father out in the real world trying to parent in ways that are loving, meaningful, authentic, and ultimately revolutionary.

Contributors include Steve Almond, Jack Amoureux, Mike Araujo, Mark Andersen, Jeff Chang, Ta-Nehisi Coates, Jeff Conant, Sky Cosby, Jason Denzin, Cory Doctorow, Craig Elliott, Chip Gagnon, Keith Hennessy, David L. Hoyt, Simon Knapus, Ian MacKaye, Tomas Moniz, Zappa Montag, Raj Patel, Jeremy Adam Smith, Jason Sperber, Burke Stansbury, Shawn Taylor, Tata, Jeff West, and Mark Whiteley.

Revolutionary Mothering: Love on the Front Lines
Edited by Alexis Pauline Gumbs, China Martens, and Mai'a Williams
ISBN: 978-1-62963-110-3
$17.95

Inspired by the legacy of radical and queer black feminists of the 1970s and '80s, *Revolutionary Mothering* places marginalized mothers of color at the center of a world of necessary transformation. The challenges we face as movements working for racial, economic, reproductive, gender, and food justice, as well as anti-violence, anti-imperialist, and queer liberation are the same challenges that many mothers face every day. Oppressed mothers create a generous space for life in the face of life-threatening limits, activate a powerful vision of the future while navigating tangible concerns in the present, move beyond individual narratives of choice toward collective solutions, live for more than ourselves, and remain accountable to a future that we cannot always see. *Revolutionary Mothering* is a movement-shifting anthology committed to birthing new worlds, full of faith and hope for what we can raise up together.

Contributors include June Jordan, Malkia A. Cyril, Esteli Juarez, Cynthia Dewi Oka, Fabiola Sandoval, Sumayyah Talibah, Victoria Law, Tara Villalba, Lola Mondragón, Christy NaMee Eriksen, Norma Angelica Marrun, Vivian Chin, Rachel Broadwater, Autumn Brown, Layne Russell, Noemi Martinez, Katie Kaput, alba onofrio, Gabriela Sandoval, Cheryl Boyce Taylor, Ariel Gore, Claire Barrera, Lisa Factora-Borchers, Fabielle Georges, H. Bindy K. Kang, Terri Nilliasca, Irene Lara, Panquetzani, Mamas of Color Rising, tk karakashian tunchez, Arielle Julia Brown, Lindsey Campbell, Micaela Cadena, and Karen Su.

*Birth Work as Care Work: Stories from
Activist Birth Communities*
Alana Apfel
ISBN: 978-1-62963-151-6
$14.95

Birth Work as Care Work presents a vibrant
collection of stories and insights from the
front lines of birth activist communities.
The personal has once more become political, and birth workers,
supporters, and doulas now find themselves at the fore of collective
struggles for freedom and dignity.

The author, herself a scholar and birth justice organizer,
provides a unique platform to explore the political dynamics of birth
work, drawing connections between birth, reproductive labor, and
the struggles of caregiving communities today. Articulating a politics of care work in and through the reproductive process, the book
brings diverse voices into conversation to explore multiple possibilities and avenues for change.

At a moment when agency over our childbirth experi-
ences is increasingly centralized in the hands of professional elites,
Birth Work as Care Work presents creative new ways to reimagine the
trajectory of our reproductive processes. Most importantly, the contributors present new ways of thinking about the entire life cycle,
providing a unique and creative entry point into the essence of all
human struggle—the struggle over the reproduction of life itself.

Praise:
"I love this book, all of it. The polished essays and the interviews
with birth workers dare to take on the deepest questions of human
existence."
—Carol Downer, cofounder of the Feminist Women's Heath Centers of California and author of *A Woman's Book of Choices*

My Baby Rides the Short Bus:
The Unabashedly Human Experience of
Raising Kids with Disabilities
Edited by Yantra Bertelli, Jennifer
Silverman, and Sarah Talbot
ISBN: 978-1-60486-109-9
$20.00

In lives where there is a new diagnosis
or drama every day, the stories in this collection provide parents of
"special needs" kids with a welcome chuckle, a rock to stand on, and
a moment of reality held far enough from the heart to see clearly.
Featuring works by "alternative" parents who have attempted to
move away from mainstream thought—or remove its influence
altogether—this anthology, taken as a whole, carefully considers the
implications of parenting while raising children with disabilities.

From professional writers to novice storytellers including
Robert Rummel-Hudson, Ayun Halliday, and Kerry Cohen, this as-
sortment of authentic, shared experiences from parents at the fringe
of the fringes is a partial antidote to the stories that misrepresent,
ridicule, and objectify disabled kids and their parents.

Praise:
"This is a collection of beautifully written stories, incredibly open
and well articulated, complicated and diverse: about human rights
and human emotions. About love, and difficulties; informative
and supportive. Wise, non-conformist, and absolutely punk rock!"
—China Martens, author of *The Future Generation: The Zine-Book
for Subculture Parents, Kids, Friends, and Others*

"This is the most important book I've read in years. Whether you
are subject or ally, *My Baby Rides the Short Bus* will open you—with
its truth, humanity, and poetry. Lucky you to have found it. Now
stick it in your heart."
—Ariel Gore, founding editor of *Hip Mama*

Don't Leave Your Friends Behind:
Concrete Ways to Support Families in Social
Justice Movements and Communities
Victoria Law and China Martens
ISBN: 978-1-60486-396-3
$17.95

Don't Leave Your Friends Behind is a
collection of concrete tips, suggestions,
and narratives on ways that non-parents
can support parents, children, and
caregivers in their communities, social movements, and collective
processes. *Don't Leave Your Friends Behind* focuses on issues affecting
children and caregivers within the larger framework of social justice,
mutual aid, and collective liberation.

How do we create new, nonhierarchical structures of
support and mutual aid, and include all ages in the struggle for social
justice? There are many books on parenting, but few on being a
good community member and a good ally to parents, caregivers, and
children as we collectively build a strong all-ages culture of resistance.
Any group of parents will tell you how hard their struggles are and
how they are left out, but no book focuses on how allies can address
issues of caretakers' and children's oppression. Many well-intentioned
childless activists don't interact with young people on a regular basis
and don't know how. *Don't Leave Your Friends Behind* provides them
with the resources and support to get started.

Praise:
"This book is mind-blowing, brilliant, and urgently needed! It is full of
useful models and strategies for creating resistance that breaks down
barriers to participation for children and people caring for children,
and integrates deeply transformative commitments to building
radically different activist culture and practice. This is a must-read for
anyone trying to build projects based in collective action."
—Dean Spade, author of *Normal Life: Administrative Violence,*
Critical Trans Politics, and the Limits of Law

A Wolf at the Gate
Author: Mark Van Steenwyk
Illustrator: Joel Hedstrom
ISBN: 978-1-62963-150-9
$14.95

The Blood Wolf prowls near the village of Stonebriar at night. She devours chickens and goats and cows and cats. Some say children are missing. But this murderous wolf isn't the villain of our story, she's the hero! The Blood Wolf hates humankind for destroying the forest, but an encounter with a beggar teaches her a better way to confront injustice. How will she react when those she loves are threatened?

This imaginative retelling of the legend of Saint Francis and the Wolf explores what it means to be a peacemaker in the midst of violence and how to restore a healthy relationship with creation. Settle in and read a tale of tooth and sword, of beggars and lords, of outlaws and wild beasts. It is a story of second chances and the power of love. This is the story of *A Wolf at the Gate*.

Also available is a family-friendly rollicking musical soundtrack CD from Jon Felton and his Soulmobile, *Songs for A Wolf at the Gate*.

Praise:
"*A Wolf at the Gate* is a simple story that evokes profound and fundamental themes: survival, hunger, war and violence, law and justice, fear, greed, and predation. In the hands of Mark Van Steenwyk it becomes a transformative parable of truth and reconciliation, the power of community, and the dazzling force of love enacted in the public square, the very heart of justice."
—Bill Ayers, author of *Public Enemy: Confessions of an American Dissident*

Girls Are Not Chicks Coloring Book
Jacinta Bunnell and Julie Novak
ISBN: 978-1-60486-076-4
$10

Twenty-seven pages of feminist fun! This is a coloring book you will never outgrow. *Girls Are Not Chicks* is a subversive and playful way to examine how pervasive gender stereotypes are in every aspect of our lives. This book helps to deconstruct the homogeneity of gender expression in children's media by showing diverse pictures that reinforce positive gender roles for girls.

Color the Rapunzel for a new society. She now has power tools, a roll of duct tape, a Tina Turner album, and a bus pass! Paint outside the lines with Miss Muffet as she tells that spider off and considers a career as an arachnologist! Girls are not chicks. Girls are thinkers, creators, fighters, healers, and superheroes.

Praise:
"An ingeniously subversive coloring book."
—Heather Findlay, editor-in-chief, *Girlfriends* magazine

"Get this cool feminist coloring book even if you don't have a kid"
—Jane Pratt, *Jane* magazine